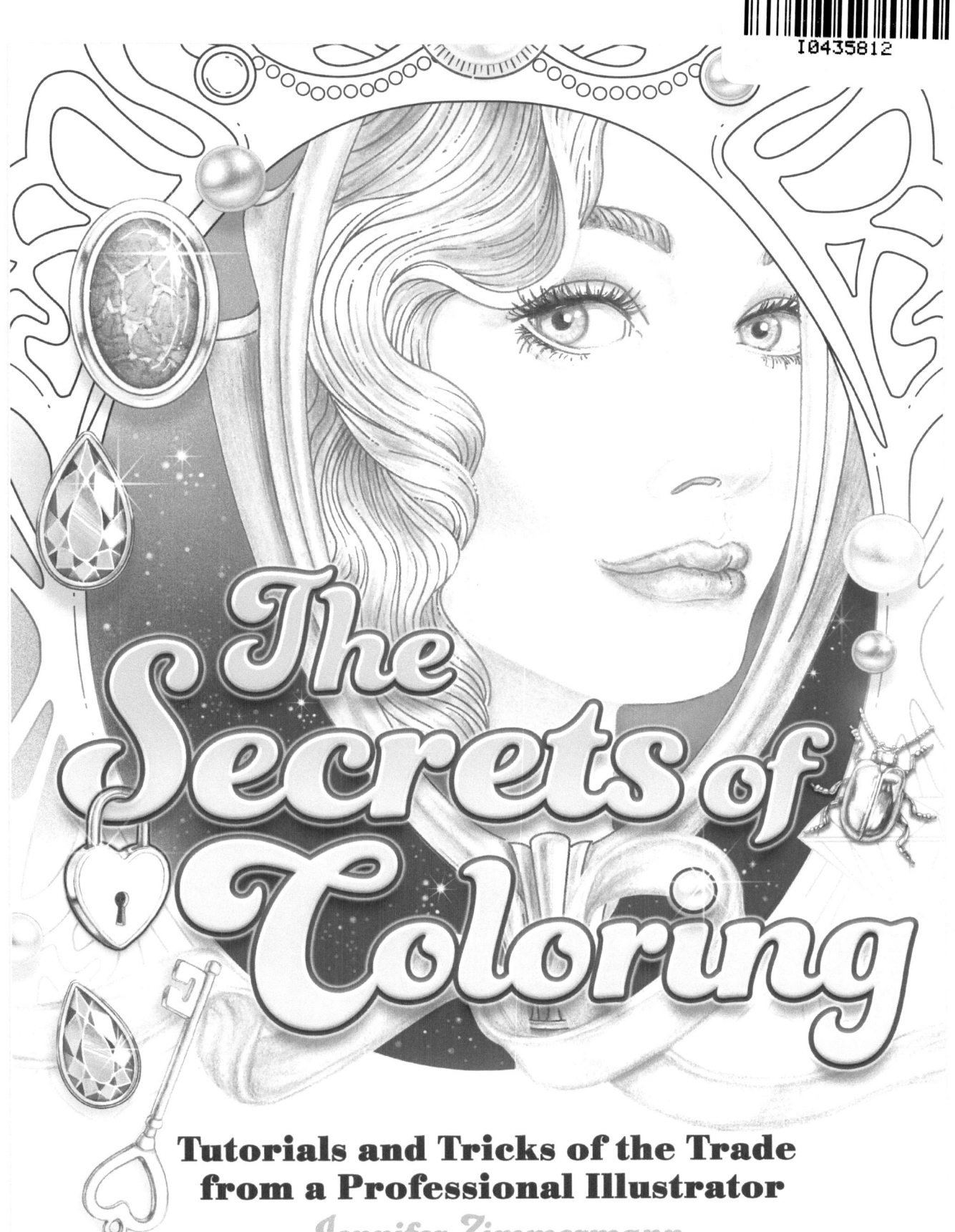

The Secrets of Coloring

Tutorials and Tricks of the Trade from a Professional Illustrator

Jennifer Zimmermann

Thank You...

To my amazing family who continues to support me, through my artistic journey...

To my fantastic administrators and team:
Elizabeth, Karen, Tina, Michelle, Jill, Mary, Cindy and Pauly

To my many friends who constantly encourage me and proudly share my art!

The Secrets of Coloring

ISBN-13: 978-0-9989292-1-7
ISBN-10: 0-9989292-1-2

Getting Started

The Secrets of Coloring is an interactive book in which you will learn about coloring and drawing supplies. You will be introduced to new techniques by testing them out first – then later apply them to adult coloring books to create finished coloring pages. You may even desire to go a step further and create or improve upon your own drawings. You will find sections to practice technique throughout *The Secrets of Coloring* and sample pages to put to use at the end of the book. You may notice a few blank pages in between. This is to prevent wet media such as alcohol-based markers from seeping through to the next page. It's important to have a nice neat book for a long time to be able to reference.

Coloring should be a mindless (yet mindful) activity, much like yoga, that lowers stress levels, brings us self-awareness, and returns us to our childhood happy places! Don't let the stress of daily life or self-comparison get you down. Many colorists strive to color like professionals but don't know how best to utilize their materials. They keep buying more materials, hoping that something will magically happen. They see others create dynamic and professional-looking pieces of art but don't know if they'll ever be able to get there. This is where I come in.

I'm not only a professional artist and illustrator with a BFA and training from some of the finest colleges and universities in the United States but also a teacher with a Master's degree in Educational Studies. I studied under some very influential artists and illustrators of our time, taking bits and pieces of knowledge from each. For over a decade I taught elementary, middle, and high school art in the public schools, and I love to share my extensive knowledge of the subject of art.

As a teacher, I have the ability to put myself in the shoes of those with very little skill or patience when it comes to art. I have mastered the art of breaking techniques down into manageable steps without pain or frustration. I pride myself on being able to help those who love art, and those who appreciate art but still struggle with being able to achieve certain effects or to create realistic and believable images of their own. It is my goal to be able to teach anyone almost anything in this book...and more. Practice, practice, practice. It does wonders.

In 2015, I became aware of the coloring book craze, and my first book was published soon after. I got involved on social media, in coloring groups, and suddenly became known in the coloring world for my pearls after releasing a written *Pink Pearl Step-by-Step Tutorial*, much like the ones in this book! I went on to create a YouTube channel where I demonstrate different techniques and host video tutorials. All this time I have received many messages from fans, requesting more and more tutorials. I have done many events such as hosting live "Color Alongs" in front of thousands of people online. I began amassing a collection of things to teach – a "to do" list of sorts since creating my pearl tutorial. I was very busy in 2016 and 2017 preparing to release two more coloring books. I never made time to put that list into motion until now.

I appreciate each and every one of my followers. It brings me much joy to see my ideas come to life through you! There is no greater reward than putting a smile on someone's face and witnessing the joy of accomplishment! I hope to continue this colorful journey and collaboration with you, and to teach you some new things along the way! I hope that you enjoy this book! Happy coloring :)

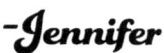

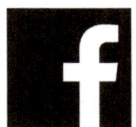 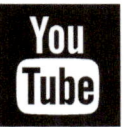   

Sign up for Jennifer's newsletter to receive occasional freebies
and stay up to date, at:

ModernColoring.com

To purchase Digital Downloads:

www.etsy.com/shop/ModernColoring

Other Books available on Amazon!
Check out **Glamourista and Glowdalas!**

Artist Page: **Modern Coloring: Jennifer Zimmermann**
www.facebook.com/moderncoloring/

Color Along Tutorials:

www.youtube.com/c/ModernColoringJenniferZimmermann

www.instagram.com/moderncoloring/

www.pinterest.com/moderncoloring/

twitter.com/moderncoloring

Amazon Author Page: **www.amazon.com/-/e/B01GNGL18Y**

Do you love this book?
__Please__ don't forget to leave a review on Amazon!
It is very much appreciated. :)

Table of Contents

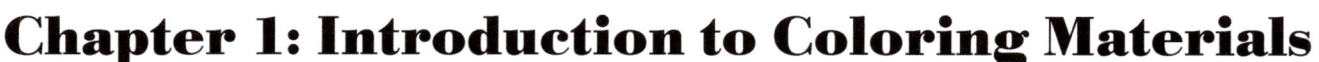

Chapter 1: Introduction to Coloring Materials

Let's discuss the best tools for use in drawing and coloring in coloring books. Most colorists use colored pencils. Why? They are versatile, portable and best of all...not messy! Plus they can last for years and years with no risk of drying out like other materials. It is essential to have a good sharpener and an eraser on hand when using colored pencils.

Other popular supplies are gel pens, which work very well for coloring those tiny areas of adult coloring books that are very difficult to get into, as are fineliner markers. A small paintbrush and some white gouache or watercolor paint works very well for tiny details and highlights. Bolder markers are great for fast coloring of large shapes, but if you plan to use alcohol-based ones you will need some blotter paper.

Newer trends in the coloring book world include eliminating the black lines from coloring book pages, adding pastel backgrounds of the sky and clouds or space, and the Bokeh effect. In addition, people now use make up, such as eye shadow for backgrounds, and glitter nail polish for shimmer. I adore PanPastel for flawless skin tones, as well as for creating certain mixed media background effects. Toned paper is quite popular with colorists these days because it brings a richness to coloring book pages. Have you tried it? Fixative sprays are recommended for finishing and protecting colorings that have had soft powder form materials added. If you foresee yourself cutting out pages from *The Secrets of Coloring*, you will need a utility knife, a straight edge or ruler, and some cardboard or card stock to protect the pages below.

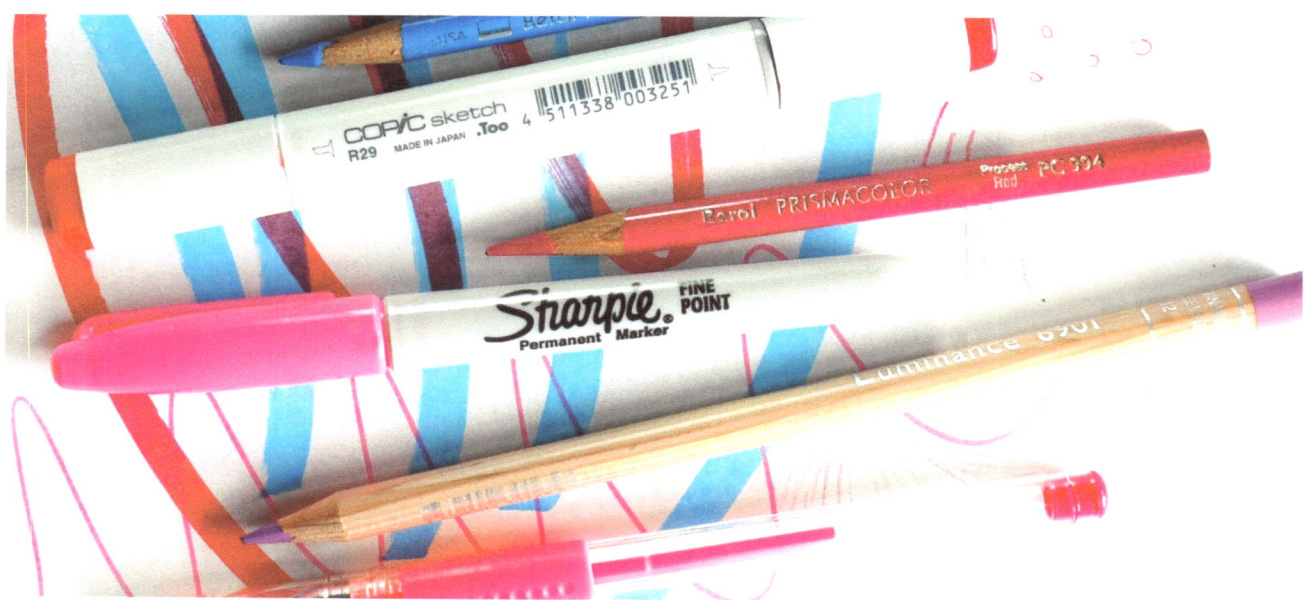

Let's not forget coloring books! Choose your favorite, but be sure to take note of the printing style (single vs. double-sided) before deciding on materials. Many artists don't mind if you copy coloring book pages from a book that you've personally purchased to other stocks of paper, and save your original book so that it can be used for this purpose repeatedly (for personal and individual use only – not to sell). However, when in doubt, you should contact the artist or publisher and ask permission or read the legal page of each book for specifics. Remember, copying onto paper for anyone other than yourself would be violating this privilege. I include a statement on the legal page of each of my books explaining the terms of use.

By the way, it is often less expensive to print something at a copy center rather than at home. I will provide an artist's permission statement at the end of this book allowing you to copy up to ten pages at a time for personal use at a business copy center. Commercial copying services don't want to risk running into copyright issues, and refuse to make copies at all, so my permission will help to eliminate that possibility.

You can find my suggestions, other useful information and freebies on my website…

ModernColoring.com. Click on the suggested materials tab under *"shop"* to find affiliate links to my favorite supplies or the *"books"* tab to find links to all of my coloring books.

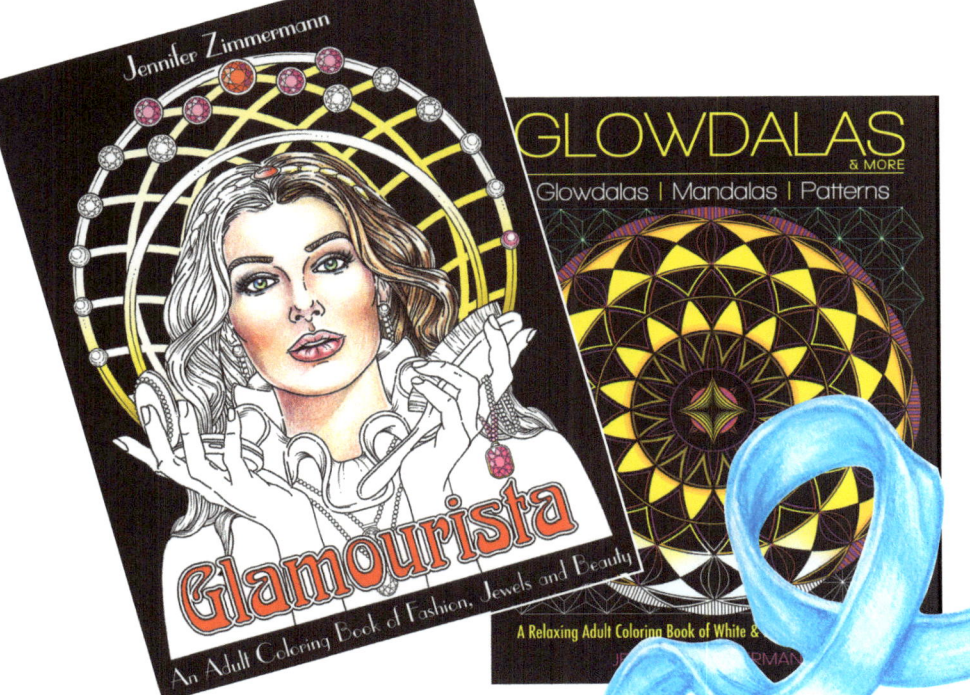

Chapter 2: Paper Types

The Secrets of Coloring is printed on a general purpose paper that works well with colored pencil and other materials such as gel pen and lighter applications of pastel. This book was not created for use with heavily applied wet mediums. However, a very small amount of gouache or acrylic paint shouldn't harm the pages, if instructions are followed. There are many varieties of paper available. Choosing a paper depends on what you plan to do with it. For example, you may be interested in copying a few pages of a coloring book to a heavier stock for use with wet media, such as heavy marker or watered-down watercolor paints.

Varieties include but are not limited to: white, hot press or smooth (such as Bristol Board), cold press or with tooth, toned (which works like an underpainting in painting – a color that shows through the top layer of material in the end), charcoal/pastel (textured), card stock, and watercolor paper. What is tooth? Tooth is the texture that paper has, as you can see in the picture below. It prevents color from completely covering a surface, so that you can still see some of the paper color. It also "grips" loose materials like pastel much better than a completely smooth paper. Some people prefer a lot of tooth, some prefer their paper smooth with only a little. *The Secrets of Coloring* is printed on a paper with an even amount of tooth.

Something else to consider is thickness and absorbency, depending on your plans. I will provide some practice pages with faux-toned backgrounds to try. Use the "toned" sample page to test out your materials. See how your pencils, markers, and pens behave differently on the next page with colored backgrounds. Be sure to use a blotter page for use with wet media such as markers.

People often ask my advice on where to start. I adore Canson and Strathmore high-end papers. Mi-Tientes paper is my favorite for pastel drawing. For copying coloring book pages, Strathmore makes a lovely toned paper that I would recommend as well. These companies have been around for a long time, and their papers are more costly than some others but are well worth the price. To do some general coloring with markers and pencils on white, I will use a Georgia-Pacific card stock. It's inexpensive, heavy weight, and runs through a printer easily – plus it has nice amount of tooth.

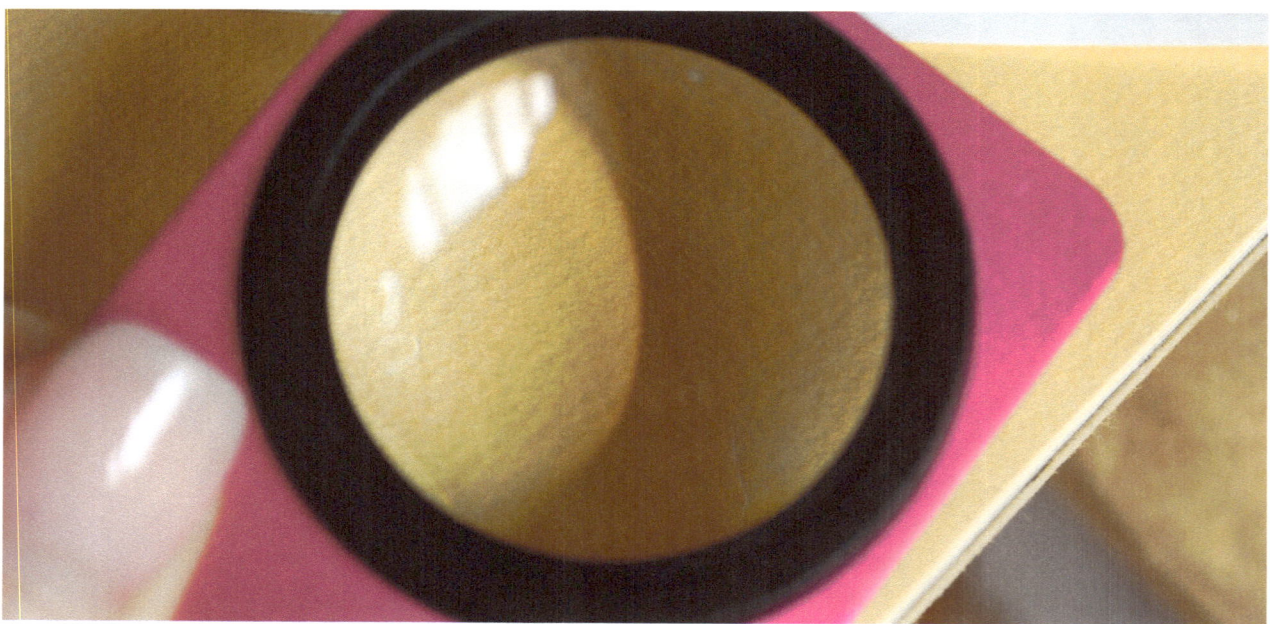

Grey

Tan

White

Use a blotter page under this page if you are going to use marker on the previous page

Chapter 3: Colored Pencils

Varieties

Pencils exist for many different purposes. In this book, we will focus on traditional colored pencils. We won't get into the discussion of watercolor pencils. There are two kinds of non water-soluble colored pencils, oil and wax – although there is much confusion in the coloring world about how they should be categorized. The most important thing to know is that choosing which to use is a matter of personal preference. Some pencils have a harder feel while others are softer. Some wax-based pencils even work similarly to oil-based ones, so determining what is right for you will vary by brand.

If you are heavy handed, I'd suggest starting with a harder pencil. If you are like me, and your hands hurt from pushing a hard lead even after a short time, or if you have arthritis, a soft-core pencil may be your best bet. Just prepare to sharpen your pencils more often.

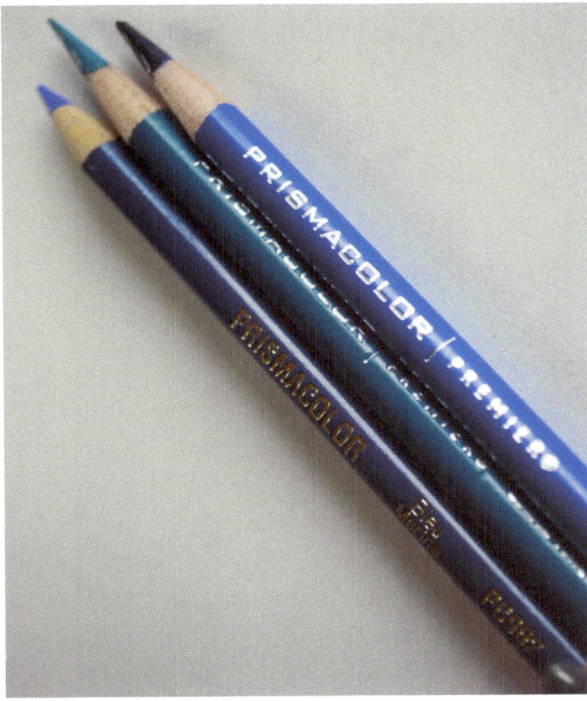

Many colorists prefer the denser oil-based pencils for tight renderings because the pencils leads are harder and hold their points well. More compact lead will also fill in the "tooth" of paper very nicely, leaving less white showing. Faber-Castell produces the very popular Polychromos line. These beautiful pencils can be bought as large sets or as open stock online and at some local art stores.

There are many brands of wax pencils, and the one that I have used for 30+ years is Prismacolor. I will use them throughout most of this book. They are soft core pencils, and I find them to be the easiest on my hands because they don't require much pressure. These pencils are available in an expansive array of colors, making it very easy to find the exact color you may be in search of! I have owned some of my Prismacolor pencils since I started drawing all those years ago, and they work as well today as they did back then.

Nowadays the line is called Prismacolor Premier. There is also a less expensive, student grade line available called Prismacolor Scholar. However, the color selection is less extensive. Oftentimes, there are terrific sales of Premier pencils online.

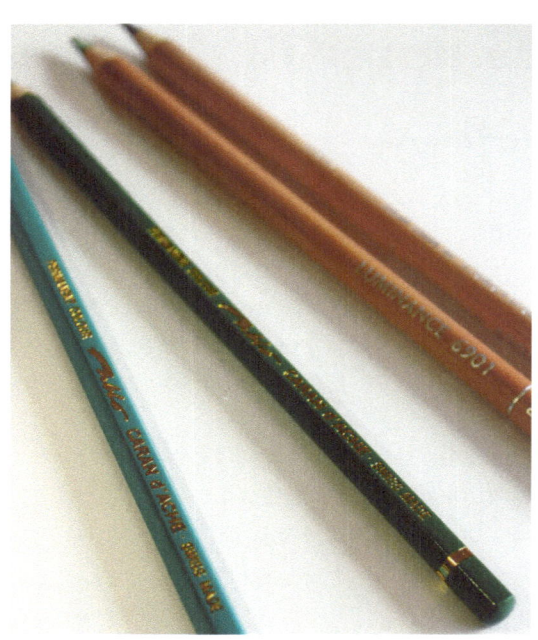

Another brand that has been around since the early 1900's is Caran D'ache. They manufacture some very sought after water-soluble pencils for artistic watercolor-like effects, as well as several lines of traditional pencils, including Pablos and Luminance (their highest end, most light-fast pencil), which I will also demonstrate with in a tutorial later in *The Secrets of Coloring*. These pencils are somewhat similar to the Prismacolor pencils in regards to consistency but have a very different feel. They have excellent layering capabilities and will smooth surfaces beautifully – like butter. There are of course many other brands of pencils, and I've only named a few. I encourage you to do a little research before you make any decisions. If you live close to an art store, I suggest buying a few open stock to test them out and discover your preferences and determine what is in your budget. At times I make announcements on my Facebook Artist Page when I see pencils go on sale. You can like my page and follow me to stay on top of things! On Facebook, just search for **Modern Coloring: Jennifer Zimmermann**.

Pencil Techniques and Terminology

Using Sharp Pencils vs. Dull Pencils

As a teacher, I've always taught my students to keep a sharp pencil. I'm pretty picky about this. However, there are some instances in which a slightly duller pencil may make your life easier and allow you to achieve a desired effect. You might notice lots of white flecks throughout a colored area. In general, however, a sharp pencil fills in the gaps of the paper "tooth" better to create a smoother looking drawing without a waxy sheen. It does take

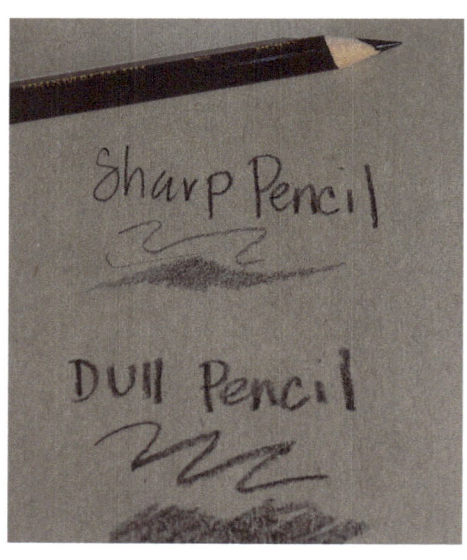

more time and effort, but like most things in life, if you don't rush through something, you'll be happier with the end result.

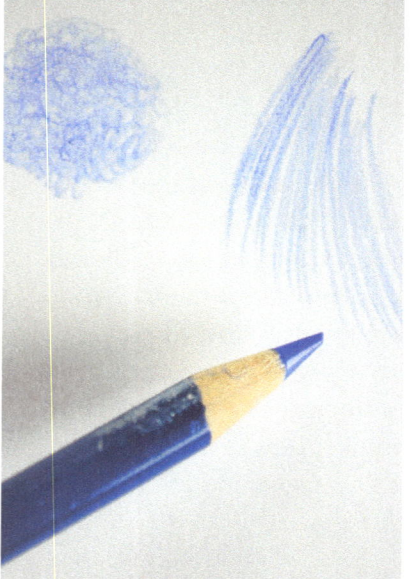

Pencil Marks…Directional vs. Circular

When teaching the how to color basics, I really only use two kinds of strokes – circular and directional. I use tiny "scrubbing" or "fuzzing" circles to fill up small spaces and "directional" movements that flow with the shape when filling larger ones. These will usually all run in the same direction as the *longest side* of the outer shape. I usually only reserve several other techniques such as hatching and cross hatching to create "implied texture" like fur when using colored pencils. Hatching comes in handy with markers and pens, as I will discuss in the next chapter. Experiment more with these techniques as you get more comfortable coloring.

Gradations

Gradations are transitions of one color into a lighter or deeper version of itself OR a blend of one color into another through pressure changes, layers, or different variations of a color.

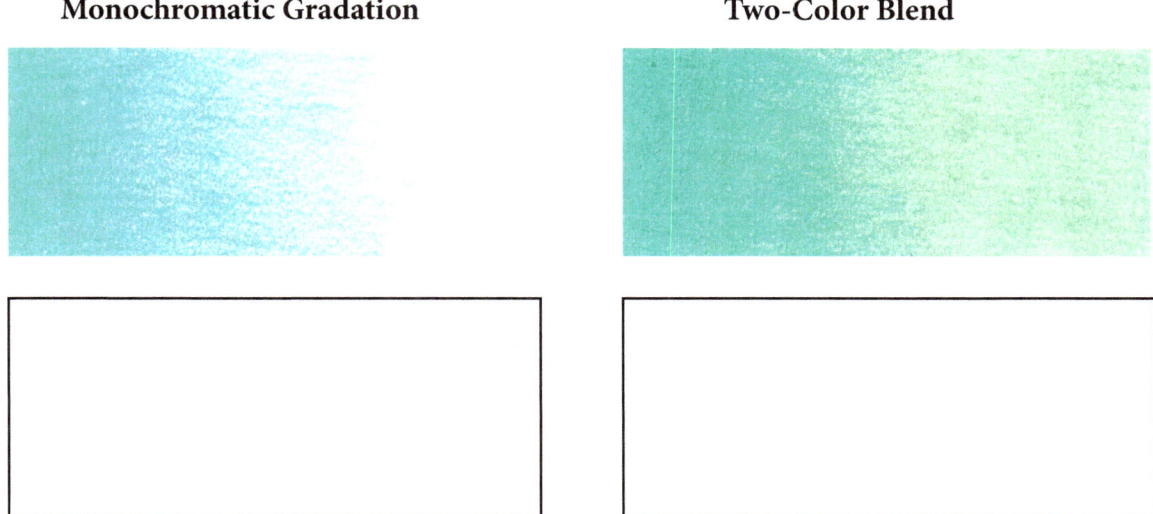

| Monochromatic Gradation | Two-Color Blend |

Try your own gradations and blends. Don't push too hard.

Pencil pressure

The amount of weight or force that is applied while drawing or coloring is called *pencil pressure*. The suggested amount is based on the brand and type of pencil or effect desired. Polychromos will require more pressure than Prismacolors, for example. Some inexpensive, or student grade pencils have very hard leads without much pigment. I find it more difficult to achieve a smooth, high-contrast drawing with these kinds of pencils. Take this into consideration when you decide to purchase your first set of pencils. I'd suggest buying a smaller set of a recommended brand over a huge set of an unknown one. You can always add to your collection, pencil by pencil.

Layers and Burnishing

As a general rule, I ALWAYS use several light coatings as opposed to heavy pressure in a single *layer*. Unfortunately, with waxy colored pencils sometimes too much is applied at the beginning, and there is no going back. Applying a lot of pressure and creating a blended and sometimes waxy or shiny surface with little "tooth" showing through is referred to as *burnishing*. It is often done with a colorless blender or lighter color. Burnishing can be very beautiful on the right project and give your work a finished look. It should always be saved for the end of your coloring, as it is difficult to erase, and the risk of damaging the paper texture, or worse yet tearing it is greater. It is very possible to be successful with moderate burnishing. However, just remember that it can easily go too far. There is something that you want to avoid known as *wax bloom* – a cloudy, white covering that can occur on the surface of paper when using wax-based colored pencils. These pencils have a tendency to build up quickly, and this is one reason that I prefer to use mixed media if a project permits (see more about this in Chapter 7).

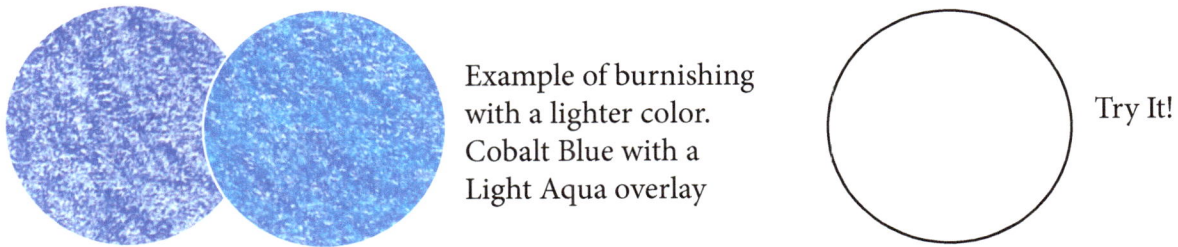

Example of burnishing with a lighter color. Cobalt Blue with a Light Aqua overlay

Try It!

Colorless blenders

These wax only blending tools can be very useful to smooth some grainy looking transitions, but I must warn you to use them sparingly. If you aren't careful in your blending, it can result in muddy looking colors or a loss of contrast. Beginners might not realize that the idea is not to coat a drawing with a blender – it is used to refine areas instead.

Very Important: Keep your blender pencil clean to avoid contamination of color! Overuse of a blender can also cause a drawing to lose its character. Blenders burnish the surface of a drawing to blend the colors, filling in most of the tooth of the paper. When a surface gets too shiny, it is difficult to see subtle transitions and nuances that make a drawing beautiful. Some people use white pencil in place of a wax blender, thinking that they serve the same purpose. Be aware that white will lighten and de-intensify your colors, whereas a colorless blender will slightly deepen and intensify the color. If you are looking to create smooth transitions, I suggest gentle burnishing with a slightly lighter color than the color below on the area in which you wish to refine. Two popular brands of blenders are Prismacolor and Caran D'Ache.

 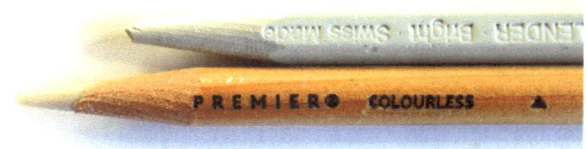

Try blending with a blender

Chapter 4: Markers and Pens

Alcohol-Based vs. Water-Based

Both marker types have advantages and disadvantages. For general coloring purposes, I prefer alcohol-based markers because of the large, clean, solid areas that are easily achieved. Blending of colors is also possible. With water-based markers, there is always a tendency to streak in open areas. However, water-based markers work well for small areas and are much safer to use than alcohol-based markers in coloring books that are printed double-sided. For these books, an alcohol-based marker will likely destroy the image on the back side of the page. However, it does depend on the paper stock on which the books are printed, as some are more absorbent than others. I always recommend testing them out in an inconspicuous area first, to see if markers bleed through (as in the bottom picture). If you are coloring in a book that is single-sided (which all of my coloring books are thus far) you can use most any marker along with a blotter page – chip board or card stock in between pages to catch any extra ink – and not risk destroying any pages. Choose what marker type to use based upon your needs. See the effects in photos to the right of both water and alcohol-based markers, on both the fronts and backs of each page.

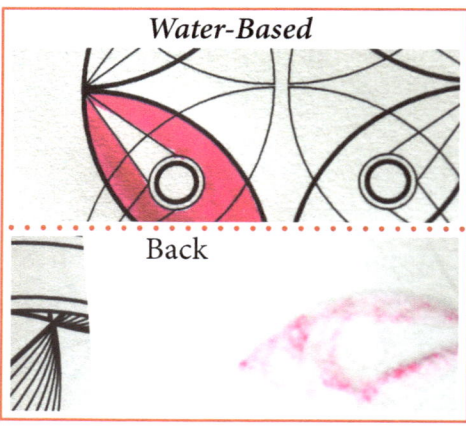

Water-Based

Back

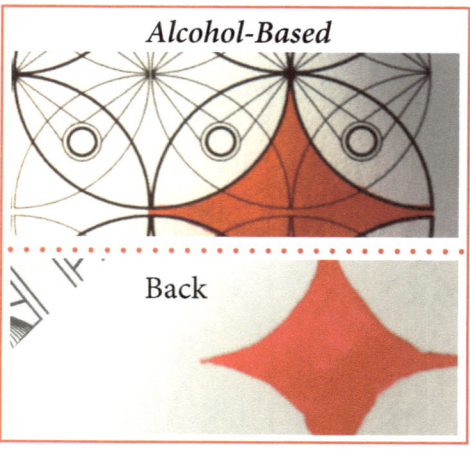

Alcohol-Based

Back

Markers & Pens: Varying Tip Types

The marker I reach for most often is a brush marker because of its many uses. Copic makes a Sketch brush-tip/chisel-tip combo marker, which comes in over 300 colors. It is easy to hold and is encased in an oval-cylinder barrel, which prevents it from rolling off of a table. It provides buttery smooth color with no "drag" and great versatility! Brush markers are fabulous for getting into tight spaces. Broad chisel tips are great for filling in large areas quickly. One of the best features is that these are refillable, and the nibs are replaceable! Copic also makes their original marker with a square plastic barrel, which has a fine tip/broad chisel tip combo. They also produce some less expensive round barrel markers called Ciao, which are smaller markers similar to the Sketch but with fewer colors available – however, these are great for the beginner. I also use Prismacolor markers which come in various combos of chisel tip, brush tip and fine tip. These are lovely markers and usually cost a little less than Copic's high-end markers. They are also often easier to find, as Copic's sometimes end up on backorder due to their popularity. In any case, you can get both of these brands as sets or sold as open stock. If you are on a limited budget and just beginning your coloring journey, Bic makes marker sets, and Sharpies come in a plethora of colors sold both individually and as sets.

I usually use directional, hatching strokes when applying marker to an open area. By this, I mean that my strokes "mirror" or follow the shape of the section I am coloring, as opposed to just randomly coloring it in or using circular strokes. The larger the strokes the less streaking.

For special effects, I enjoy stippling on certain projects – by making tiny dots to fill up a space (often confused with Pointillism which was an actual movement in art where dots were painted strategically to achieve an overall appearance of color). See an example on the next page. For stippling or outlining a shape, I use water-based fineliners, such as Maped Graph'Peps or Staedtler Triplus. For rich black permanent lines, I prefer to use waterproof Pigma Microns or Copic Multi Liners.

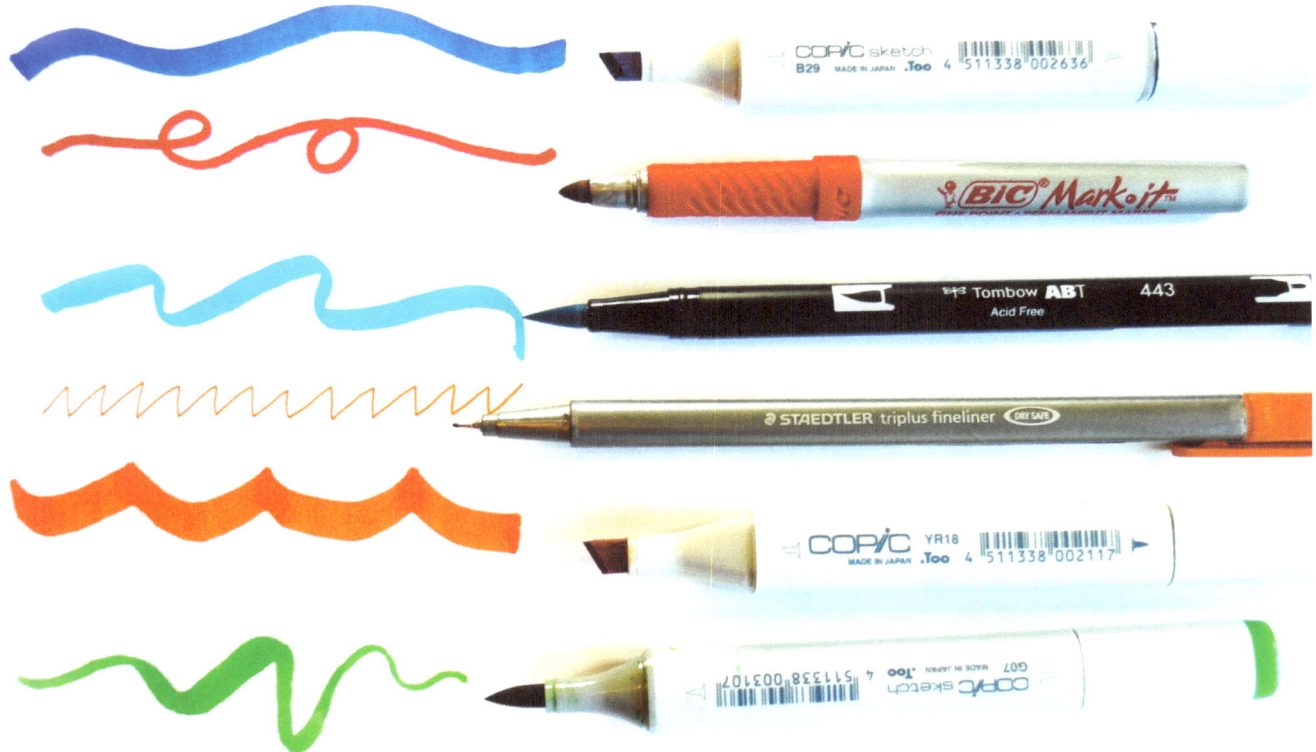

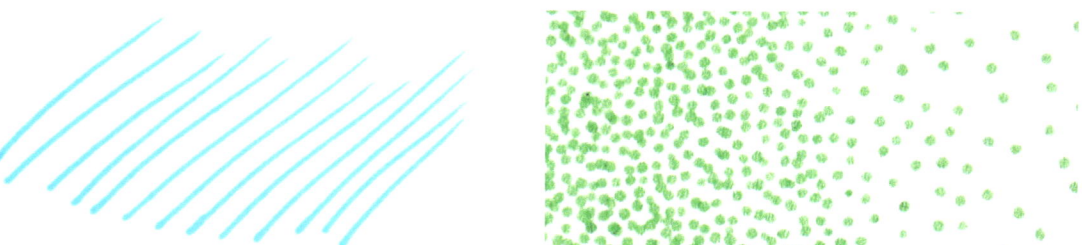

Hatching   Stippling

Gel pens

Gel pens have many different purposes. Some are opaque and cover over dark surfaces easily. Others come in metallic and glitter form too. For adding a bit of twinkle I love my Gelly Roll Stardust pens. For adding highlights to colored pencil drawings I most often reach for my Uniball Signo because of its opaque milky consistency. Test your gel pens on the toned sampler page and use them on the coloring pages in the back of this book.

Chapter 5: Other Necessities

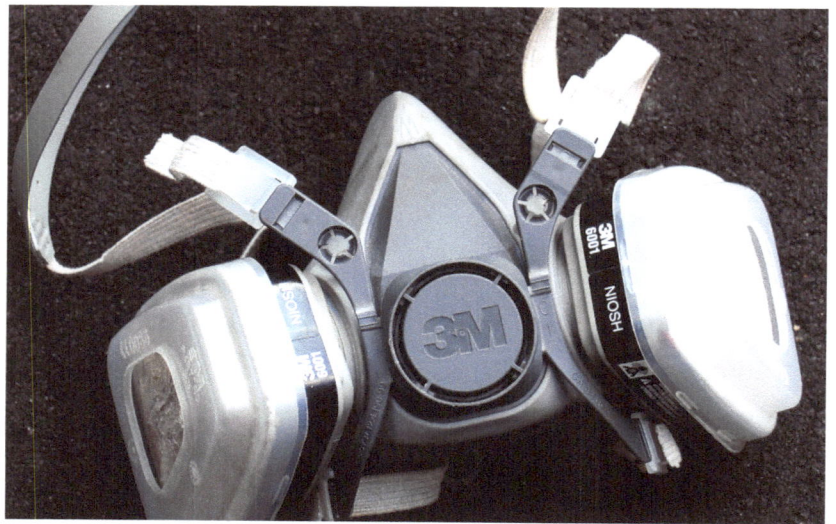

Fixative, Mask, Ventilation

These are important items to have on hand if you plan to use pastels or even eye shadow on your backgrounds! Fixative will not make it rub-proof, but it will help prevent the pigmented dust from falling or brushing off. Some people report having negative experiences, such as darkening of the colors in a drawing, so I always recommend testing it out on a rough drawing with the same colors first. This way you will understand how it will behave. When I use fixative, I spray my work at the very end, but it can be used intermittently if it is the "workable" type. I have used Krylon workable fixative for years, so it is safe to say that I'd recommend it for most pieces, however, many artists have had success with SpectraFix, which is a non-toxic and non-aerosol fixative made especially for pastels. Some people even mix up their own fixatives and store them in simple spray bottles, although I would recommend a lot of experimentation if you are going to go that route. In any case, after it is dry, I recommend placing your art behind acetate or glass to prevent it from getting destroyed. It is important to follow the directions on the can carefully.

Test spray your can a few times before spraying your masterpieces, and keep an appropriate distance to avoid drips. Any brand of aerosol spray fix or even spray paint could sputter, so go lightly, and discard the can before you hit the very end. Keep your nozzle clean too. You must also use a well-ventilated area, or simply go outside, when using a product such as an aerosol fixative. A charcoal mask is recommended (as pictured).

Erasers

Although colored pencil isn't meant to be erased like graphite is, if you use lighter pressure when drawing and coloring to begin with, it is easier to remove unwanted color. For small mistakes and subtle lightening, I would recommend a kneaded eraser or a white rubber eraser and a white eraser pen. It is important to keep your erasers clean to avoid color contamination.

I love to use erasers to gently pull out areas of colored pencil…not necessarily to erase them, but just to lighten them up and to smooth the color. This technique works best with kneaded erasers. They start out square, and once manipulated, immediately look like gray chewing gum! To use them for this purpose, take a piece the size of the area you'd like to lighten. Push it down with all of your weight on the drawing, being careful to cover the entire shape. Then gently pull it up from one side to the other. You will see some of the "lifted" color on the underside of the eraser once you remove it from the drawing. It is important to clean the eraser before using it again, to avoid color contamination onto another drawing. To do this, "knead" the eraser by stretching and folding the dirty parts inward! Vôila…it's like new!

I also use an eraser pen that I have dubbed my "secret weapon"! It has a white eraser so it doesn't leave a trail of color on my art. It is tiny so it can get into small spaces. I use this to "pull" highlights and to clean up little boo-boos. It is called a Tombow Mono Zero. It is an amazing tool!

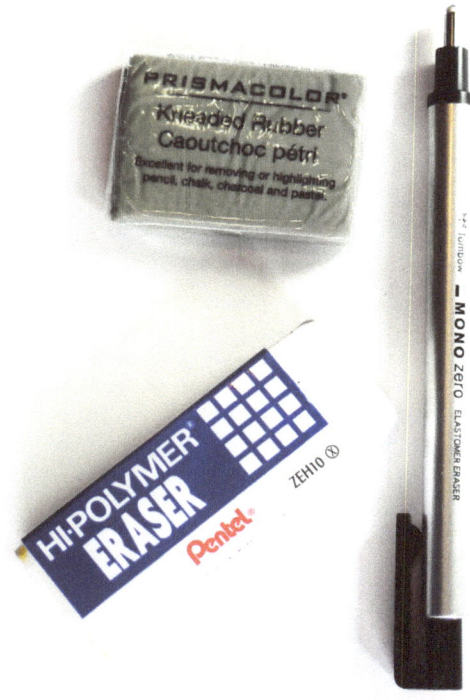

Pencil Sharpeners

At times I will use my old electric sharpener very carefully. Oftentimes I start a brand new blunt pencil with it. After the initial sharpening I prefer to use a manual sharpener. The benefit is that more of the pencil is preserved since I have more control, so it will likely last longer. I like my T'Gaal sharpener a lot – it's a popular one amongst colorists, but I also love my Maped Galactic 1-Hole Sharpener! It has a special eject button for broken leads.

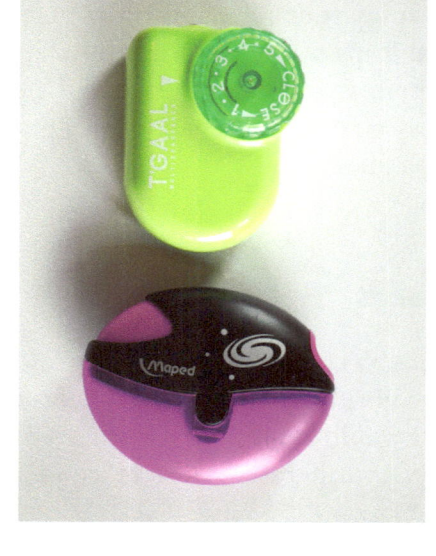

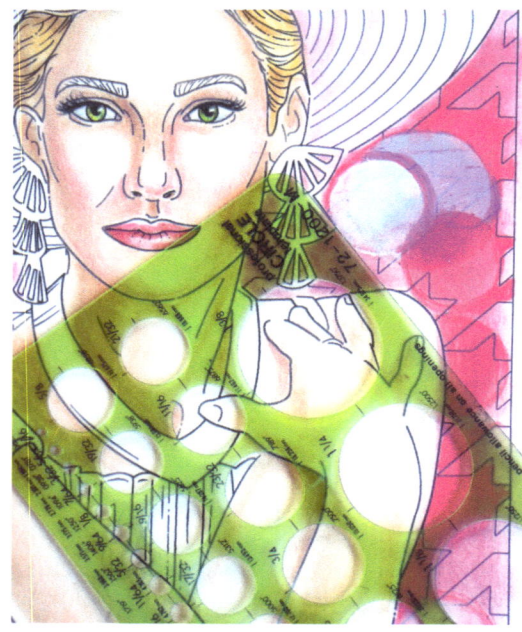

Stencils & Templates

Drafting stencils can come in handy when adding background details. It is easy to fill in a large space using a repeating pattern (such as the Bokeh effect). You can cut out your own in card stock, or purchase a repeating-shape sheet or a whole set that is made of a durable plastic.

PanPastel/Chalk Pastel

If you enjoy the look of soft smooth backgrounds or want to learn special effects such as Bokeh and stamping, you may want to invest in some pastels. I adore my PanPastels with Sofft tool because of their versatility and ability to transform drawings into almost life-like images due to the smoothing they provide.

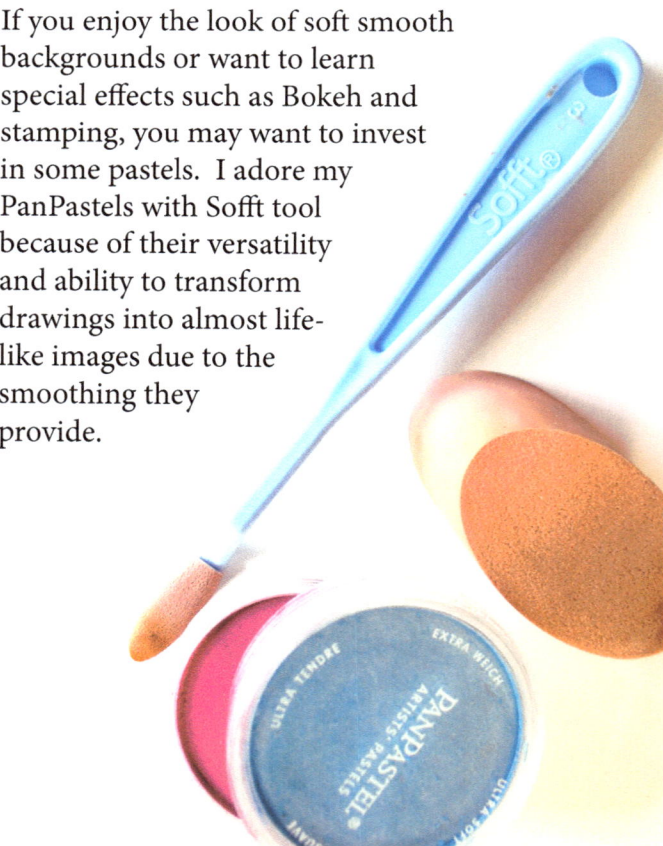

Paint Brushes

You may want to invest in a few fine paint brushes for painting tiny details such as highlights as opposed to drawing them. You can also use them to smooth out gel pen lines, but you must always be careful to clean them properly after use.

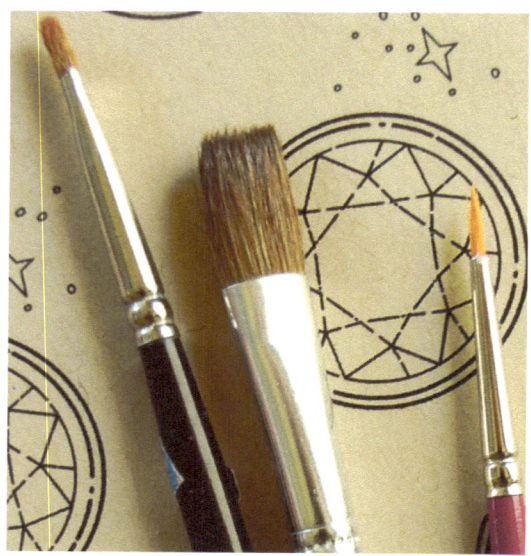

Chapter 6: Non-Traditional Materials

Have you tried...

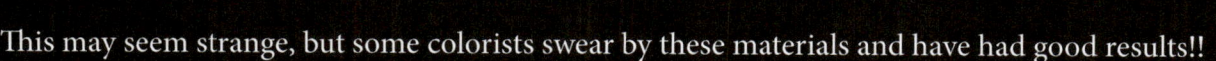

* *Vaseline or baby oil to mix and smooth colored pencils*
* *Hairspray in place of fixative*
* *Eye shadow in place of pastels*

This may seem strange, but some colorists swear by these materials and have had good results!!

Experimenting is fun...just remember to use at your own risk!

There's nothing wrong with trying something new and different. I am always encouraging my students to push further – think outside of the box.

If you are on a strict budget, these materials may even work really well for you if you aren't concerned with the longevity of your art. If you are simply looking to inexpensively and quickly create coloring pages or drawings for the sole purpose of taking snapshots to share on social media (see Sharing chapter), or just to de-stress, then go for it! If you plan to gift someone with a beautiful drawing that you'd like to last for years without worrying about fading or yellowing, then I'd suggest sticking with traditional art supplies. No one knows the long-term effects of these non-art supplies on our art.

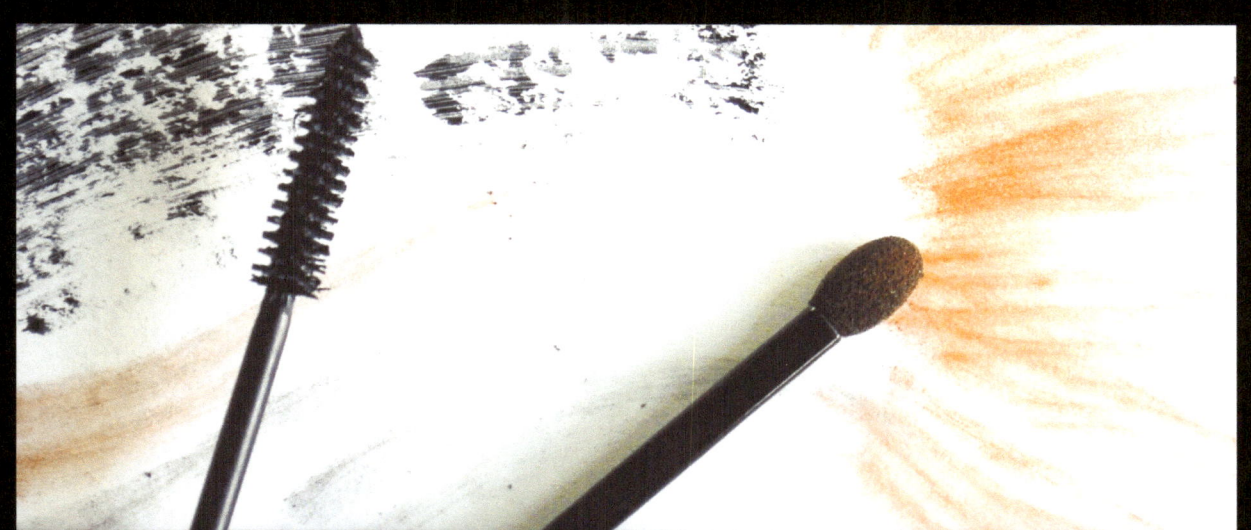

Chapter 7: Time-Saving Tips, and Techniques for Maximum Impact

DO use mixed media! One very important illustrator's trick that I learned in art school is to use a light layer of marker under layers of colored pencil. The result of this process is threefold:

1. Smoother, richer color because the tooth of the paper is completely saturated by the marker.
2. There's significantly less wax build up – the top layer of colored pencil sits on above, making it pop!
3. The drawing or coloring is completed in much less time too! It's a win-win-win. It also lessens the chances of wax bloom, which was explained in Chapter 3, Colored Pencils. Of course, as stated earlier it is important to know, if you are using a coloring book, if it is double-sided and to test the paper for bleeding.

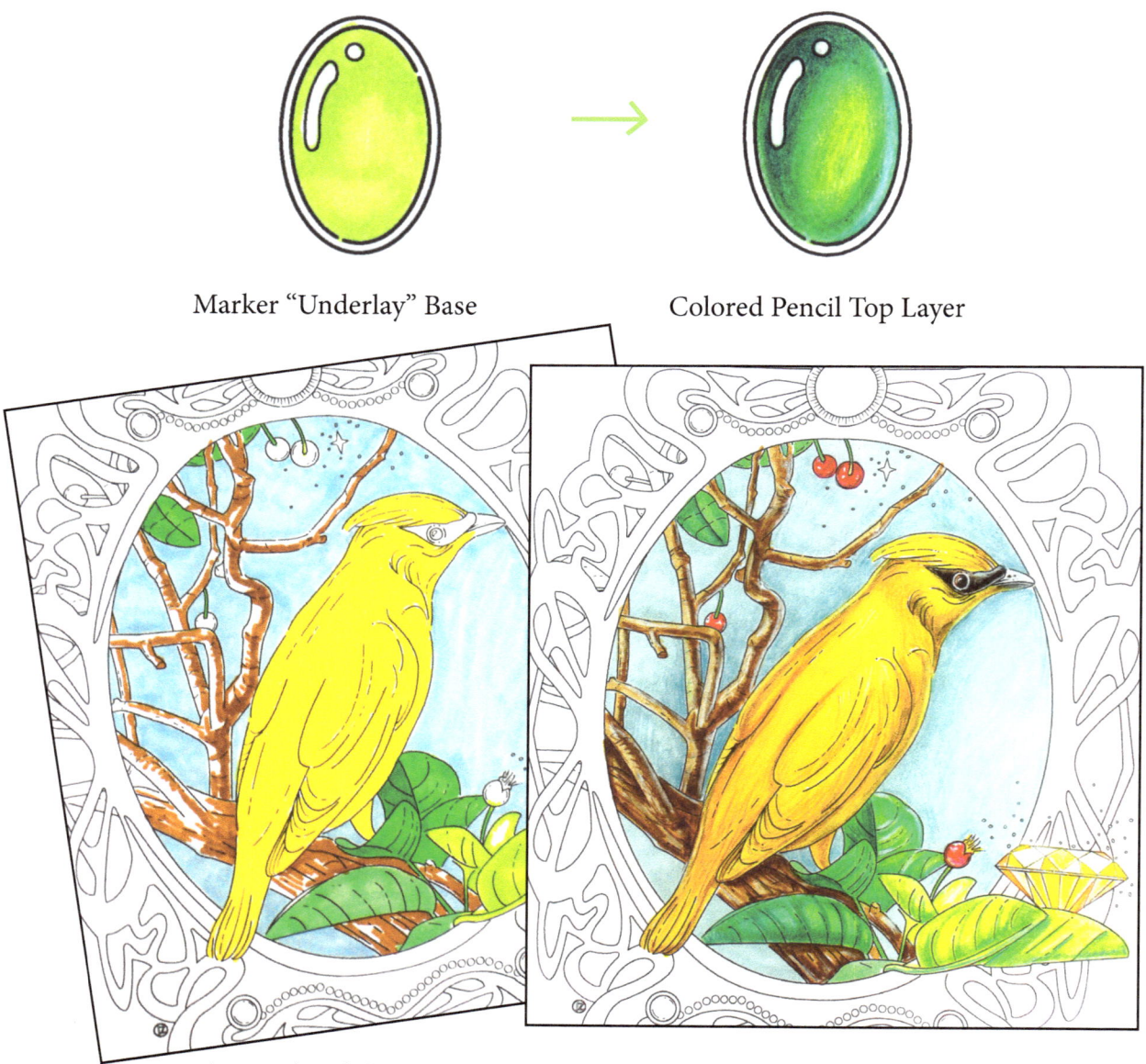

Marker "Underlay" Base Colored Pencil Top Layer

A completed drawing with a marker base and colored pencil top layer.

* *DO use larger tools!* Use larger tools for larger areas. If you are trying to cover a huge space with a fineliner, it will take an enormous amount of time (not to mention, wreak havoc on your wrists). Instead, use a large marker and do details in fineliner over top.

* *DO rotate your page as you color!* Most realistic drawings are colored so that the lines are often directional to go with the shape of the objects being colored. I often color upside down. :) It is impossible to create a smooth texture without turning your paper. Rotating saves a lot of time and allows you to get into tiny spaces without getting into uncomfortable positions. It makes for effective coloring!

* *DO stay organized!* Keep all of your coloring supplies in one area. It's best to have a system of organization in place so that you don't need to go looking for things when you need them. Cups work well for pencils but not as well for pens and markers – it is best to store those horizontally so the ink doesn't dry out. Bins and drawer sets are always nice to keep your space tidy. Keep your coloring pages organized! If you like to remove them from books, you can easily place them within plastic sleeves in three-ring binders on shelves once they are completed. Keep your WIP on a clipboard, for easy reach.

* *DO have sharp pencils ready!* You can initially "pre-sharpen" your pencils with an electric sharpener and just sharpen the points as they dull with a small hand-held sharpener.

* *DO experiment!* Try new mediums. Get inspired! Or just give yourself a break and use crayons! Crayons can be used for coloring large spaces too. Plus it's fun to feel like a kid again... and very affordable as well.

* *DO compare yourself with yourself, and no one other!* Never compare your skills to others. It's not healthy. But get in the habit of looking back at your old work. Compare it to your new work. After several tutorials you will gain confidence. This book will help! You will be amazed at your progress.

* *DO take a break! Don't throw it away!* Most of my coloring friends will agree. If it's not going well...STOP. Come back later. Don't toss your art! You wouldn't believe what I've come close to throwing away but didn't – thankfully. Sometimes it's good to let your eyes adjust and come back and review your progress at a later point. You might be surprised.

* *DO use reference!* There is nothing wrong with using photo reference to assist in making something look realistic. Professional illustrators do it! They often hire photographers to shoot pictures for them. There are several websites with no-cost royalty free photos that are available for personal use.

* *DO save space and put a smile on someone else's face!* Are you looking to get rid of clutter? Perhaps some of your colored pages or books that you just don't care for? You can use them in many crafts, like making bows for gifts...or better yet, donate them to local nursing homes and shelters or to Facebook groups that collect them for the purpose of distributing them to cancer patients and other medical facilities to brighten the days of their patients. Some of these groups also allow exchanging of books between members.

Chapter 8: Coloring Simplified

Whatever supplies you are using, as a general rule of thumb, I always recommend starting off with your lighter colors and then working your way to darker ones. It is much more difficult to work backwards in most cases, and it can be very challenging to remove mistakes.

Parts of Light – Drawing with Dimension (Form)

Form is the illusion of dimensionality. The following lesson is the single most important one that I learned in art school. New artists very commonly place their shadows incorrectly! Learning where to place highlights and shadows will make your drawings come to life! I took this lesson with me as a student and shared this knowledge later as a teacher. I've taught this drawing theory to every age group that I have worked with. Light defines objects in space. Without it everything is flat. If you take anything with you from this book, let it be this. If realism is what you are after then you must understand the "Parts of Light" and learn the terms, as I will apply them to other lessons in this book. Please keep in mind that highly reflective surfaces and those that are translucent will throw these rules right out the window. These guides will apply to the majority of opaque, organic forms you wish to color. I will diagram on the commonly used model of a sphere for the simplest explanation:

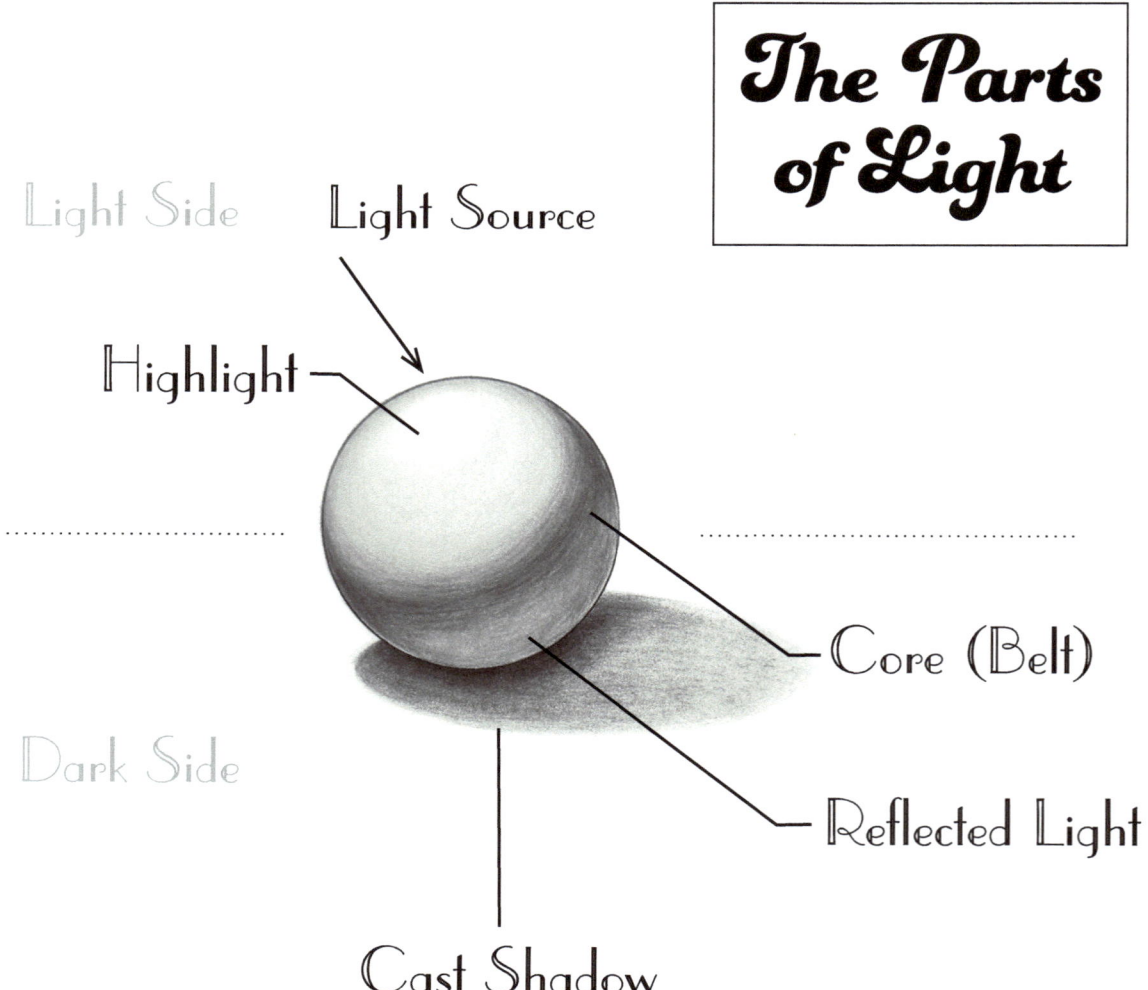

Light Side   Light Source

Highlight

Dark Side

Core (Belt)

Reflected Light

Cast Shadow

The Parts of Light

We must first start with a source of light. When we talk about using a direct *light source*, as opposed to a diffused one, this is what you need to know:

After determining where your light will be coming from (arrow), note that the sphere is divided into two distinct sides – the *light side* and the *dark side*. The *highlight* is the lightest section of the *light side*. It is the point where the most direct light is received. The darkest part of the whole object itself (not including the *cast shadow*) is the *core shadow*, or as I call it, the "belt". The *core* is what divides the two sides but ultimately rests on the Dark Side. It is not at the bottom edge of the sphere!! That is where the *reflected light* should go. *Reflected light* is light that has bounced off of a surface or another object back onto the sphere. It is lighter than the *core* but darker than anything on the light side. Finally, you must not forget to add a *cast shadow* on the opposite side of the object from where the light is coming on to the surface on which the ball or object is sitting. Unless the ball that you are drawing is a very dark gray or a black ball, the darkest part of your whole drawing will likely be right under the ball where your *cast shadow* begins. If your *light source* is on the upper left (as in the diagram), then your shadow will be on the lower right and vice versa. This will help to plant your object on to a surface and give it believable form and dimensionality.

Extra: Learn and memorize this phrase that I learned in college from one of my toughest yet most influential teachers – my illustration professor, Gerry...

"The lightest light in the dark is always darker than the darkest dark in the light."

This statement means that even though it is important to add *reflected light*, one must keep the dark side dark enough to "tuck under" or it will look flatter by competing with the light side. It may take a while for this to sink in, but it really holds true.

Now, think about all of the objects you draw or color. Go back and look at your oldest work. Where is the shadow? Is there a light source? Do the objects look like they have form?

. . . .

Lime Green Sphere

On the next page you'll find a step-by-step tutorial on creating a Lime Green Sphere. Following the tutorial is a colored pencil practice page.

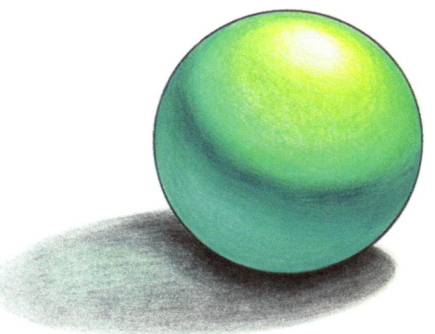

You will need:

-Prismacolor Premier colored pencils:

Chartreuse 989	Cool Grey 70% 1065
Spring Green 913	Cool Grey 20% 1060
True Green 910	Indigo Blue 901
Peacock Green 907	Black 935
Parrot Green 1006	Blender 1077

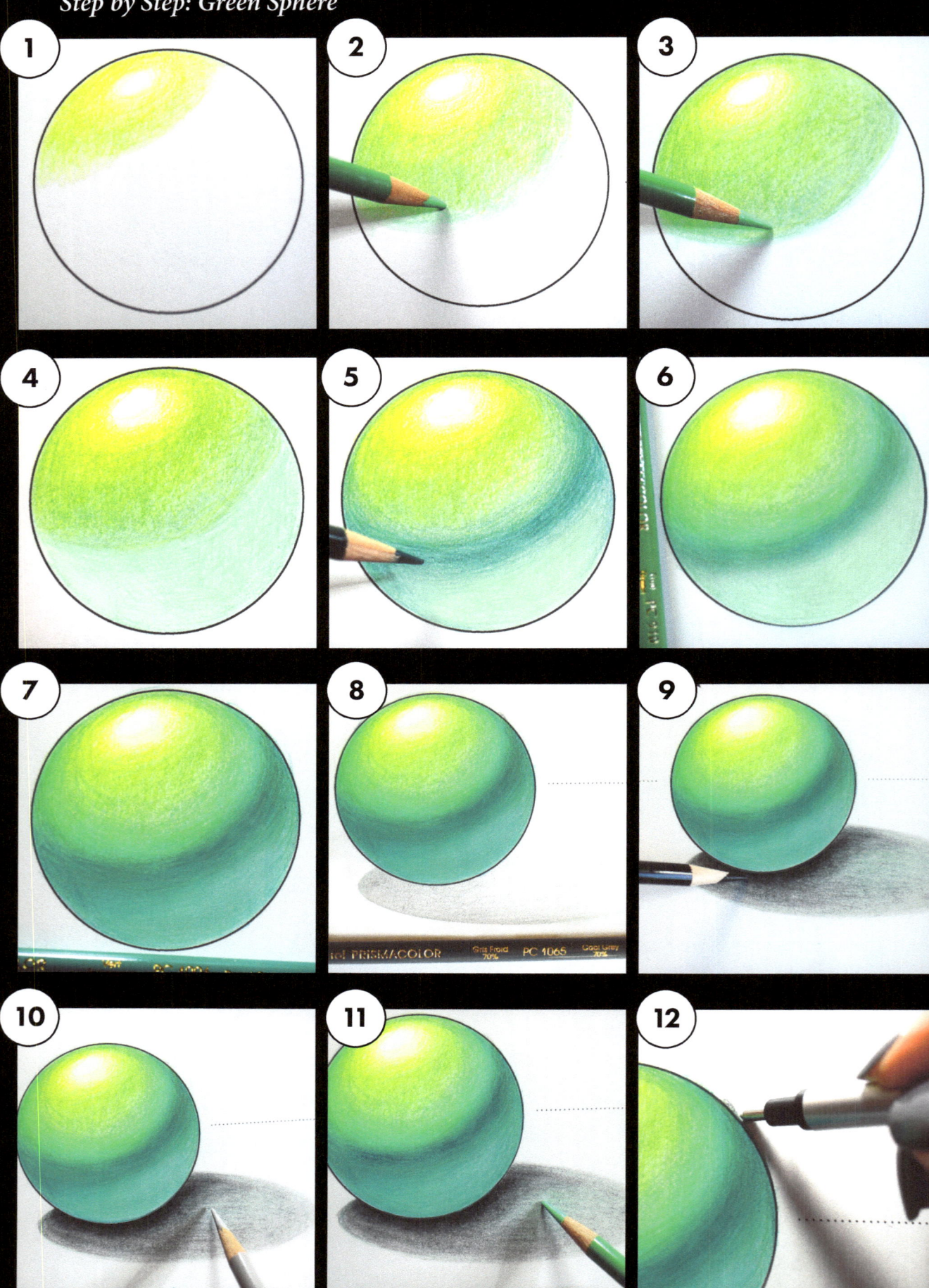

1. I start off leaving a white space where the *highlight* should be (the lightest spot of the whole sphere). I circle around it outward, using light pressure with Chartreuse, then with Spring Green away from the *highlight*, being careful not to cover up the first color. Only the Chartreuse should circle the white. I use some small circular motions to fill in this area.

2-3. Next, I work down toward the center of the sphere curving down in the middle. I add in True Green, 910, blending the two colors, but not covering up all of it – Then as I continue downward I add True Green until about the mid-point. I then add a second layer. I use more circular motions as well as longer "U" shape strokes across the sphere from side to side.

4. I add a light layer of True Green to the bottom half of the sphere, being sure not to go too heavy.

5-6. Across the center of the sphere I begin to lightly add a cooler, darker green called Peacock Green 907 from side to side, forming a "belt" as I call it across the "belly" of the sphere. This is the *core*. I smooth it out by burnishing it with 910 slightly.

7. I then darken the bottom half of the sphere with Parrot Green 1006, blending it into the core as well. I darken the core again, as needed with 907. The bottom crescent is called the *reflected light*.

8-9. I lightly use the darker grey 1065 to create an *ellipse* shape for the shadow. I fill it in, keeping the edges on the right soft and blurry. I use Black right under the sphere itself, blending it to the right just a little.

10. I use the lighter grey 1060 on top to smooth out the color of the main part of the *cast shadow* and add a hint of 910 too. (Shadows often have a bit of color reflecting into them from the objects casting them).

11-12. A touch of Indigo Blue 901 over the *core* blended with 907, helps deepen just a little. I use my Mono Zero eraser to clean up little boo-boos and to pull a little more white into the *highlight* and it is complete!

**Now, if it's not perfect, don't fret. Try again. It gets better each time. I promise.

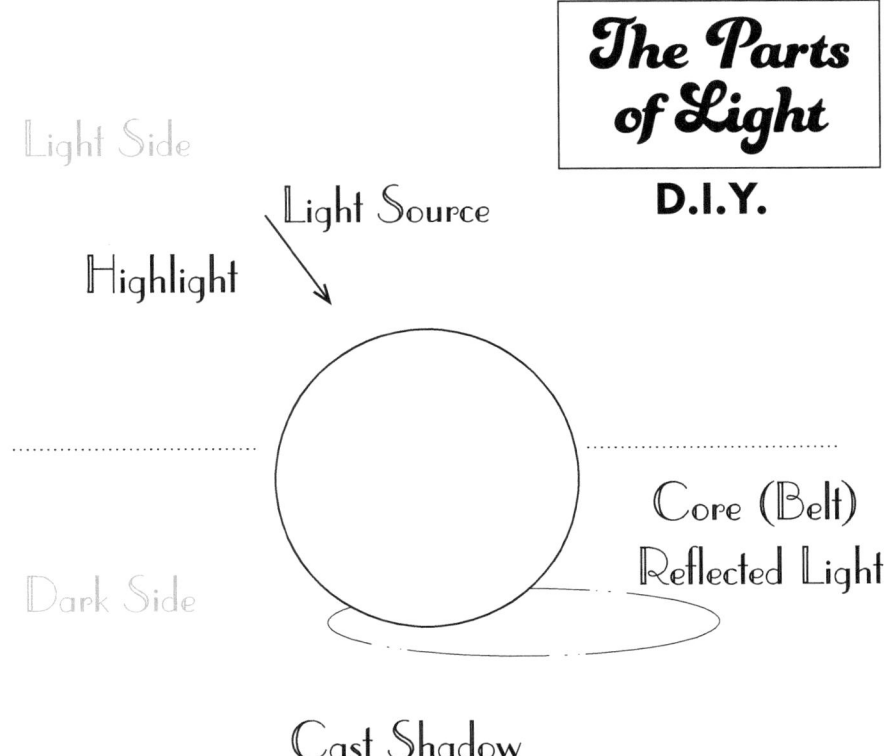

Use a blotter page under this page if you are going to
use marker on the previous page

I will demonstrate color theory using the Primary Color, Magenta, so it is understandable how it is affected by other values and colors.

Value - The lightness or darkness of a color.
Value can be measured on a scale from 0-100%, with "0" representing white and "100" representing black. Every color has a value, but sometimes it is difficult to compare values of colors because of their intensity or saturation.

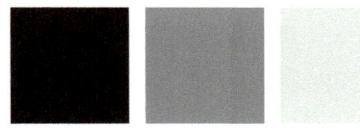

Hue - Another word for color

Tint - A hue plus white
A color can be lightened and made less intense by adding white

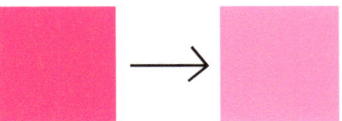

Tone - A hue plus gray
A color can be neutralized with gray, to keep the same value, but change the intensity or saturation. Colors can also be neutralized by using their color-wheel opposites, otherwise known as their "complements"

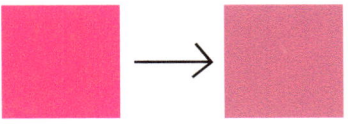

Shade - A hue plus black
A color can be darkened and made less intense by using black. If the goal is to keep the some of the intensity of a color while darkening it, instead of black, use a darker version of the same hue

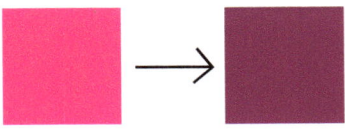

Color Temperature - A hue's "visual temperature"
Cool vs. Warm - warm colors bring objects forward, while cool colors make objects recede. If you want an object to look 3-D, consider where you place colors

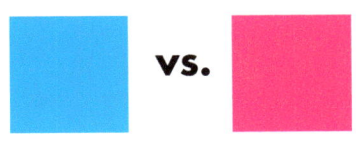

Color Intensity/Saturation/Chroma - the brightness and pureness of a color, full strength
Color intensity will change if tints, tones and shades are added

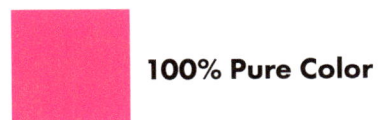

100% Pure Color

CMYK Color Wheel

This is the same special color wheel that I've taught for many years. Instead of the standard Primary Colors: Blue, Yellow, Red, you can see the names are a little different. (C) Cyan, (M) Magenta, and (Y) Yellow are very specific versions of Primary colors. They are in their purest form and truly cannot be mixed by any other colors. This is why my color wheel looks a lot brighter than most! This wheel yields all colors. In fact, your ink jet printer probably prints such vivid photos by using these exact ink colors...plus Black (known as K). You can make neutrals by mixing opposites across the wheel, otherwise known as complements, and much more. Make your own color wheel in the back of the book!

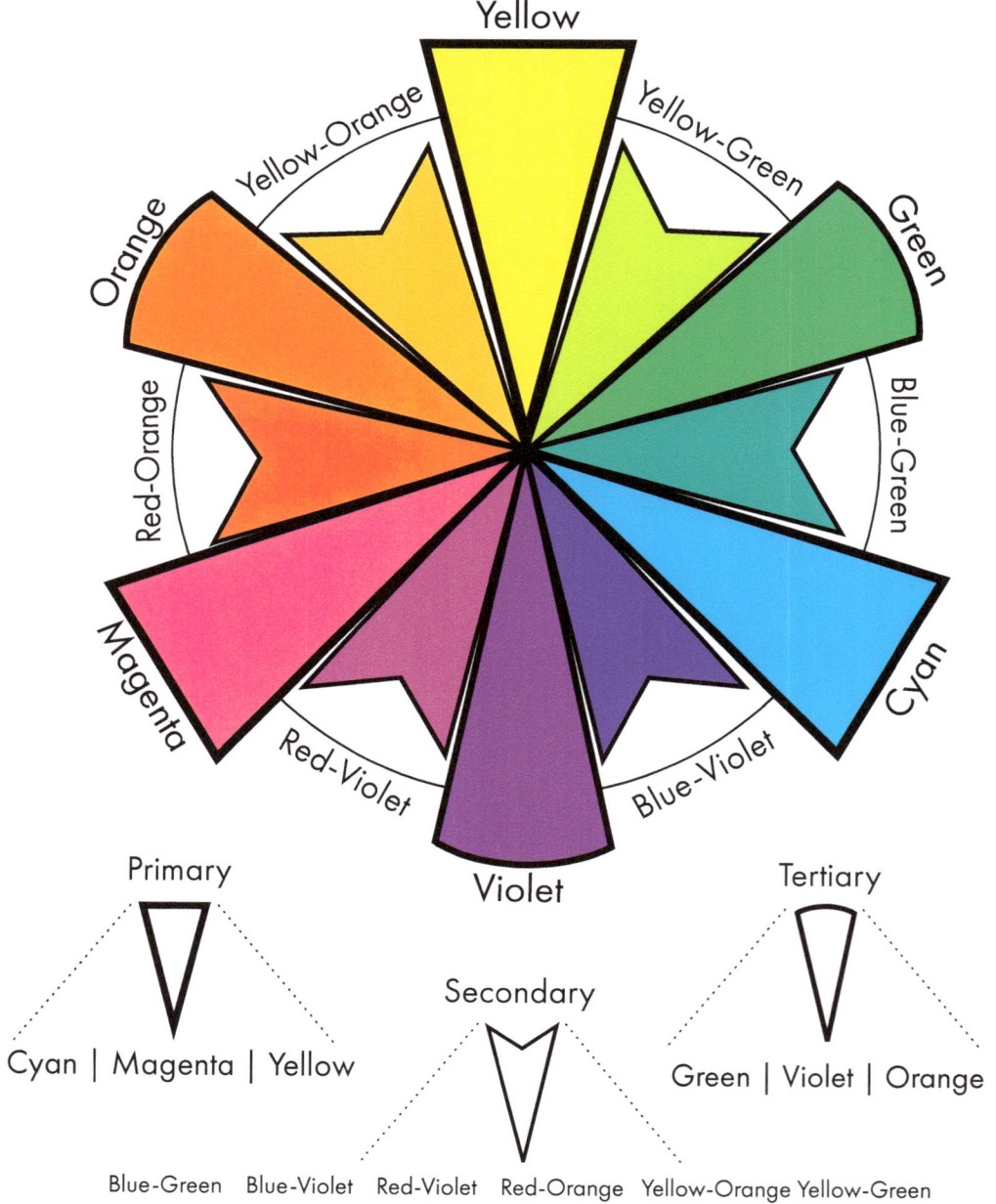

Color Temperature's Effects

Color has visual temperature. Greens and blues are cool (think of the ocean being cool). Reds and yellows are warm (like the sun or fire). When deciding upon colors to use, think about what your desired result is. Try this: study the pictures below. This bird coloring page has been colored twice. It is almost exactly the same with exception of the color and intensity of the bird, the gem, and the berries. Can you see how the effects are different? Try squinting and looking at both, one at a time. In which picture does the bird stand out more? Where is the first place that your eye goes to in either coloring? Why do you think this happens?

In the yellow-bird version your eye was likely drawn to the yellow bird or gem, or better yet the red berry! You may not have noticed the blue bird first in the blue-bird version. The leaves all the way to the right in the foreground are one of the warmest colors, as is the tree -- they stand out. But wait! Green is still a cool color! How can that be? Green is just not as cool as blue is. Warmer and more intense colors have a tendency to jump out at us. It's all relative. Artists use these tricks all of the time to direct your eyes! Were you drawn to the cover of this book? Why do you think?

warmest

warmest

Which of the three circles is warmest?

Color palettes

There are many color palettes that artists use to create certain moods or to serve a certain purpose. Bold, bright colors command attention. Complementary colors are often used in advertising to lead your eye to a product. Cool colors are soothing and calming. Warm colors create energy. Beyond that there are many combinations of colors that are actually related "scientifically" by plotting them on the color wheel. Here are a few commonly used palettes: Monochromatic - one color + black and white; Complementary - two colors across the wheel; Analogous - neighboring colors; Triadic - three equidistant colors.

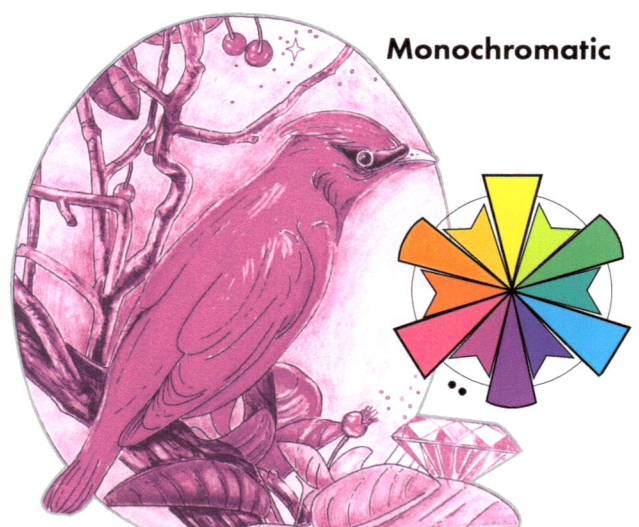

Monochromatic

Red-Violet + Black + White

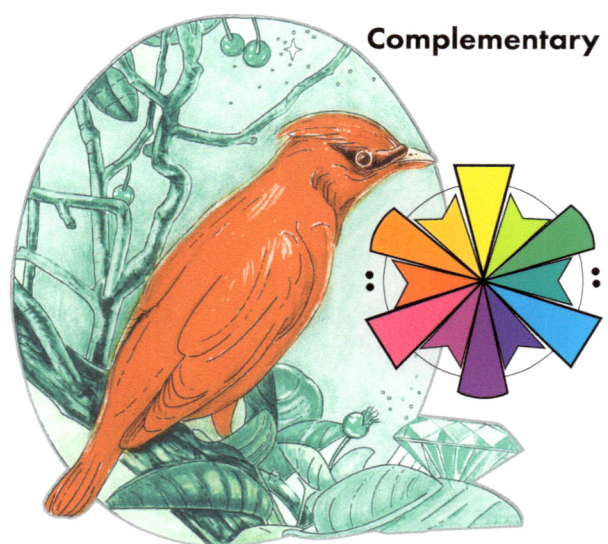

Complementary

Red-Orange + Blue-Green + Black + White

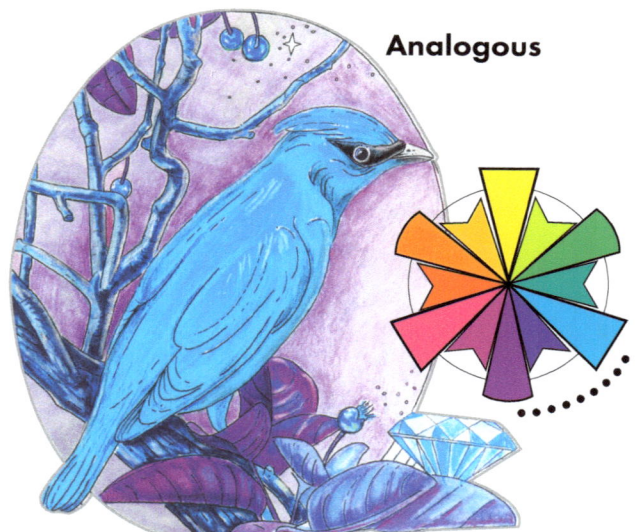

Analogous

Violet + Blue-Violet + Cyan + Black + White

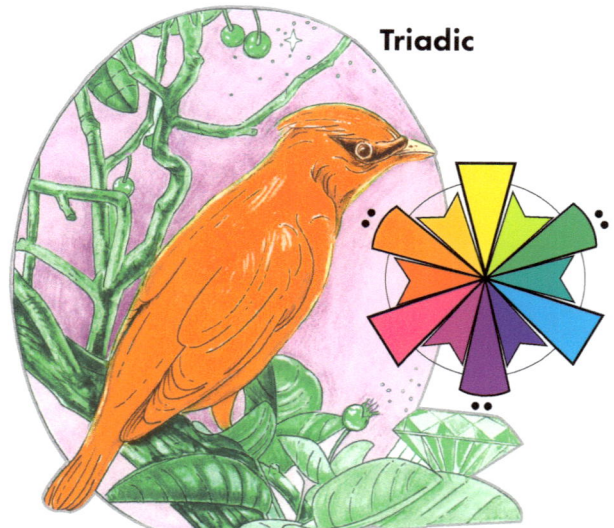

Triadic

Orange + Green + Violet + Black + White

For more in-depth possibilities, it's easy to go online for color inspiration. Many palettes are available for inspiration. There are several websites on which you can search for palettes. Try **www.design-seeds.com** or **colorpalettes.net** Be sure to read the terms of use for each.

Try coloring the bird using a few different palettes. The backside of this page is not printed to prevent damage in the event that you should choose to use markers.
It is recommended that you use a blotter page beneath it.

Palette Name or Type:

Colors Used

Palette Name or Type:

Colors Used

Use a blotter page under this page if you are going to use marker on the previous page

Chapter 9: An Illustrator's Secret Techniques and Tutorials

Creating Realistic Pictures by Adding Extra Dimension

Increase the richness, depth, contrast and add shadows to your colored picture with black pencil or deep, rich hues such as Indigo Blue to make your images jump off the page! Raise your own bar.

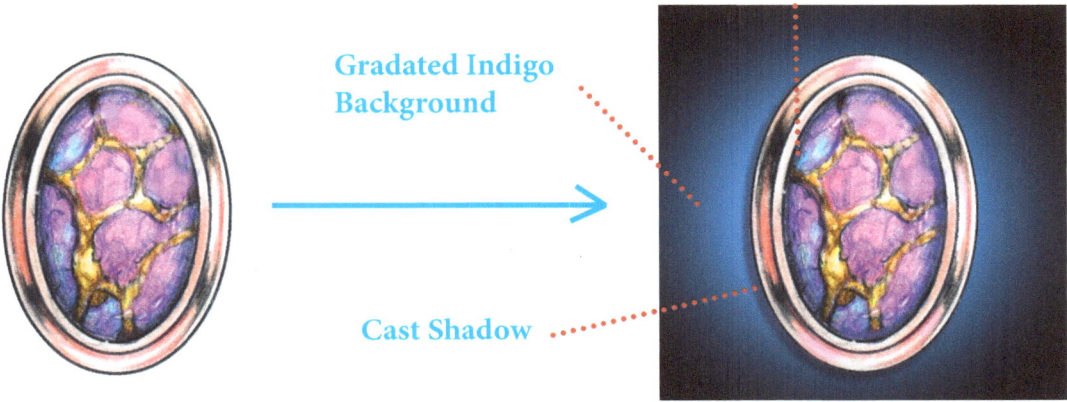

Cast Shadow

Gradated Indigo Background

Cast Shadow

Adding White Embellishments

Take it even a step further – add "pings" and reflections for a professional and finished look!

Use a white gel pen, such as a Uniball Signo, draw a cross hair or "plus" shape following the steps below, where you would see a shine. "Dot and blot" it quickly with either your finger or preferably a Precision Tip Q-Tip cotton swab. Add another layer of the same shape or just a dot in the center – but this time don't blot it, so it stays bright. Another "cross hair" can be added on top at an angle for that additional gleam. Practice! Doesn't it jump off the page?

OR

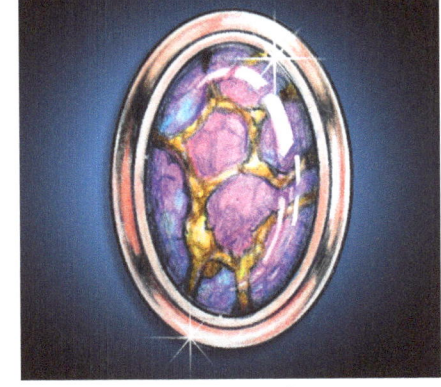

Use a very small amount white gouache/watercolor tube paint – a low-sheen opaque paint, and a very fine paintbrush, and paint your "plus" or "cross hair". The benefit: you can control the thickness of the line especially with a tiny brush.

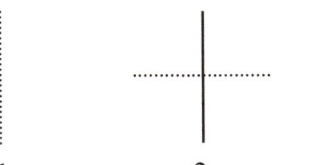

1.   2.   3.   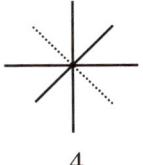 4.

See the *Mojave Turquoise tutorial* later in ***The Secrets of Coloring*** to learn how to add these reflections! Want to create rose gold? There's a tutorial for that too.

Erasing Black Lines

A significant trend in coloring right now is "erasing black lines" and replacing them with white outlines – or camouflaging them altogether with colored gel pen or some opaque paint to make the harshness of outlines disappear!

This can either be decorative, as in the first picture, or it can be used to take a coloring book line art drawing to a whole new level by removing the flatness that outlines create – ultimately making it look more like an original piece of art or even an oil painting!

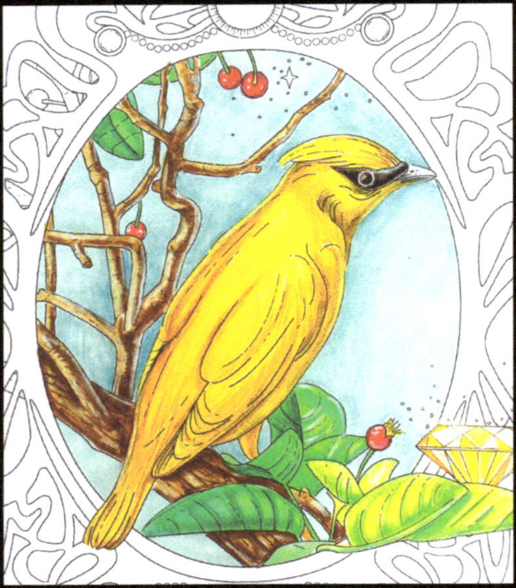

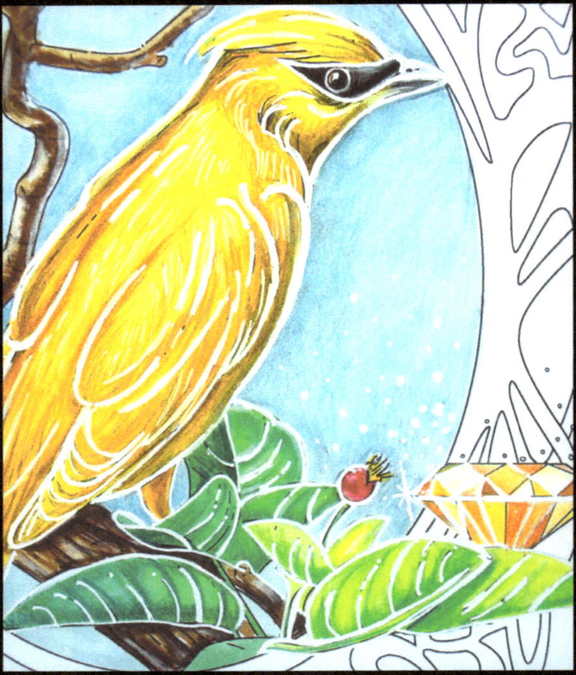

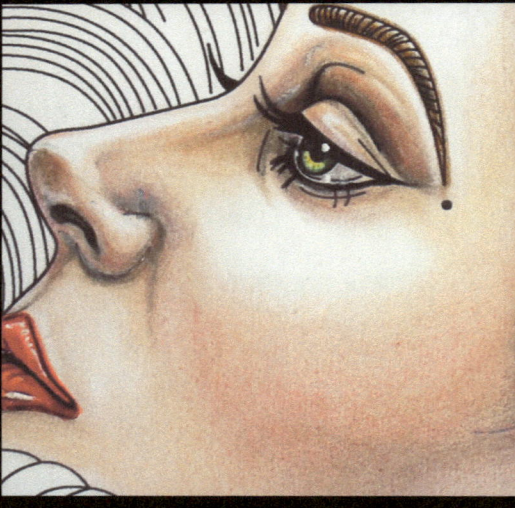

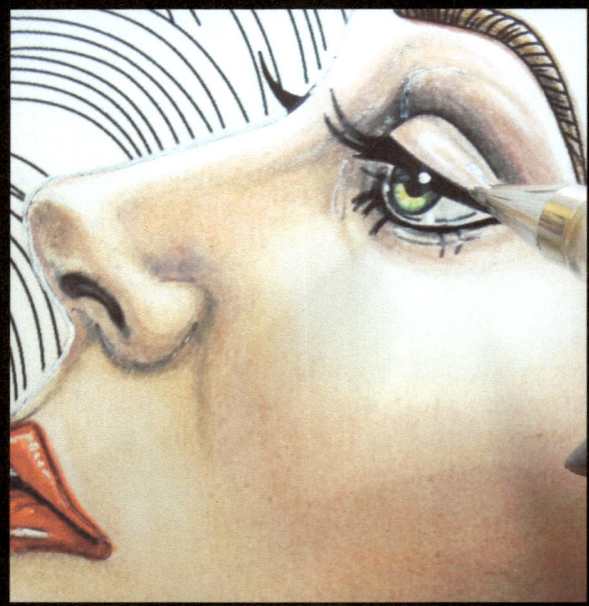

White gel pens are different by brand. I would suggest an opaque one for this technique such as a Uniball Signo.

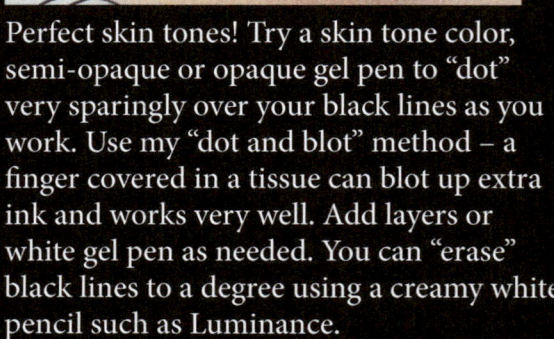

Perfect skin tones! Try a skin tone color, semi-opaque or opaque gel pen to "dot" very sparingly over your black lines as you work. Use my "dot and blot" method – a finger covered in a tissue can blot up extra ink and works very well. Add layers or white gel pen as needed. You can "erase" black lines to a degree using a creamy white pencil such as Luminance.

Did you know?

You can also print a page on a copier on a lighter setting so as not to have totally black lines. This way they are easier to cover up.

Do you prefer small spaces to color? Do you have some books with larger spaces that you don't know what to do with? Well if you don't want to donate them, customize them before you color them! Embellish them with doodles! You can fill any space with black permanent lines in different thicknesses. Try different patterns or just get creative and add designs where you see fit. You can even "tattoo" a portrait coloring page. :)

The key is to use an ink that will stay put and not smear when using your other mediums. I often use a Micron, Copic, or Faber-Castell pen for this purpose, as mentioned in the Introduction to Materials. You can certainly embellish with colored fineliners too! Just don't plan to use any wet media over them. You can always fill in your doodles with colored pencil afterwards as in the example below.

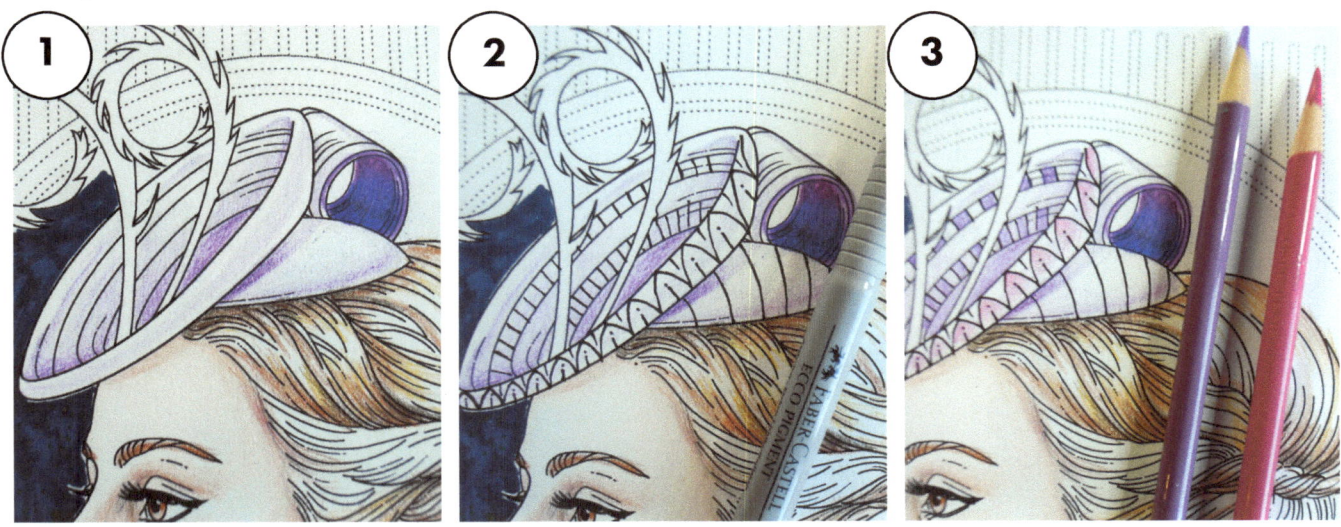

Glitter Pen Embellishments

Another neat trick is to use a layer of marker and/or colored pencil and top it with a layer of glittery, transparent gel pen for a rich, sparkling effect. This works well for jewels like the emerald cut stone from *Glamourista,* or the *Mojave Turquoise tutorial* veining from this book. It works great for fairytale scenes! Another perfect use is on or in a white space next to a dark background, as in my *Glowdalas* book example below.

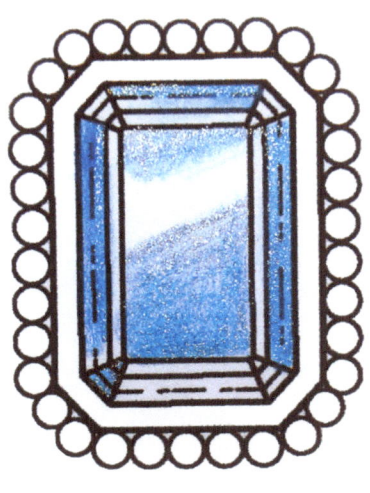
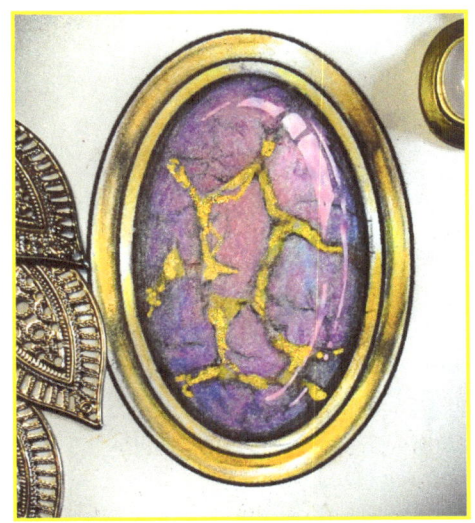
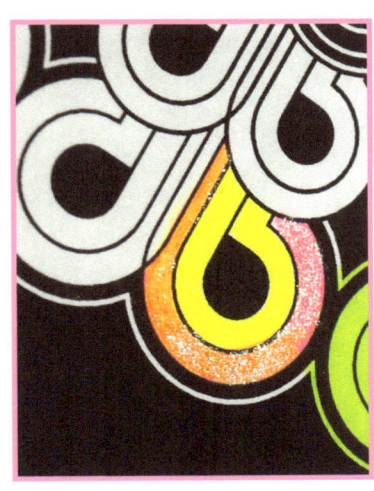

Make a Glimmering Ruby Slipper with Glitter Pen Embellishments

Use a handful of markers and some glittery gel pens to create this effect on the line art at the end.

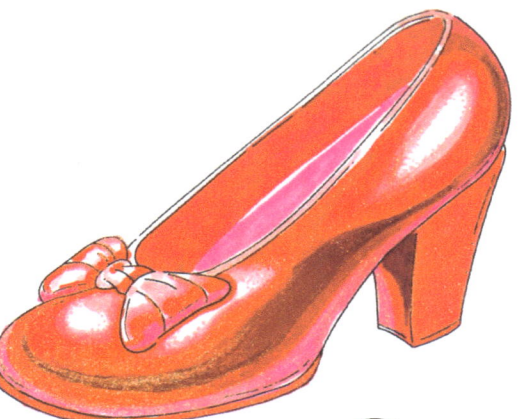

You will need:
- A pencil
- Markers, preferably brush tip, alcohol-based
- The "Glimmering Slipper" line art page
- Coordinating colored gel pens or just one clear gel pen.
- A flat brush to evenly spread the gel, and a little water.

On the line art page, I map out where the different parts of light will go, as below. Use *very, very* light pencil and mark your shoe as I've marked mine, but leave out the color names. :)

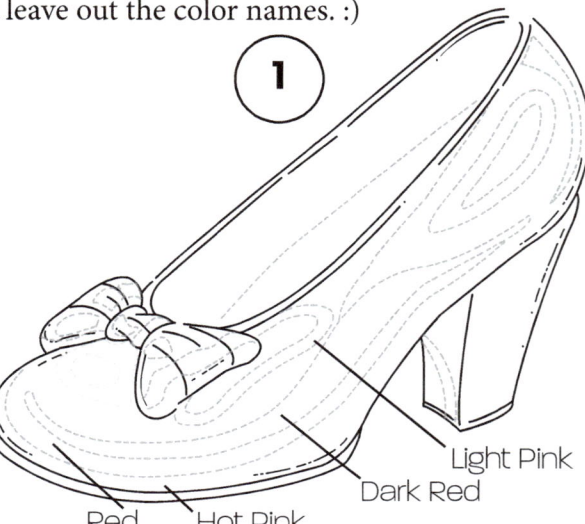

Light Pink
Dark Red
Red   Hot Pink

2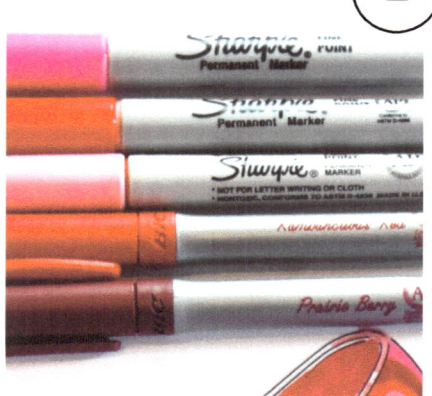

I select a few markers within a family, such as all violets, with varying degrees of darkness. I've chosen red for rubies. You can choose any color you wish, as long as you have all of the matching materials.

3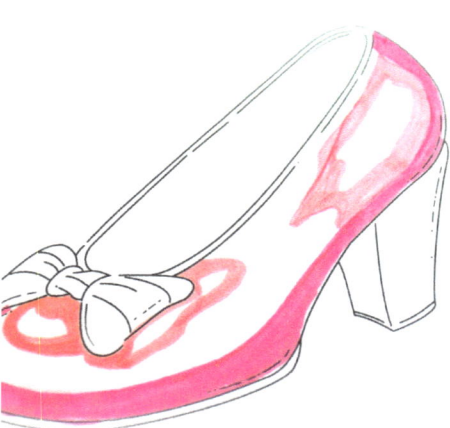

Leave your brightest highlight white then use the next lightest color to surround it, in my case, light pink. I use directional strokes to circle around each section or use lines that bump right against each other without overlapping. I follow with medium and dark markers. To create dimension, I use a dark hot pink color for the inside of the shoe and reflected light on the edge of the shoe. I add some stippled dots along the edge of each white highlight to visually blend them into the pink and make it less stark and do the same with some areas of other colors on the shoe. I allow it to dry completely.

4 Once dry, working quickly, I add a layer of clear glitter gel pen, such as Gelly Roll Stardust over the top of the lightest color, leaving out the white sections. I use a slightly damp, flat brush to spread it evenly. I either use only the clear pen itself or a coordinating color to match each shape. In this case I also chose red and dark pink to vary the sections.

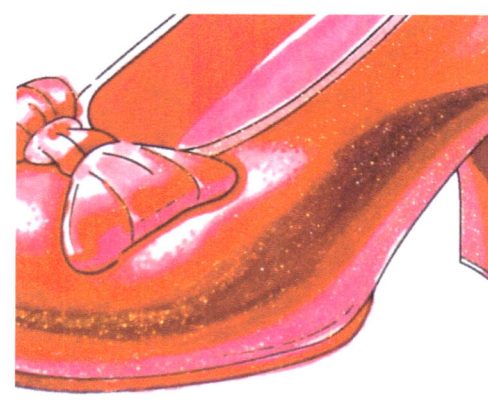

Now it's your turn to test your markers and gel pens in the space below. Let the marker dry thoroughly before using the gel pen. Try different combinations and see what the results are before moving on. When you are ready, make your own masterpiece out of the "Glimmering Slipper" line art in the back of the book. Remember to place a blotter page beneath this page and the line art page if you plan to color with marker or other wet media.

Mixed Media Embellishments

Think outside of the box – find some non-traditional bling such as rhinestones, nail art studs, or decals to use as a finishing touch! Take your creativity to the next level and go for some bold and unique touches such as fabrics! Using lace or tulle with a touch of glue will certainly dress up your coloring.

Did you know? *You probably will want to cut any pages with 3-D embellishments out of your books so that they don't permanently imprint your surrounding pages.*

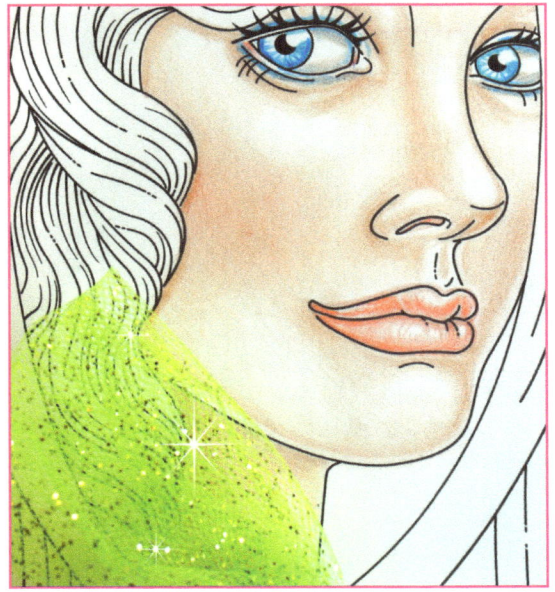
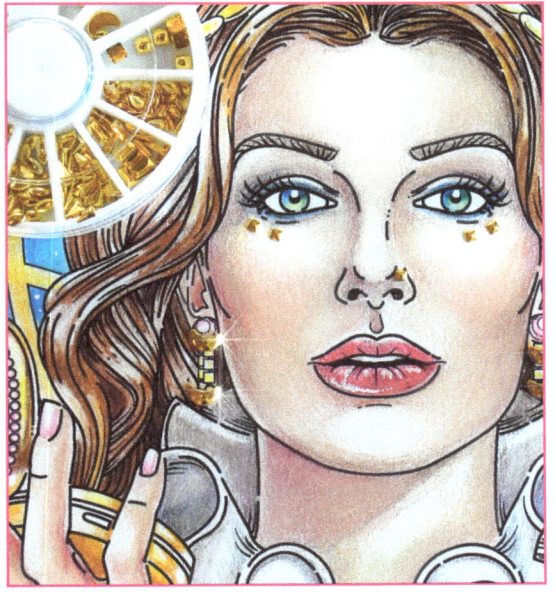

. . . .

Step-By-Step Tutorials: Backgrounds

Creating dynamic backgrounds is huge part of coloring today, but the backgrounds don't necessarily have to be created using the same materials as the rest of the drawing. In the following lessons, we will create the illusion of dimension, as well as some amazing otherworldly effects.

Simple, Green Glowing Colored Pencil Background

You will need:

- Prismacolor Premier: 1004, 913, 912, 920, 992
- Kneaded eraser   (optional)
- Colorless blender (optional)

Tip: Don't Be Afraid to Rotate the Page!

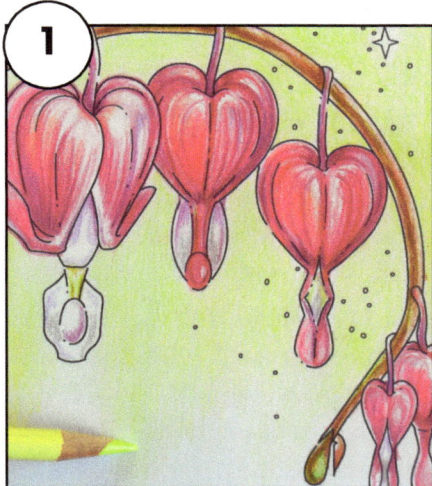

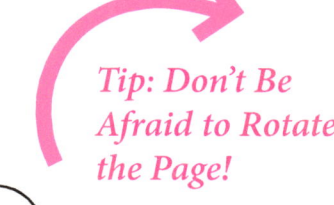

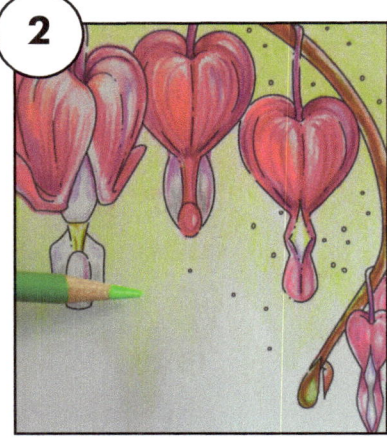

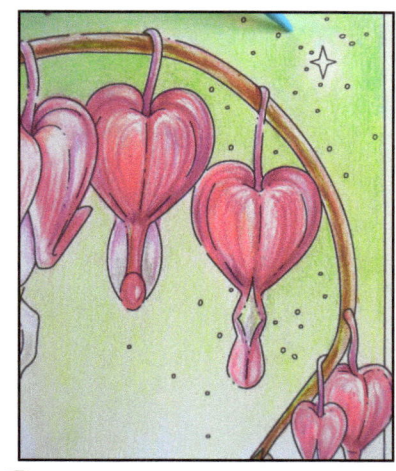

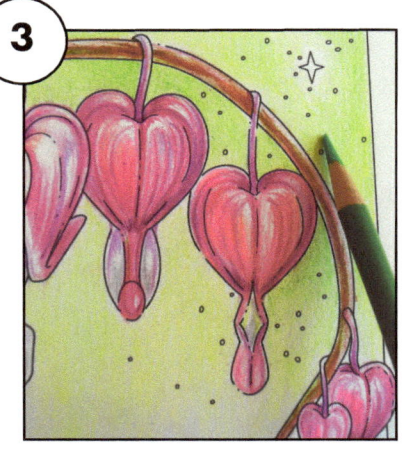

I lightly fill most of the background with an even gradation layer of Yellow Chartreuse 1004, using both vertical strokes and small circles in hard to reach places. I fade the gradation into white near the bottom. I leave the edge uneven intentionally to make it interesting.

From the bottom of the left most flower upwards, I use vertical strokes with Spring Green 913, to layer over the first color. I take it to the top edge and avoid the little stars.

Apple Green 912 is used on the background, from about the middle of the flowers upwards to the top edge, leaving some of the Spring Green uncovered.

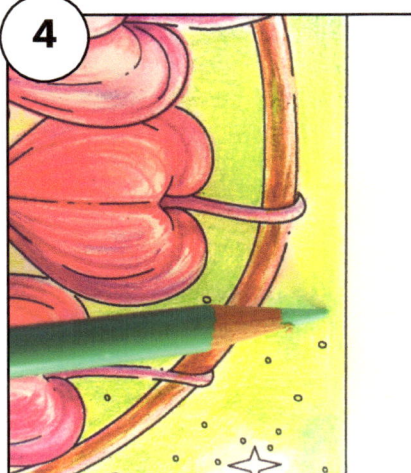

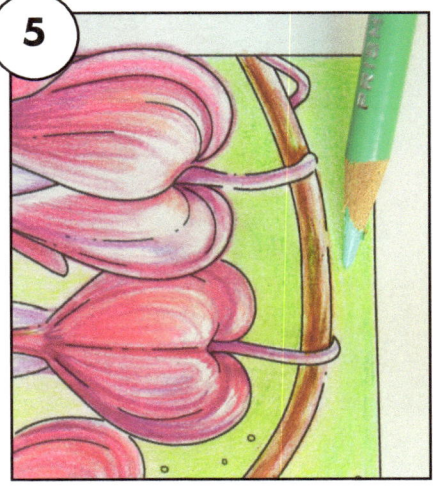

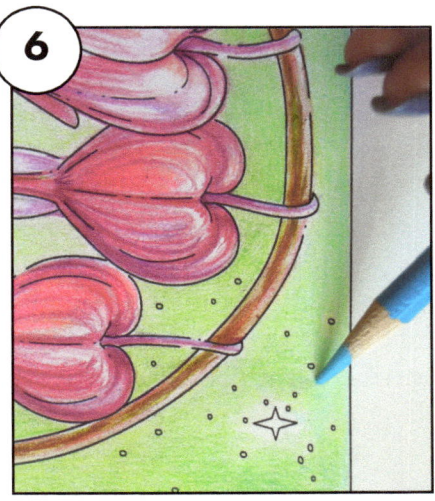

I rotate the page. I Light Green 920 is used just above and below the branch (left and right in this picture), gradating it more heavily towards the top of the image – avoiding the large star.

I turn my page like this frequently to get into small spots more easily.
Here the Light Green is really starting to bring it to life :)

Finally, a hint of Light Aqua 992 on top of the Light Green near the top of the page (the right in this picture) will really give it some beautiful, subtle variation and make the star pop out! If you wish, use a colorless blender to smooth.

The Bleeding Heart Flower lesson is a little further into the book

Mixed Media Nighttime Sky with Glowing Stars and Illuminated Moon

This lesson uses a combination of mediums to create a real glow! Set off your beautiful drawings with a vivid celestial backdrop or use on a coloring page with a blank background.

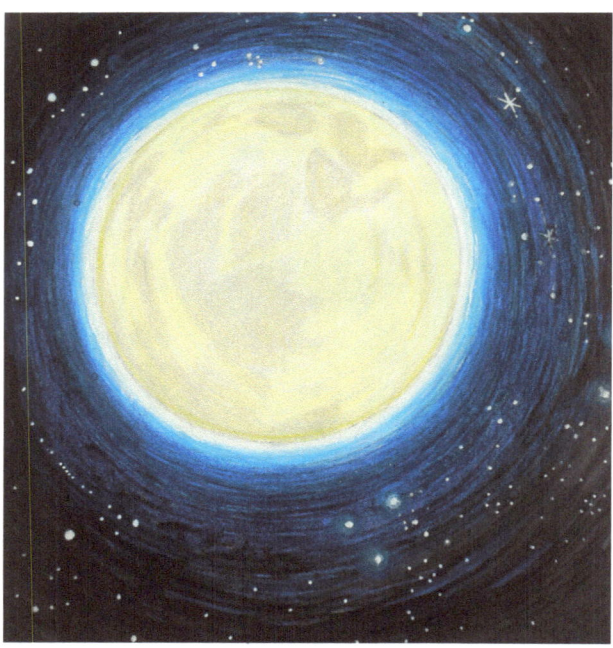

You will need:

- A blotter page

- To draw/trace a circle on a blank page or download the bonus "Luna" line art page at ModernColoring.com/freebies. To access, enter the secret code found on the backside of one of the last pages of this book

- Ultramarine or Cobalt Blue, Medium Blue and Black brush tip markers (preferably alcohol). I used Copic Sketch in B23 & B29 and a Black Fine Tip Sharpie (although a brush or chisel tip would be easier)

- A range of 4-6 blue colored pencils that vary in darkness, 1 yellow and 1 light grey pencil, white and black pencil. I used Prismacolor 902, 903, 919, 133, 1100, 916, & 1052. You may also choose to use a colorless blender for a smoother gradation

- A good white gel pen, such as Uniball Signo

I lay down a layer of light to medium blue marker around the perimeter of the circle, using tick or hatch-like strokes, leaving a small white gap around the circle. I add another "band" of hatch marks as I complete the circle moving outward filling up sme of the page.

Next, I "visually blend" by using hatching of the darker blue lightly, overlapping the first color a little, as I move outward to fill the frame – everywhere but the moon shape.

With black I use the same method over part of the darker blue. I make long directional strokes that circle around the moon. I fill in large empty white areas with the same type of stroke. The darkest colors should be near the edges of the paper.

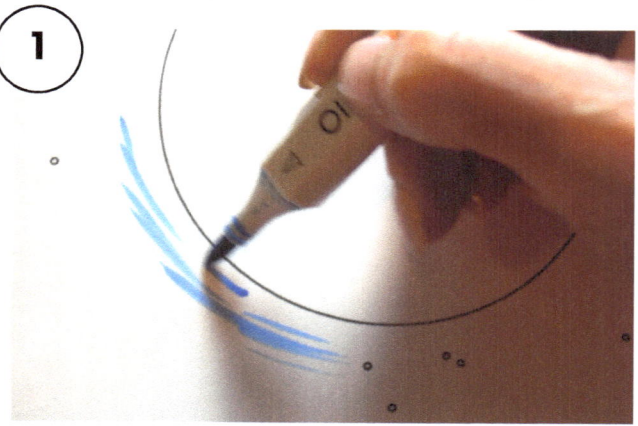

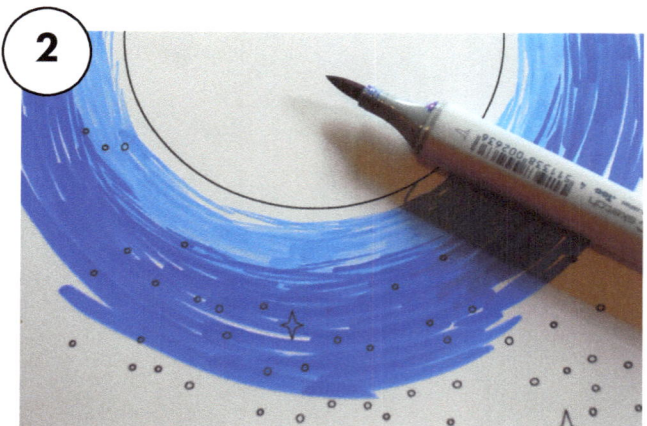

Did you know?
You can use more black rather than the dark blue for a higher contrast sky.

I choose my most vibrant dark blue pencils, in the same color family as the blue markers, to go over those areas and blend the hatch marks, leaving the white gap around the moon alone. Using directional strokes "circling" out away from the moon, I use a light vibrant blue softly, right up to the gap leaving about 1-2 mm of white still showing. Use a white pencil over the edge next to the gap to smooth and lighten just a bit.

Then I fill in the spaces furthest away from the moon with black pencil using the same directional strokes. It helps to apply a colorless blender to smooth the gradation.

I resist the temptation to push really hard. Taking time is key!

Next, using a very light hand, I color with my yellow to define the edges of the moon and gently fill in the circle as I move inward. It's good to go a little heavier in some places than others to make it interesting. I introduce the 30% Warm Grey to very lightly go over the bottom part of the edge of the moon, just to define it, but don't just "outline" the whole moon. Finally, use your white pencil to blend together while lightening.

Optional: For more detail, grey can be used to lightly outline the shapes of craters on the surface of the moon (it helps to look at some photos for reference) and lightly fill them in. Blending with white pencil will make it look smooth and give it a glowing effect.

I use a white gel pen to go over the gap where I may have gotten too close on either side! I cover up the hard outline of the moon too. Here I have dotted tiny stars with a gel pen.

You may want to try using a Precision Tip Q-Tip cotton swab to "blur" some by dabbing once gently, then go over them again with one tiny dot. Keep your pattern random. Vôila!

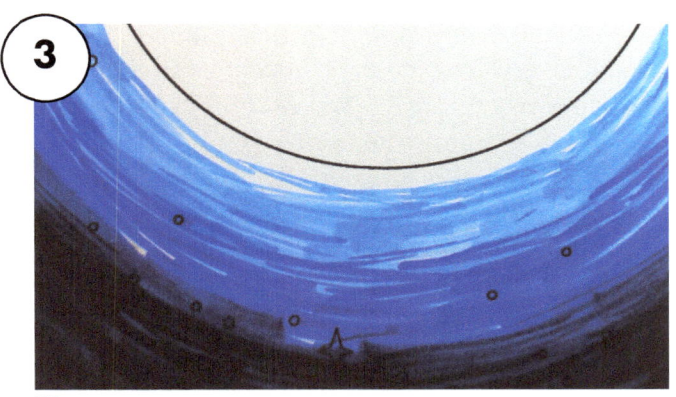

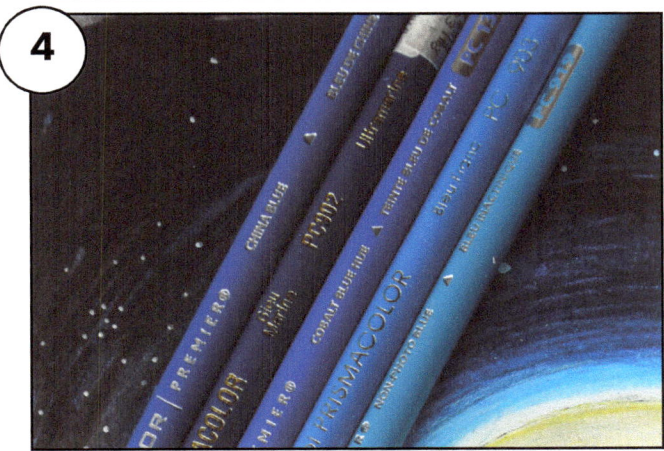

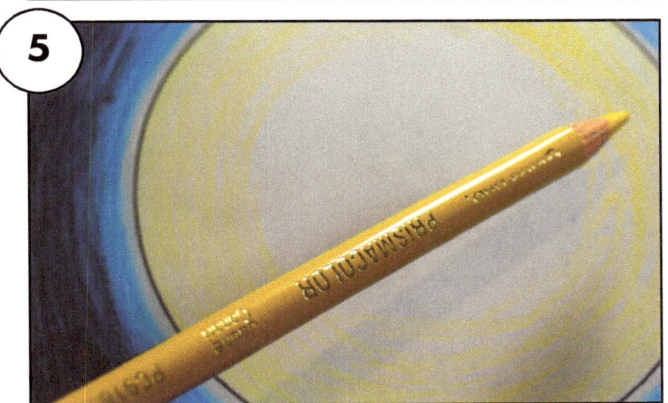

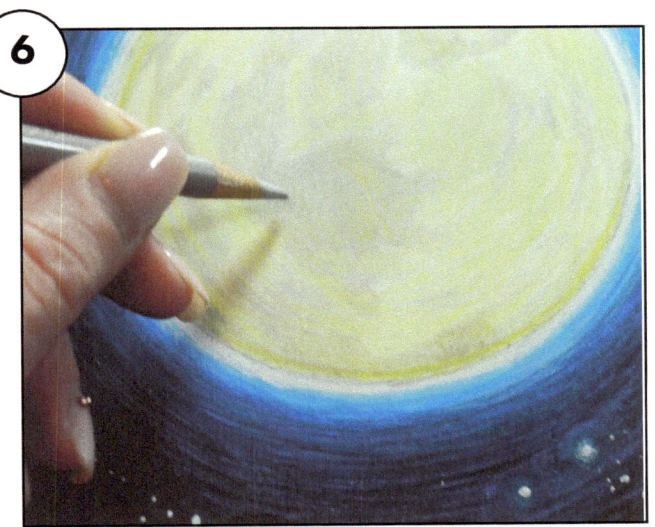

PanPastels are some of my favorite coloring tools. They are really unique in that they provide a relatively dust-free, creamy powder coating to a surface. They fill in space quickly, can be easily manipulated or added upon, and they can be "lifted" or "pulled" too. They work great as a base and give everything a smooth glow!

Pastel/PanPastel and Kneaded Eraser "Lifted" Clouds with Daytime Sky

This works great on coloring pages with empty backgrounds. Try this on already cut-out animal or portrait coloring book pages, after completing the subject first, for a really cool outdoor feel!

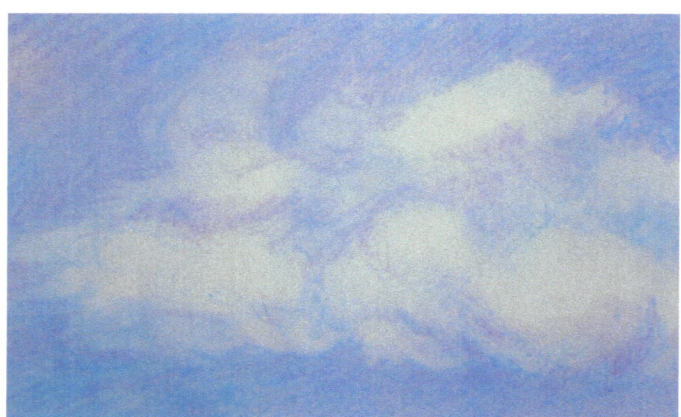

You will need:

- PanPastels in 2-3 colors – I am using a Pearlescent Blue and Violet Tint. Add another darker color if you'd like more contrast (or sub chalk pastels and a utility knife)
- A sponge or tissue (I am using a Sofft sponge)
- A kneaded eraser
- Coordinating colored pencils to add detail to your background as needed. I am using Light Cerulean Blue 904 and Parma Violet 1008, both Prismacolor.

I lay down a layer of PanPastel, using at least two colors in patches. Next, I blend the colors a bit with my Sofft sponge tool, making sure that there is still some differentiation between the colors.

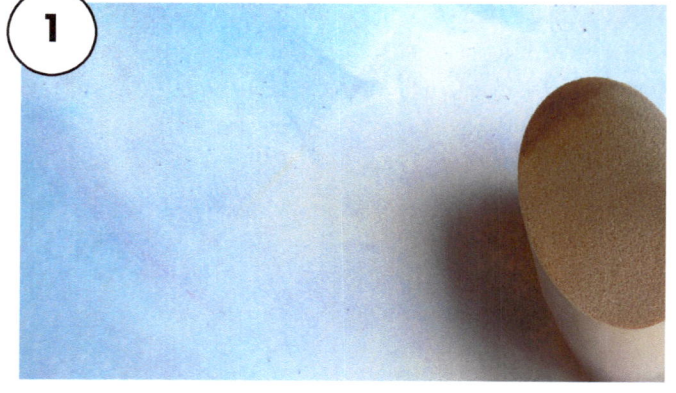

(1)

Did you know?

You can use regular pastels as a replacement, but you will need to scrape some of the chalk dust on to your paper with a utility knife, instead of drawing the color on, for smoother consistency – and blend it with a sponge or tissue.

(2)

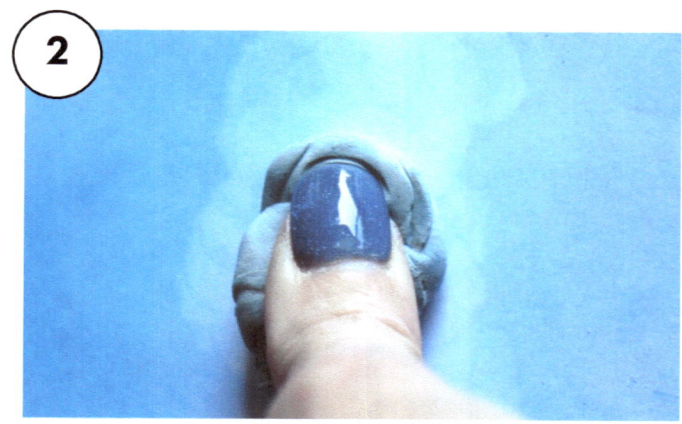

I squish my kneaded eraser into a round shape, checking that it is clean first (see Chapter 5, Other Necessities for more info).

Using my body weight, I push the eraser down where I want to begin the first cloud. I gently pull it off of the paper. Notice the imprint of pastel on the back of the eraser. It won't turn the paper completely white, but it will lighten it.

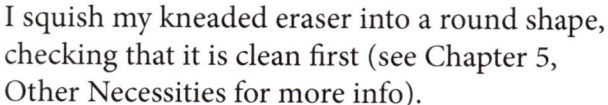

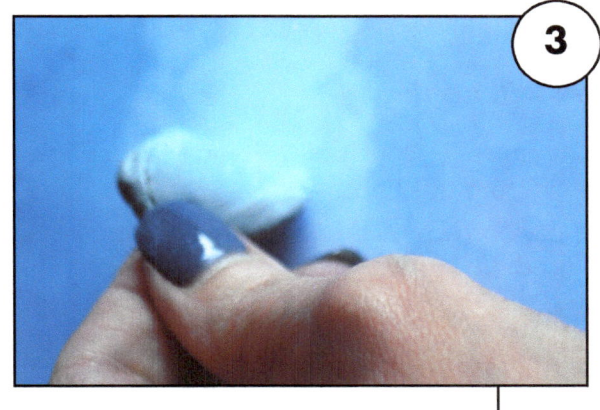

3

I can alter the shape as needed to pick up or "lift" the color off in several pulls in the shape of the cloud. I knead to clean the eraser in between and reposition it next to the previous eraser mark.

I continue adding clouds to my background, making them smaller as I move downward if I'm trying to convey distance. If I can't seem to lighten my cloud enough by "lifting" once, I try this: clean the eraser really well and on top of the same spot use a swift, sweeping motion in only one direction while holding down the paper securely with the other hand. I don't rub the eraser back and forth, or it may tear the paper. To ensure success, I make sure to clean the eraser in between sweeps.

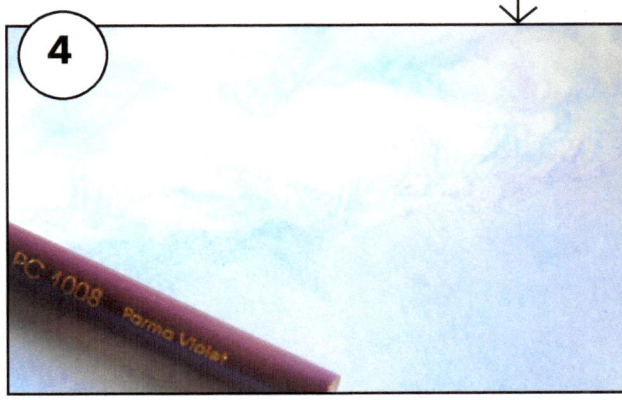

Next, I use some colored pencil in between the "puffs" of the cloud to create more dimension. (You can shade around the clouds if you like them to stand out more being careful not to outline them). I add more colored pencil to the background if I want more detail.

4

5

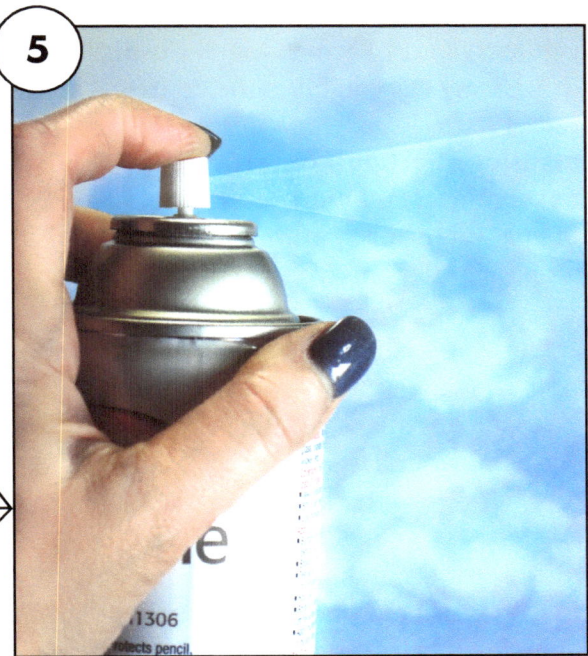

If you wish, you may spray fix your drawing if it is complete to prevent it from getting damaged. Be sure to read Chapter 5: Other Necessities, for more information.

PanPastel, Stamp and Marker Shimmering Wallpaper Background

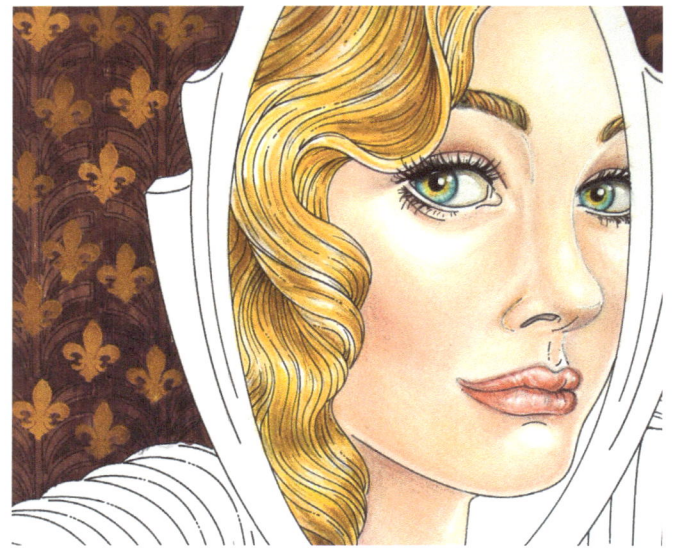

This works great on coloring pages with empty backgrounds.

You will need:

- To remove or copy the "Mirror, Mirror" line art page from this book
- A dark brown marker, preferably alcohol-based. I used Bic Marking Woodsy Brown.
- A stamper of your choice. I used a fleur de lis made by Recollections, purchased at Michael's.
- VersaMark Watermark Stamp Pad
- Gold or other color PanPastel
- Some dark colored pencils such as Prismacolor Black Grape or Black – if you want to accentuate the background shapes.

You will probably want to cut this page (or any other PanPastel page) out of your book or simply make a copy to work from. PanPastels, although not nearly as messy as regular chalk pastel, will leave a trace of powder that you won't want on your other pages.

I lay down a layer of brown marker using long hatching marks as you fill in the entire background. I try to keep overlapping to a minimum, using directional or vertical lines to fill in most of the area. I did a second layer around the shapes on the background to make it darker than the shapes themselves.

After allowing to dry, it's time for your desired stamp(s) and the watermark stamp pad. The pad is made of a sticky substance that attracts PanPastel powder base. It is clear, so be careful not to stick your fingers in it and get it all over.

Slowly, I press the stamper into the ink and begin to stamp a pattern. It's important to keep the stamper at the same angle and a similar distance between applications. I don't push too hard, but always make sure that the whole raised design is being stamped each time.

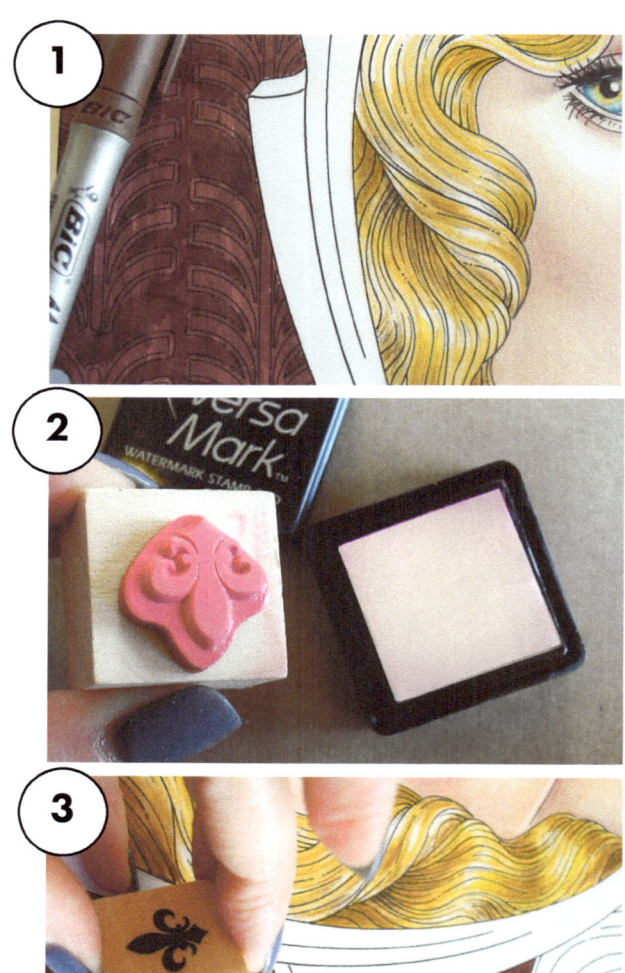

Once the entire background pattern is stamped, I use a Sofft knife or sponge to apply a layer of PanPastel. Dipping the bottom into the pan, I rub it gently in circles on the paper until it covers each shape. Blow off the extra powder.

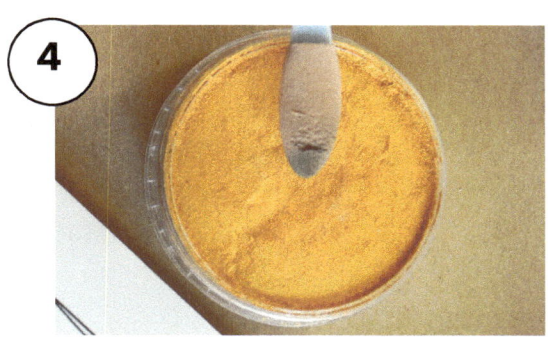

Now if you'd like to perfect each stamped design, use a dark colored pencil similar to the background and trace around the edges to clean it up. You might choose to gradate the darkness away from each shape into the background for more drama. You may decide to use spray fix on this page to keep the powder completely in place.

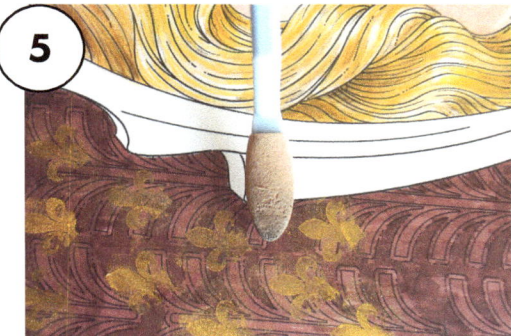

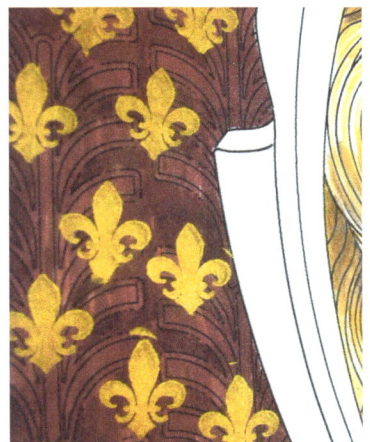

A perfect detail from a completed background!

Did you know?

You don't need to overload your sponge. It doesn't take a lot of powder!

Step-By- Step Tutorials: Living Things

PanPastel, Marker, Colored Pencil Portrait Tutorial (next page)

This is a multi-part tutorial for basic skin, lips, eyes, and hair. You can use the same line art as in the previous tutorial.

You will need:
-A pale yellow marker (I used a Spectrum Noir chisel tip in TN2 color)

-Various Sofft Knives and PanPastels (if desired):
   Burnt Sienna Tint, Red Oxide Tint, Burnt Sienna Shade and Yellow Ochre

-Prismacolor Premier:
   927, 939, 928, 1017, 1092, 1031, 956, 140, 1061, 1002, 945, 920, 105, 1065, 1034, 1098, 948

-Kneaded eraser
-Uniball Signo white gel pen
-Black waterproof pen such as Copic, Faber-Castell or Micron (optional)

PanPastel "Underlay" for Basic Skin Tones – Creating Buttery Smooth Skin

This is an in-depth step-by-step lesson combining a PanPastel base with Prismacolor pencils. If you don't have PanPastels and Sofft tools I would recommend skipping them altogether and using only colored pencil. You will need one marker if you have it.

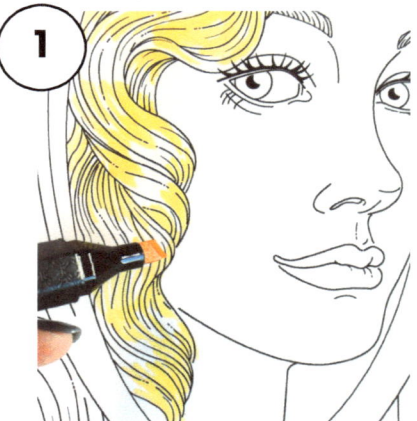

I first use a Spectrum Noir marker on hair, everywhere except the reflections (middle areas that bend outward). I leave them white.

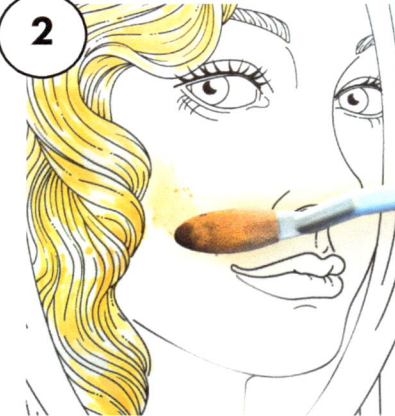

I then begin laying down my first color on face, Burnt Sienna Tint, with my rounded Sofft tool, blending in different directions.

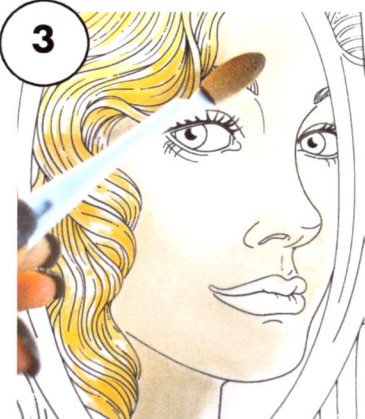

I cover up most of the face except area under eyes, top of nose, and neck side where highlights go. The white space creates a little drama.

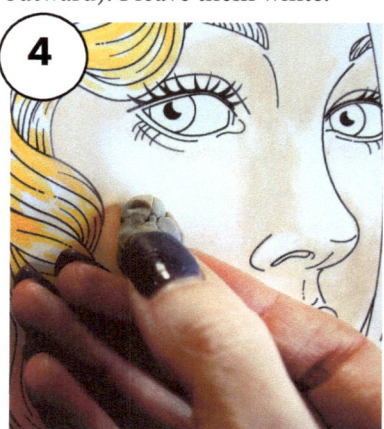

When I'm done blocking in color, I use a kneaded eraser to smooth transitions to highlight areas – get rid of harsh edges.

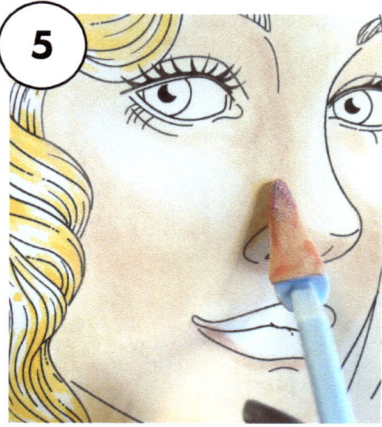

Next, I use my Red Oxide Tint and pointed Sofft sponge tool to develop the nose shadow. For this I use a downward motion.

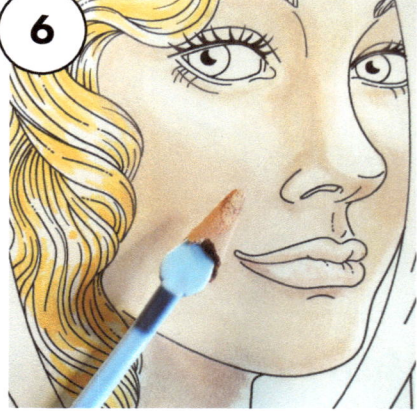

I then deepen the shadows under the jaw and eyebrows, under the lips, and add a few soft details on the bottom edge of both lips and cheeks.

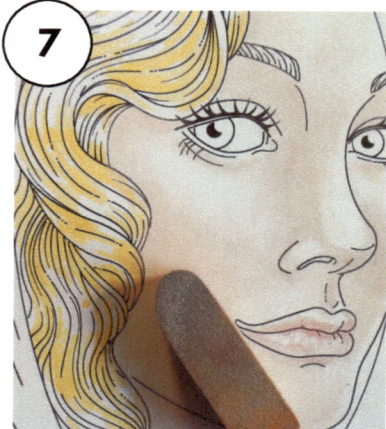

The Sofft finger shaped sponge is great for smoothing and softening. I sweep it in the direction of each feature, as if it were 3-D.

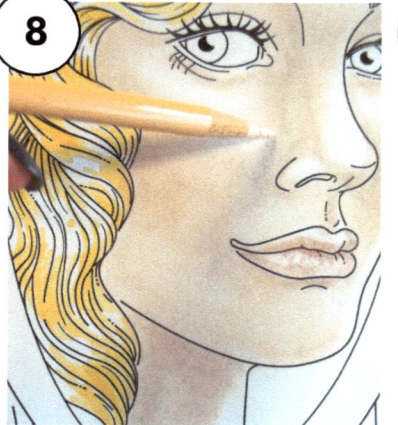

Now it is time for colored pencil. Starting with the lightest, Light Peach 927, I blend all around covering the PanPastel using little circles to smooth it. I then create and deepen a jawline shadow and the neck, using a light hand, with Peach 939. Side to side on the jaw and under it.

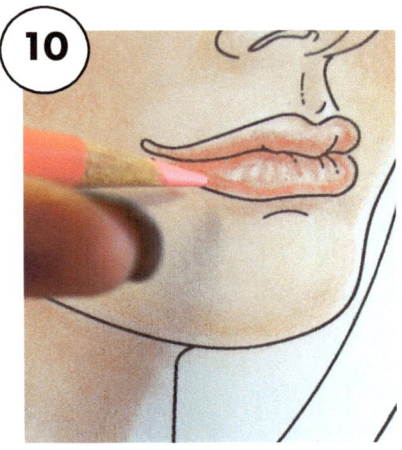

10 Lips start to take form when Blush Pink, 928 is added close to the bottom edge (core shadow) leaving the very edge lighter. I also add almost-vertical lines from center of lips downward.

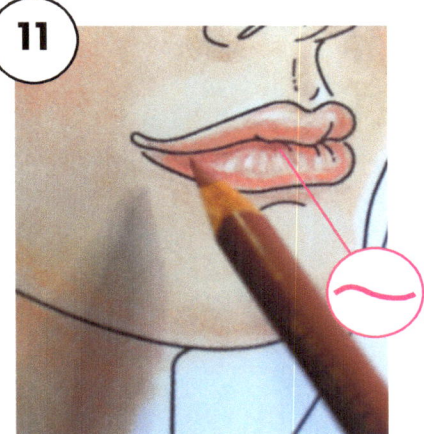

11 Next I introduce a little Clay Rose, 1017, under the top lip as a cast shadow on to bottom lip. It is simply a line that runs parallel to top lip, in between the lips.

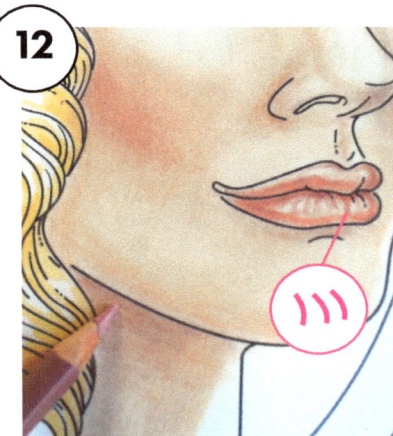

12 I deepen the almost vertical lines on bottom lip and add 1017 to the jaw and on the neck to darken the cast shadow and "push it back", so the face stands out more.

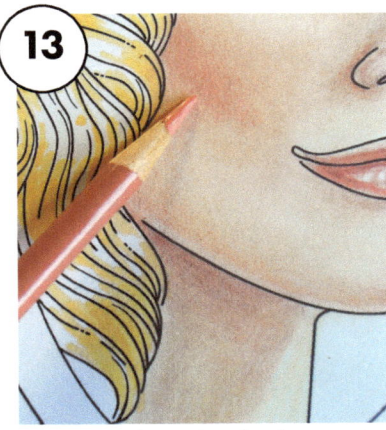

13 Going back to the cheek area, I use Nectar 1092 to add color and blend out a cheek bone. I soften my pressure as I move up closer to the eye.

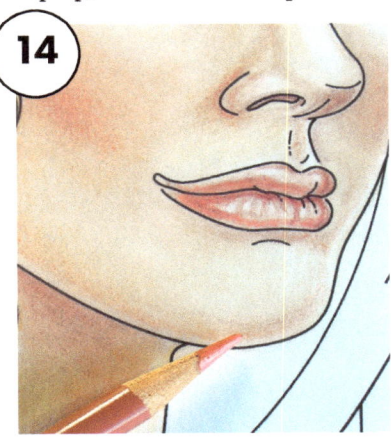

14 A darker core shadow on the bottom of the chin and far cheek rounds out the face. Nectar is a great medium tone for this.

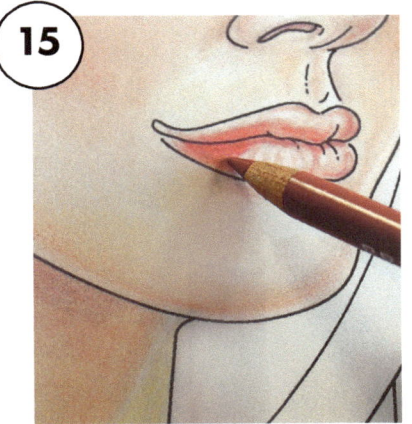

15 I create more dimension by using a touch of Henna 1031 on the left side of the mouth and I deepen the lip shadows just a touch.

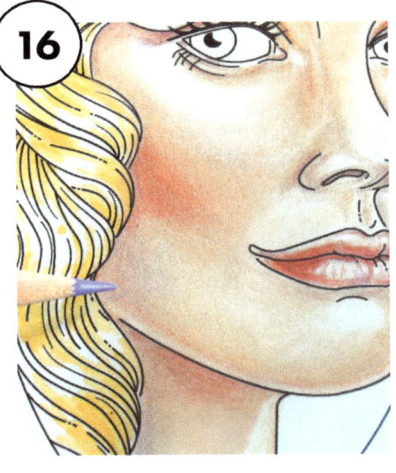

16 Perhaps the strangest addition is Lilac 956. I use it in the shadows where no direct light hits, such as where the hair meets the face, the crease of the eye, and on neck. I blend everything with all of the lighter colors again as needed. Real skin has some cool tones to it!

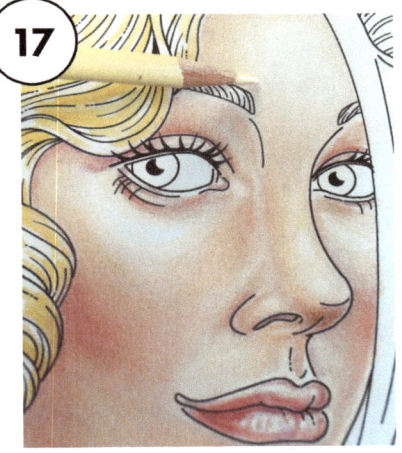

17 Eggshell 140 is then used to warm up the overage of white highlight areas, by filling in some of the tooth. I minimize the forehead highlight by circling from the outside in towards the middle to blend it, but leave the center (the white paper) alone.

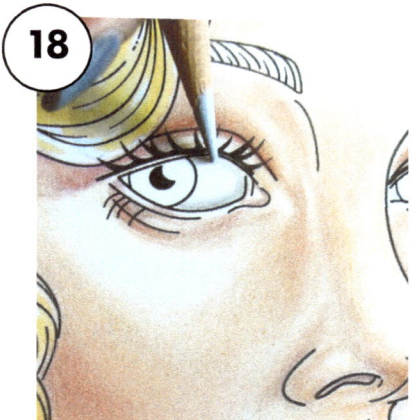

18 Eye whites are not just white. They need shadow! I create the shadow by adding Light Cool Grey 20% 1061 under the top lash line and at the bottom half of the eye by blending.

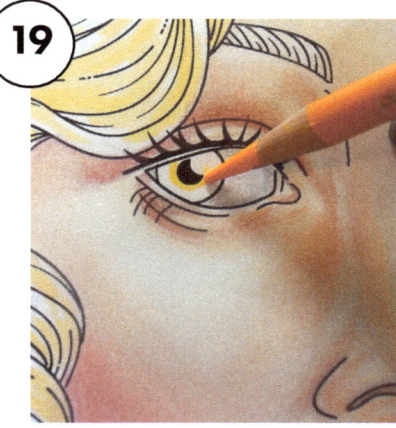

19 I am making a multi-colored eye with an amber and blue-green iris (colored part of eye). Start by circling the pupil (black part of eye) with Yellowed Orange 1002.

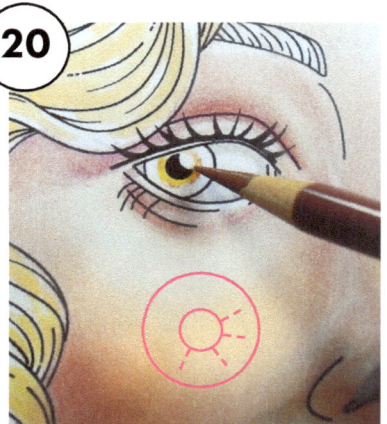

20 Next I add some flecks of brown on the edges and draw a few "skinny spokes" with a razor sharp pencil towards the pupil with Sienna Brown 945. Don't overdo it.

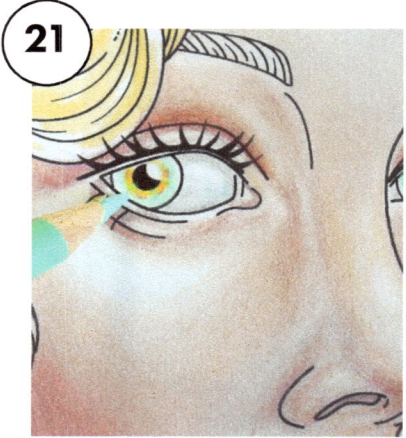

21 I selected a bright, intense green called Light Green 920 to fill in the rest of the iris. I add a few skinny spokes inward with this color too.

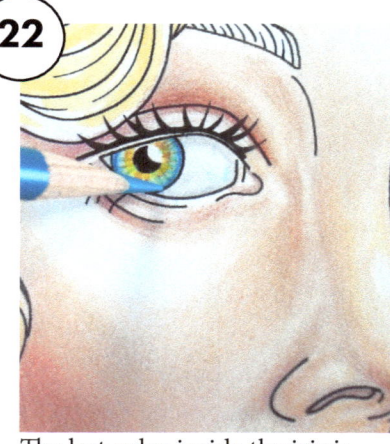

22 The last color inside the iris is Cobalt Turquoise 105, and it goes just inside the outer black line of the iris, adding a handful of thin spokes inward.

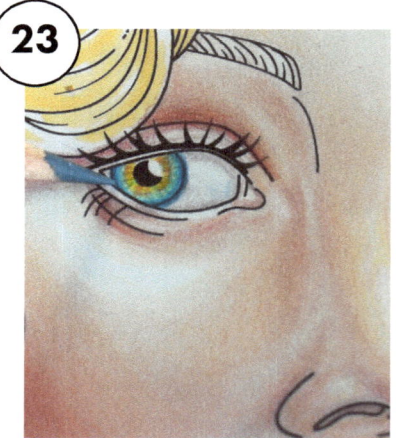

23 I fuzz the black line using a 70% Cool Grey 1065, right on top of it and add a few spokes inward with a very sharp pencil.

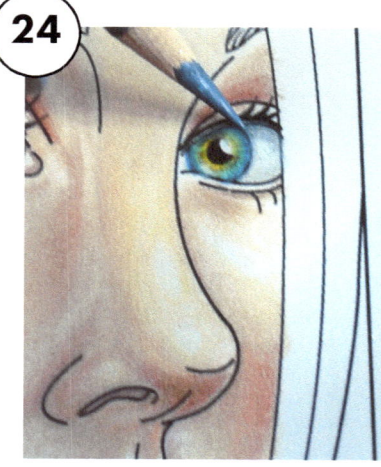

24 I use the same Cool Grey to deepen the cast shadow from the top lid and lashes onto the eyeball, and subtly increase the shadow on bottom edge.

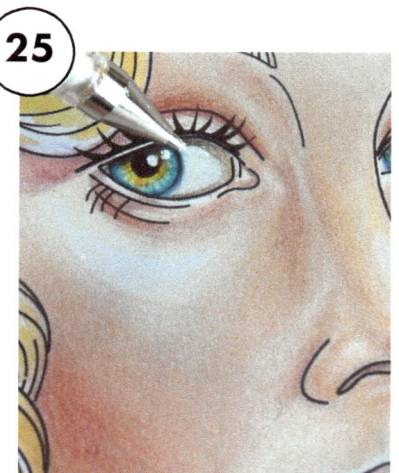

25 Finally, I add a few white reflective highlights right under the top cast shadow of the eye. Doesn't it bring this face to life?

Optional: "Remove " black line art lines by "dotting and blotting" them with a white gel pen, a little at a time. You can sometimes cover them up a little with skin tones. Add more eyelashes with a Micron or Copic black pen.

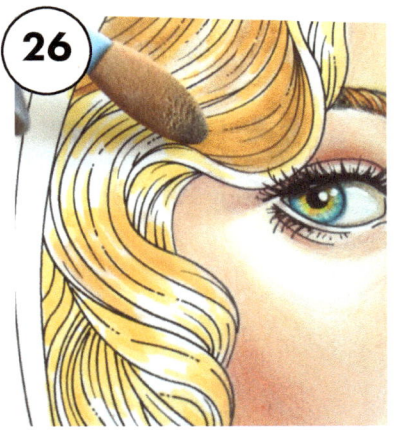

26 I begin filling in the hair with my Sofft rounded sponge knife and a combination of Burnt Sienna Shade and Yellow Ochre PanPastels, mainly in the large areas that dip downwards. This will create shadow.

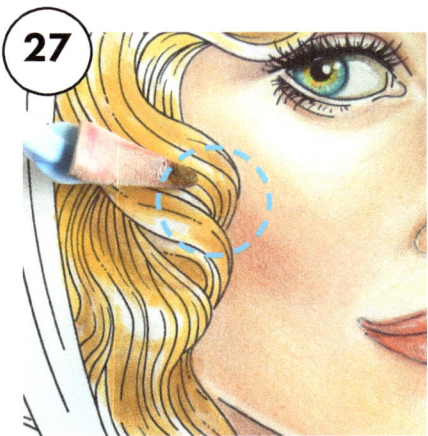

27 I switch to my pointed knife to get into some smaller spaces that "tuck under" into other parts of the hair. I use this tool to blend along the strands of hair, curving in the same direction which they are drawn.

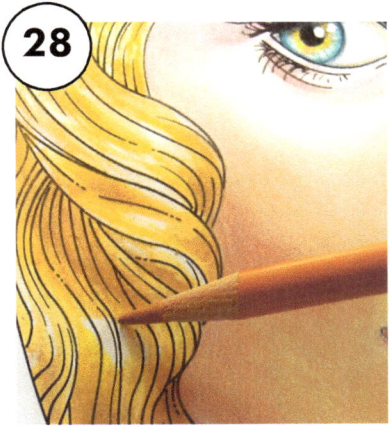

28 Once the PanPastel is complete, I use my second lightest pencil, Goldenrod 1034 to add more warmth to the hair, using small circular motions, being careful to avoid the white areas of reflection. I use a sharp pencil to also draw just *a few* individual strands that overlap the white reflections to break up the white space.

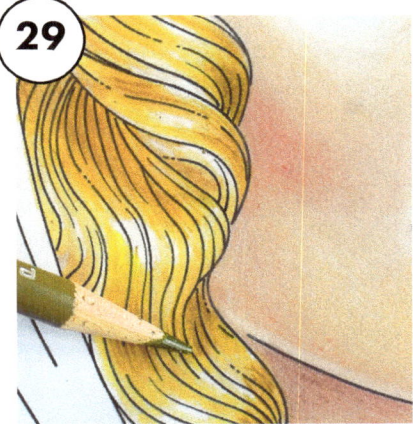

29 I use a medium tone, cooler color called Artichoke 1098, next, to get into the shadow areas, mostly using vertical movements.

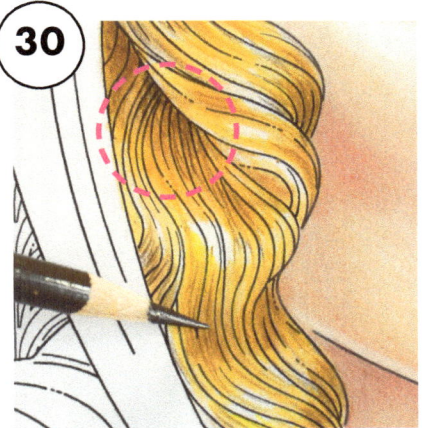

30 The last dark color is Sepia 948 for the upper edge of each shadow and a few of the darkest strands.

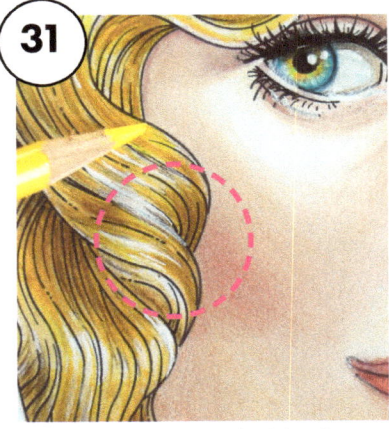

31 Now I go back in and add a few white gel pen highlights and flecks of Canary Yellow next to the highlights.

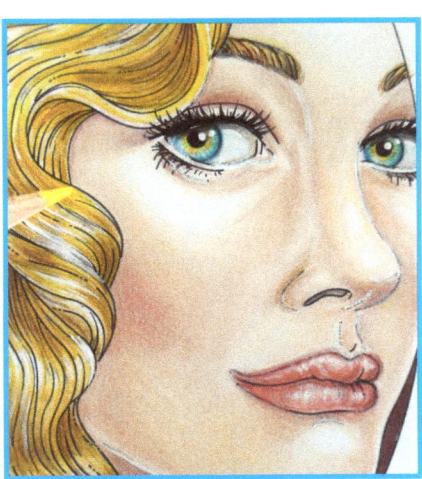

I add my finishing touches to the skin, which includes "erasing" the black lip lines with my gel pen, and fuzzing around them with the lip color pencils again. She is complete! Complete your mirror (see tutorial) and the sofa as you wish. Read up on spray fix in Chapter 5, Other Necessities.

Did you know?

Sofft knife covers are washable? Just use a little mild soap and water with warm water and watch the color come out.

Links to these products, as well as other recommendations can be found under the Shop tab at ModernColoring.com.

Colored Pencil Skin Tones on Toned Paper – Skin Only

This is a method of creating smooth, glowing skin tones. You can use any colored pencil, but I am using Caran D'Ache Luminance and Faber-Castell Polychromos – favorites among very skilled colorists.

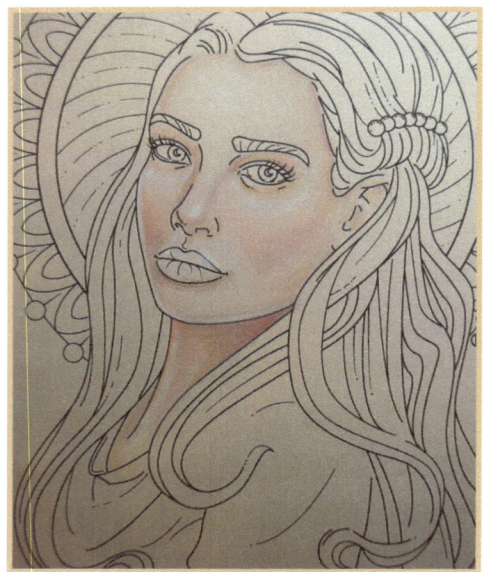

To see a time-lapse video of the completion of this page, please visit my YouTube channel.

You will need:

- The "Ayla, Beauty" toned paper line art page
- Caran D'Ache Luminance in 872, 836, 862, 866, 872, 242, 571, 001
- Faber-Castell Polychromos in 189, 130, 134
- Kneaded eraser to lighten (optional)
- Mono Zero eraser pen (optional)

1

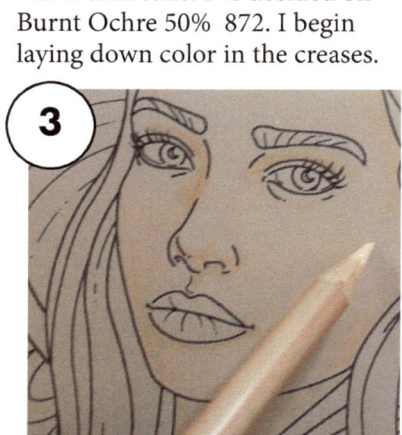

First I start with a medium value warm skin tone. I've decided on Burnt Ochre 50% 872. I begin laying down color in the creases.

2

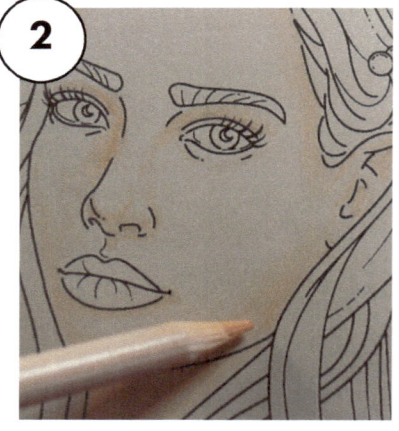

I continue with Brown Ochre 50% 836 under hair line, in ears and where the jaw starts to turn down away from the light.

3

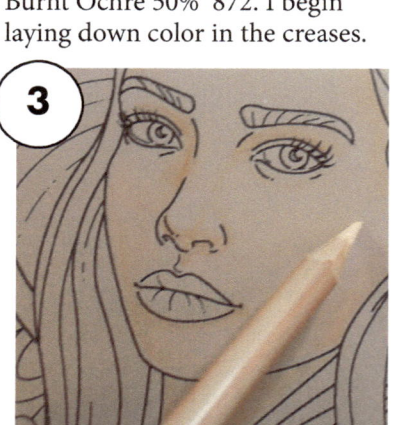

Next I add some lighter value Burnt Ochre 10% 872 throughout the rest of the face, in a light layer, connecting the other areas.

4

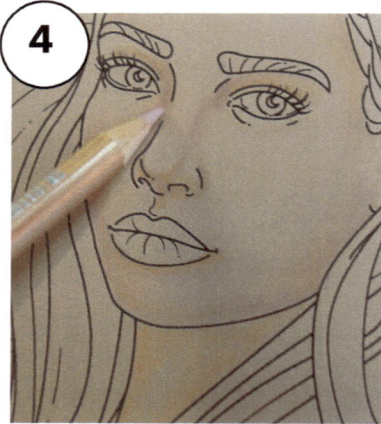

The I blend in the shadow areas with some Burnt Sienna 862. This will go on either side of the bridge of the nose, on jawline and neck.

5

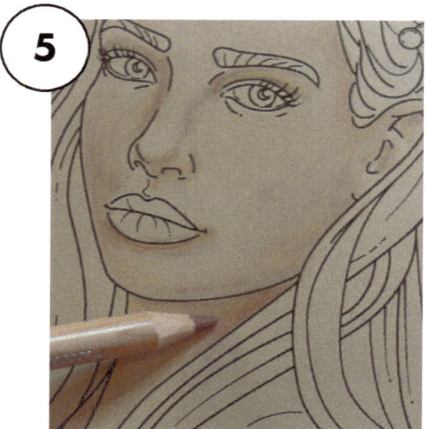

I then deepen shadows under the eye brows and the lips, and especially under the jaw and down the neck, with Burnt Sienna 50% 866.

6

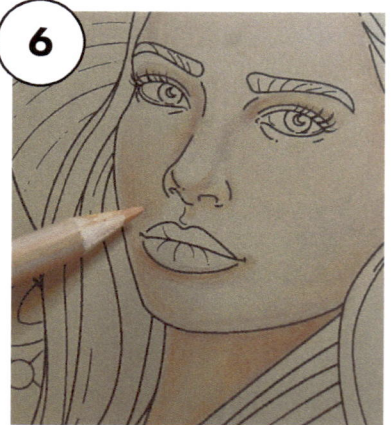

Back to the 872 to blend and raise the color on the cheek on the left a touch.

7

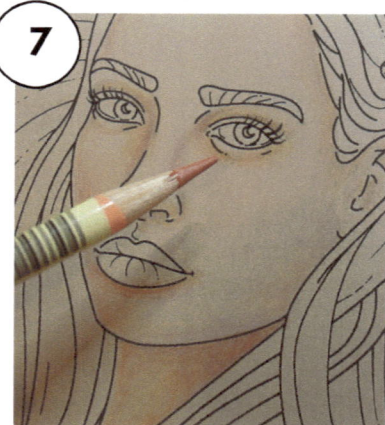

The next step is to introduce a small amount of PC Cinnamon 189 under the eyes to create lower lid pockets.

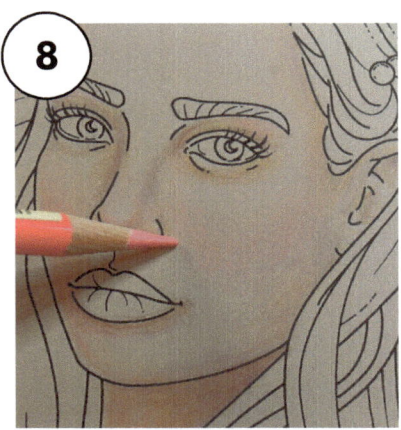

8

I love the subtle blush warmth that Anthraquinoid Pink 571, mixed with PC Dark Flesh 130 gives the cheeks and eyelids. I color in small circles in a "U" shape on the cheek.

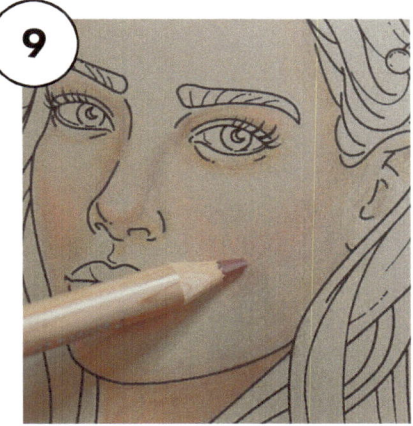

9

I finish off the cheek using 866 again. This time I only use the pencil under the cheek, to carve in a cheek bone.

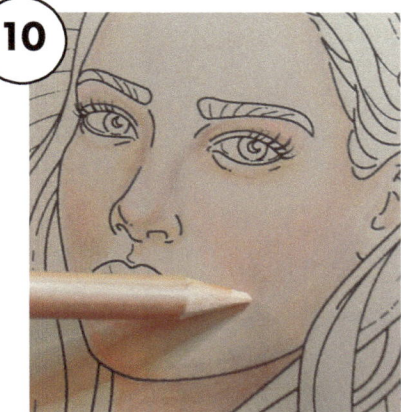

10

Back to the 872 to blend the darkest part of the cheek into the side of the face. Things become magical in the next step, when I introduce a touch of lighter color.

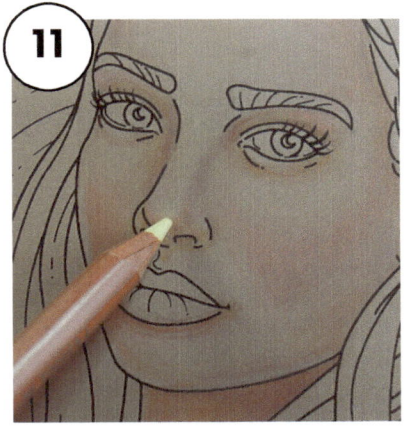

11

First, a layer of Primrose 242 on the tip of the nose and under lower eyelid down to the top of the cheek. Again, creating the "U" band of lighter color. I go over these areas once again (towards the center of each) using White 001. I've also applied a little to the edge of the face, on the left.

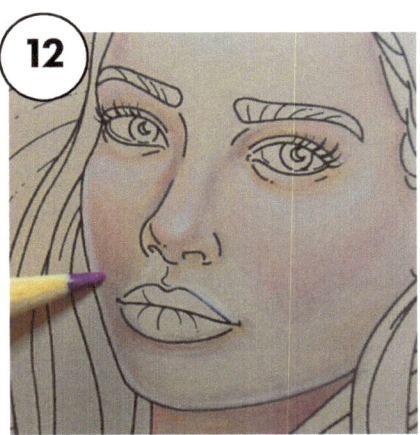

12

The final touch is a little PC Crimson 134 on the left side lower portion of the face between the cheek and lips. This is an intense color – apply it with a feather-light touch.

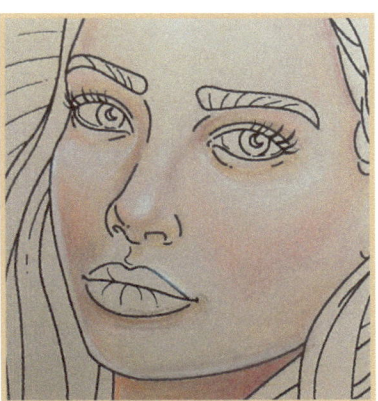

Now, try using this technique on your other portrait pages. Get inspired by what you see on social media!

*This version of "Ayla, Beauty" was colored by my friend, the incredibly talented **Maria Pain** of Norway. Maria is the person that introduced me to the creamy white Luminance pencil. She uses it to cover up some of the dark lines when coloring. Maria colors many portraits on toned paper, in a method similar to the tutorial above – her colorings are absolutely otherworldly! The end result is flawless skin that looks like it was painted with oils.*

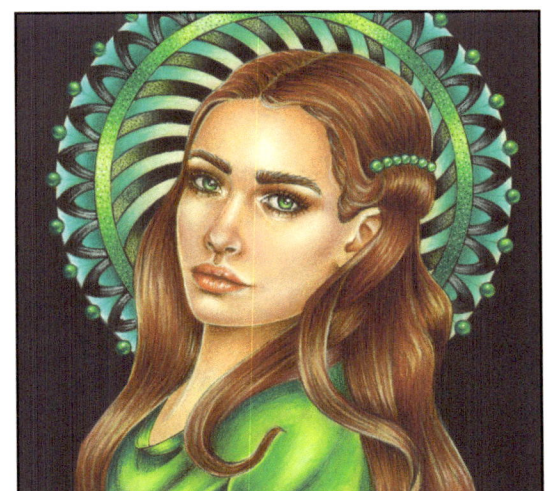

To see more of Maria's work, follow her on Instagram and like her Facebook page!

Insta: **mcrpain**

Facebook: **Maria Pain Coloring**

The Secrets of Coloring

Coloring Animal Eyes, Scales, Fur and Armor:

If you look closely, animals have such different eyes! Some have huge pupils and some small; some are slit while others are round. Some fur is short, some long. In the following lessons you will discover various key characteristics of each species. You can use this invaluable information when you color any animal or draw your own.

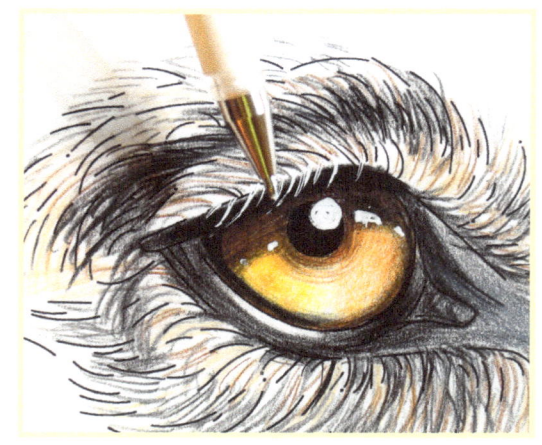

Wolf

You will need:

- The "Animal Eyes" line art page
- Prismacolor Premier:
  916, 1002, 943, 1082, 935, 1065, 140
- Kneaded eraser to lighten (optional)
- Mono Zero eraser pen for mistakes (optional)
- Uniball Signo white gel pen
- Black waterproof pen such as Copic, Faber-Castell or Micron (optional)

Did you know?

When you color hair or fur, remember that the thickest part is at the root; it gradually narrows. Placing your pencil at the root – lifting it off the page gradually will replicate this effect.

1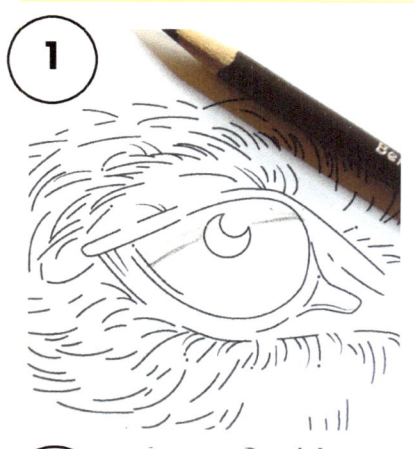

I begin by placing a thin curved line where my cast shadow will go. I skip over the pupil for now, but will end up coloring over it a little later. I grab my closest brown. Any brown will do as we will be covering it up. Keep it light.

2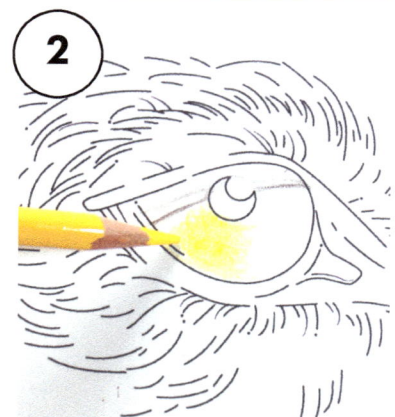

Next, below the line I draw, I add some Canary Yellow 916 on the left side of the pupil using small circles. This will be the brightest part of the entire iris (opposite the highlight), as light will shine through it.

3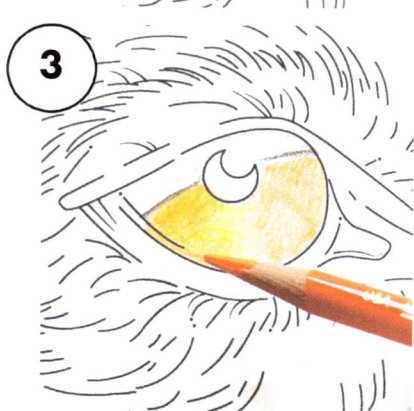

I then add a little Yellowed Orange 1002 all the way to the left, overlapping the yellow just a little. I also fill in the whole right side very lightly, so as not to fill the tooth of the paper completely.

4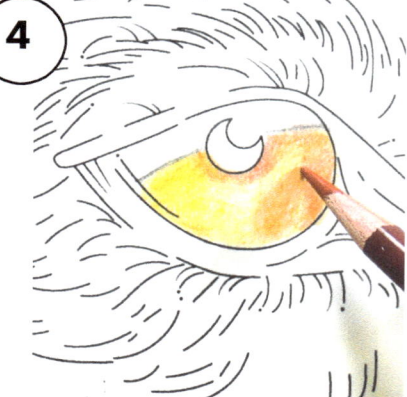

Next, I add a bit of contrast by circling under the pupil shape and coloring the right edge with some Burnt Ochre 943. I try to blend it a bit so that there is a soft transition between colors.

5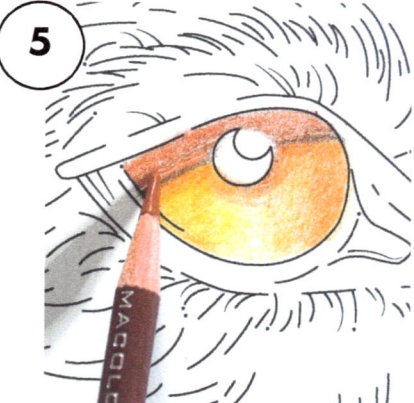

I then fill in the whole top portion of the iris with the same pencil, using a light hand.

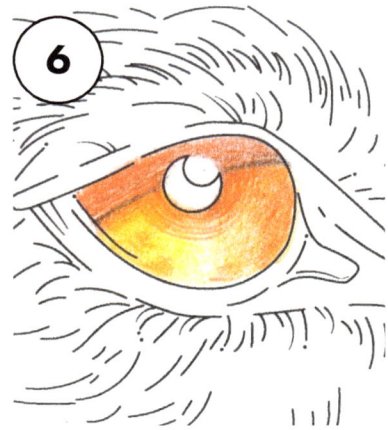

Now, to give the eye a little character, I add some patches of the 943 on the yellow area.

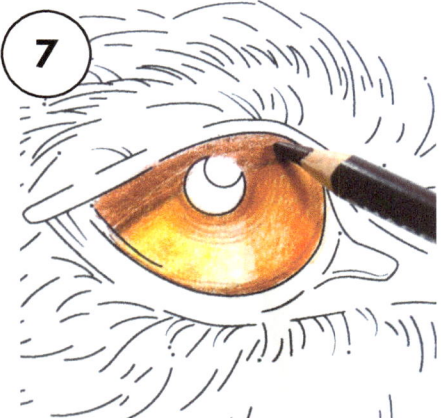

It is time to add more contrast. Chocolate 1082 is a warm brown, and will blend well here, only above the pupil. Don't try to fill it solid. It looks nice with the rusty tones showing through.

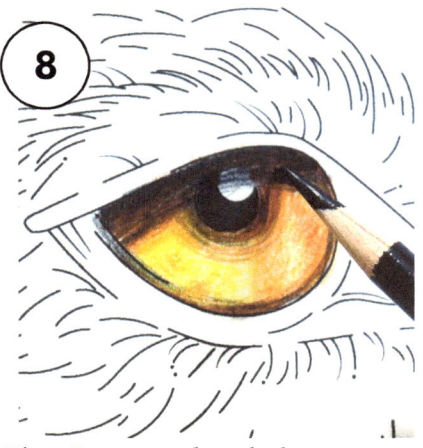

Then I go over the whole area with Black 935 – slowly building it up. You can use pencil or a black pen to fill in the pupil, like I did, for solid coverage. I also use black along the bottom edge of the iris.

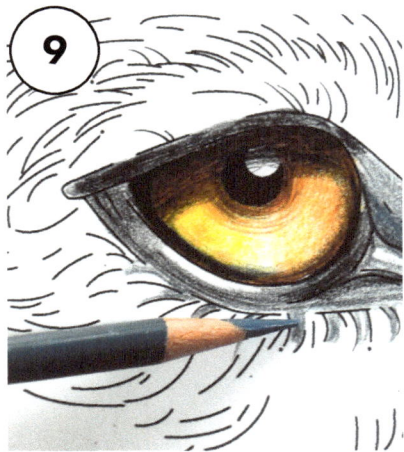

I fill in the whole area surrounding the eye with Cold Grey 70%, 1065. I leave the area directly below the yellow as white for a highlight. I blend with little bent hatch lines of a sharp pencil downward into the fur, in a few spots.

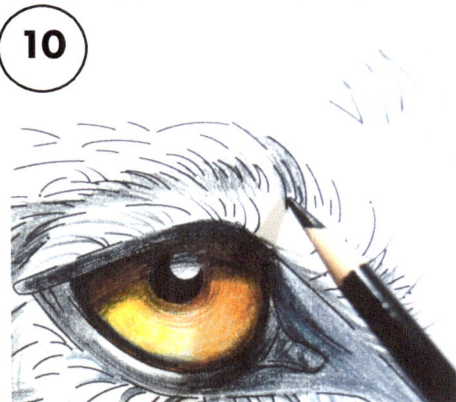

I use my Black again to create shadow in the fur above the eyelid – traveling up and down with zig-zag strokes towards the left.

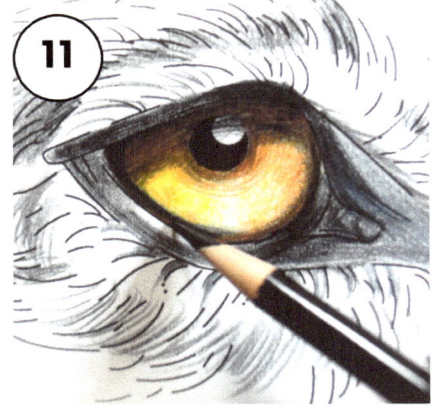

I crispen the black edge of the iris, the tear duct to the right, and add black zig-zags under the eye, in the fur.

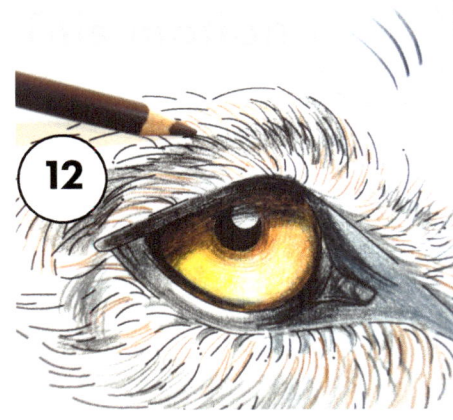

Time for some warmth with the 1082. I use quick bent hatch marks, with a bottom-up motion, for each piece of fur above the eye. I use the opposite motion below the eye.

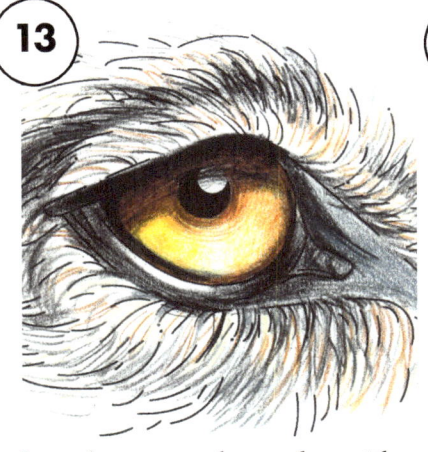

I gently go over the strokes with some Eggshell 140 to connect the fur strokes and add some warmth.

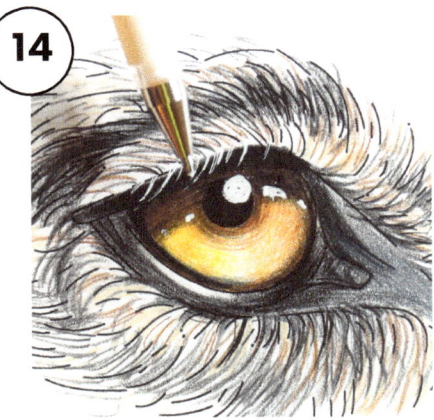

I use a white gel pen to place a few white eyelashes over the shadow. To do this, I start at the edge of the eyelid and hatch quickly downward. I also add in a few highlights where the shadow ends, so it pops!

Snake

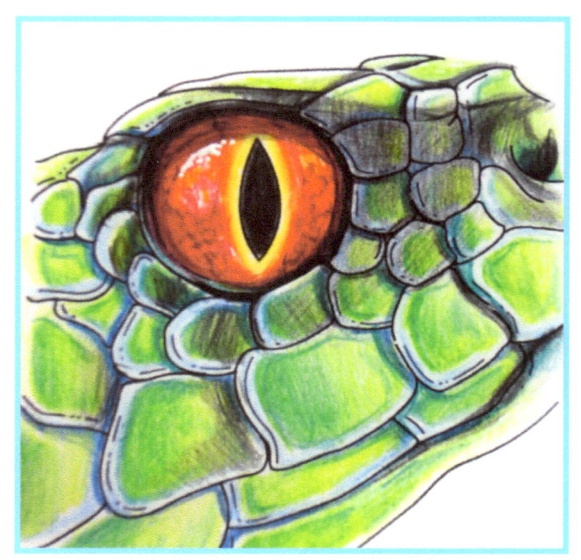

You will need:

- The "Animal Eyes" line art page
- Prismacolor Premier:
  904, 913, 912, 907, 901, 916, 122, 1002, 924, 937, 935
- Kneaded eraser to lighten (optional)
- Mono Zero eraser pen for mistakes (optional)
- Uniball Signo white gel pen
- Black waterproof pen such as Copic, Faber-Castell or Micron (optional)

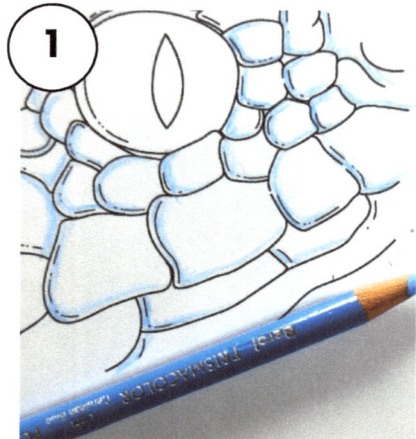

Step 1 is to use my Light Cerulean Blue 904 to add a lighter tinge on the edges that some reptile scales have. Note that I am mostly adding to the left side of each.

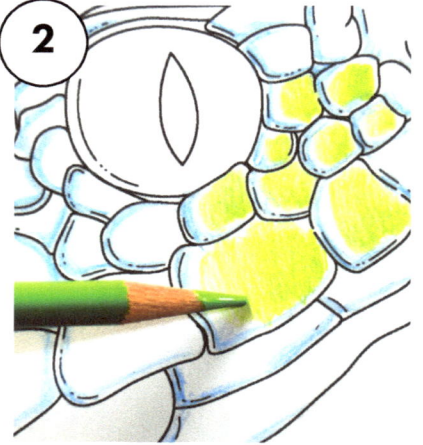

Next, I use Spring Green 913 to fill in each scale, heavier on right and lighter pressure as I travel left. This will prevent filling up the tooth when I later use dark colors.

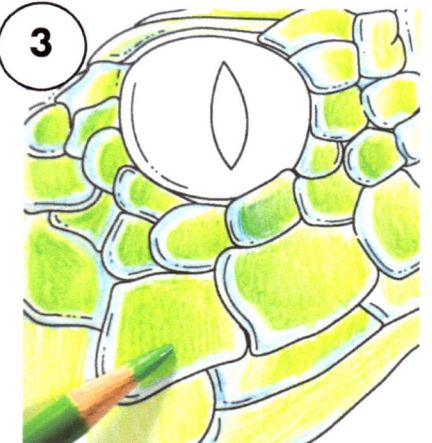

Then I deepen the left side of each scale, fading towards the right within, using Apple Green 912 – creating a smooth gradation with very little pressure.

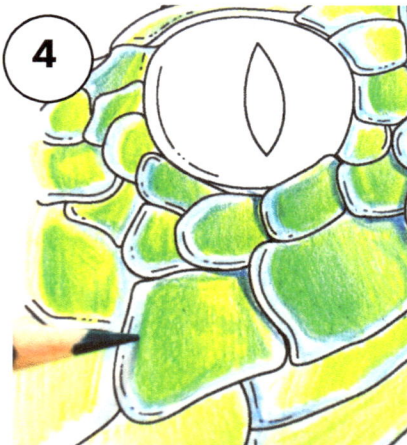

Now I add Peacock Green 907 on the left edge of the green of each scale, feathering it towards the right about 1/3 of the way.

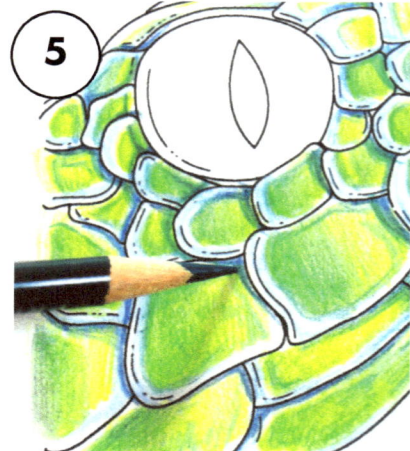

It's easy to immediately create dimension with the scales by placing a thin Indigo Blue 901 cast shadow to the left of each scale.

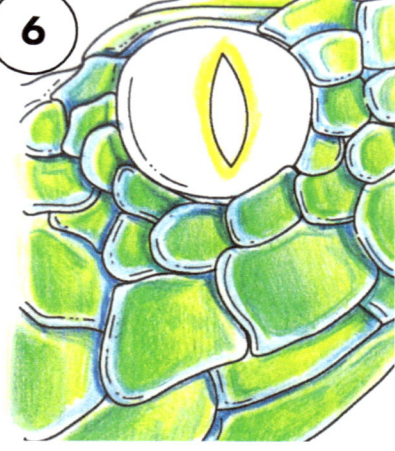

Now time for the eye. Canary Yellow 916 is used to create a ring around the pupil. In reptiles, this is often football-shaped.

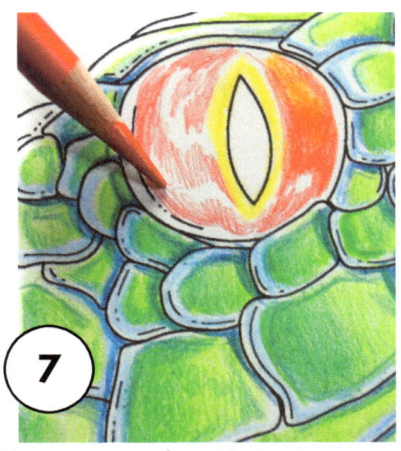

7

To create a red eye I give it some detail. I start by making up and down zig-zag marks, leaving white in between, with Permanent Red 122. Use a sharp pencil!

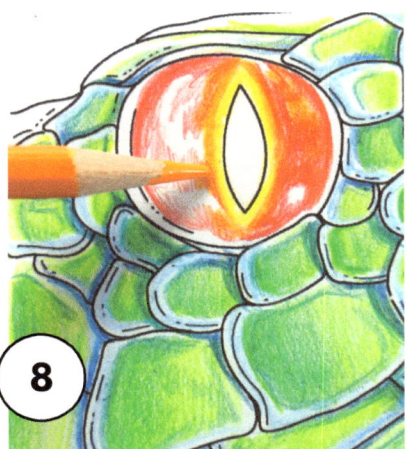

8

Now I can blend outward from the yellow ring with a little Yellowed Orange 1002. I also fill in a few of the white gaps with this color.

This motion

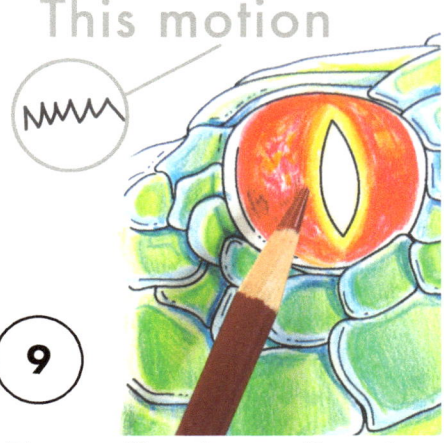

9

The eye still needs more dimension, so I use smaller up and down zig zags with a darker red, across the eye in rows in Crimson 924.

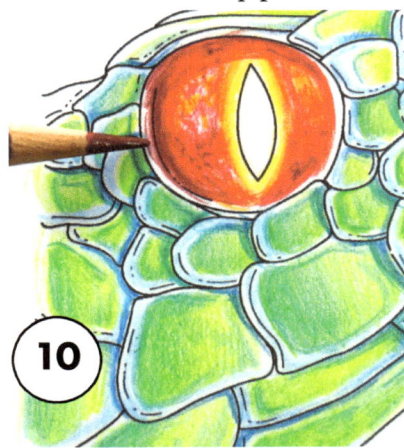

10

I use Tuscan Red 937 on the left side of the eye, in a "C" shape to create a core shadow. I also use it to block in a cast shadow at the top of the eye, under the brow.

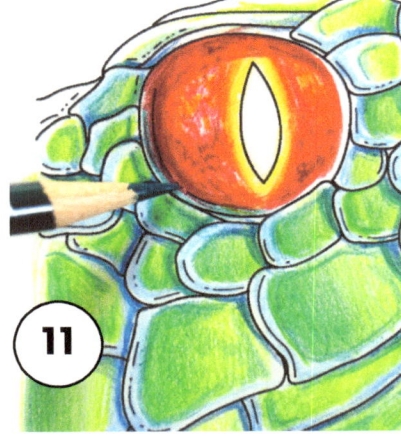

11

Under the red eye, I lightly use some 907 on the inner rim of the lower eyelid. This will act as reflected light.

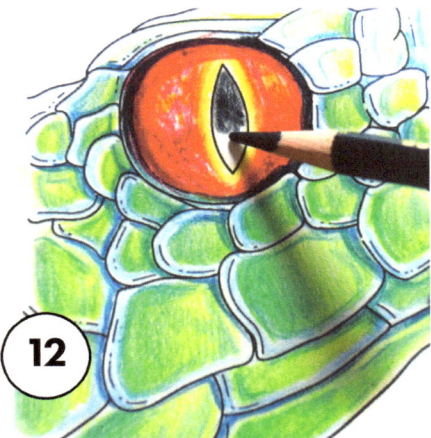

12

I fill in the pupil with Black 935 or if you wish a black permanent pen with blotter paper underneath.

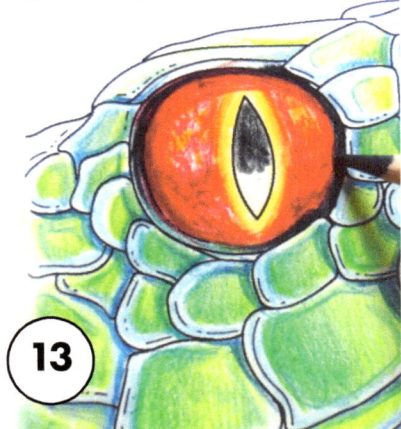

13

I create a circle with Black 935 around the perimeter of the eye, except where the green reflected light is on the lower left. I also add some to the cast shadow.

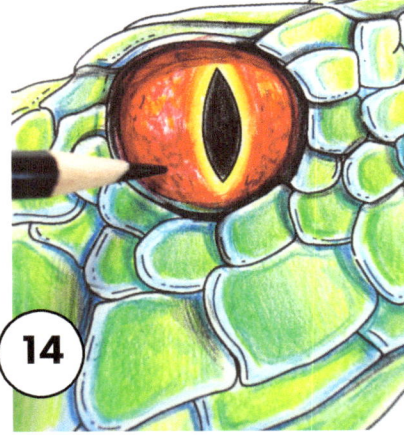

14

I add some tiny Black flecks on the lower half of the red part of the eye. It is imperative to use a very sharp pencil. Don't blend.

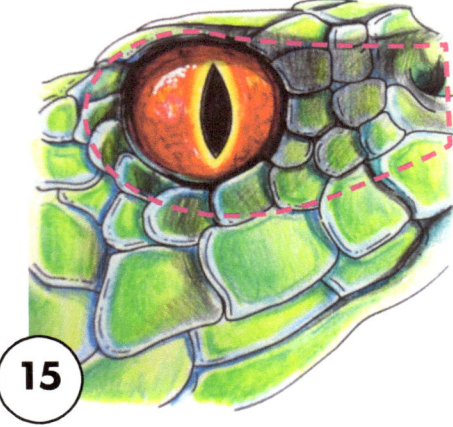

15

Very lightly I add a layer of Black starting from under the brow, around the eye (except the eye and white areas), fading downward. Deepen nostril and mouth line. I make dotted gel pen highlights where the shadow starts.

Cat

You will need:

- The "Animal Eyes" line art page
- Prismacolor Premier:
  940, 916, 1003, 943, 1098, 918, 948, 920, 908, 935
- Kneaded eraser to lighten (optional)
- Mono Zero eraser pen for mistakes (optional)
- Uniball Signo white gel pen
- Black waterproof pen such as Copic,
  Faber-Castell or Micron (optional)

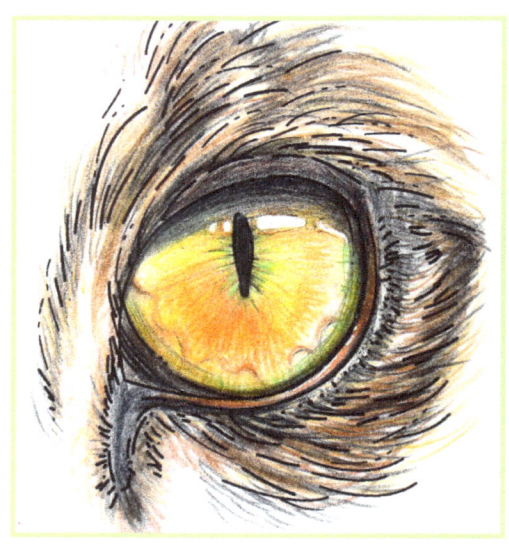

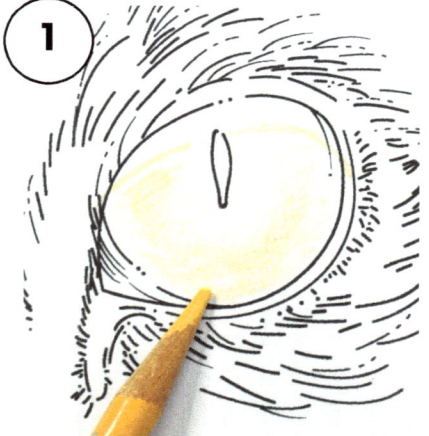

1

I begin by drawing a light colored arc from the left to the right side of the eye over the pupil. I fill in the bottom section with Sand 940. Leaving white space in the middle.

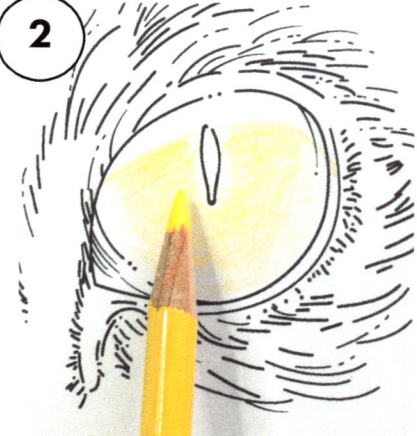

2

Next, I intensify the middle of the eye with Canary Yellow 916, filling in most of the white space.

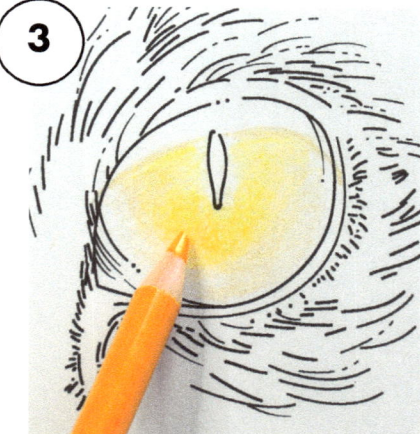

3

Then I deepen the color just below the pupil, starting with Spanish Orange 1003.

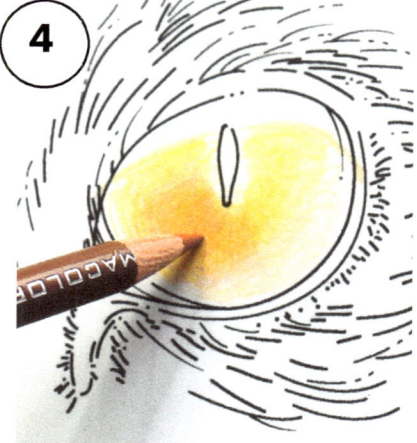

4

On top of that I introduce some Burnt Ochre 943, blending in circles. I don't go quite up to the pupil.

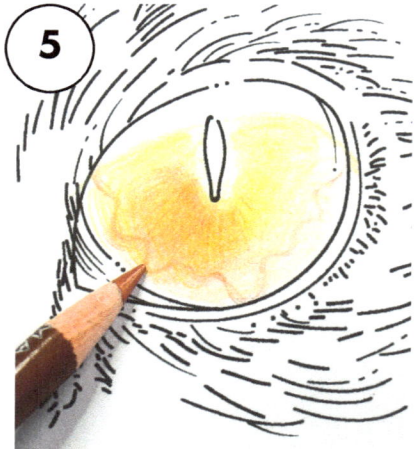

5

Then, with a razor sharp point, I draw a wavy line for variation in the iris. This makes it look real!

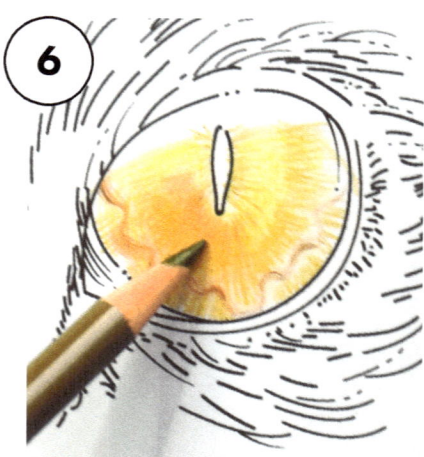

6

Now, I use a razor sharp Artichoke 1098 pencil to create short "rays" going outward from the pupil, and a second row that extends to the edge of the iris.

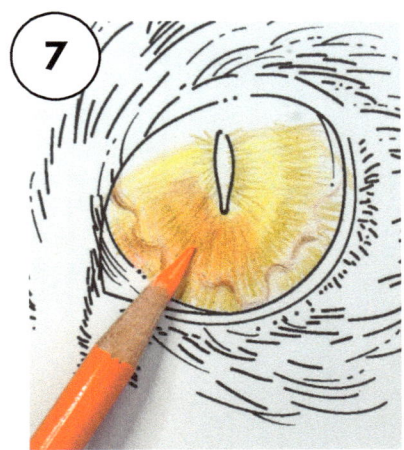

7

Now I intensify the brownish splotch with some Orange 918, and bring some to the left edge too.

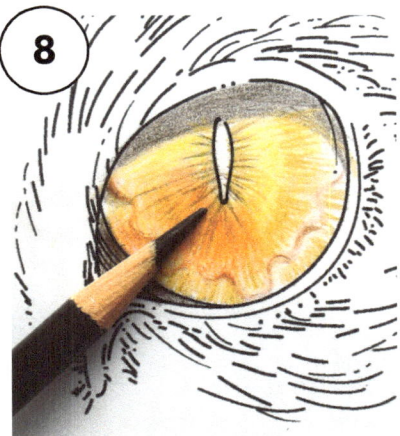

8

I then use a super-sharp Sepia 948 to darken the center "rays" and add the cast shadow from the eyelid above, and skin below.

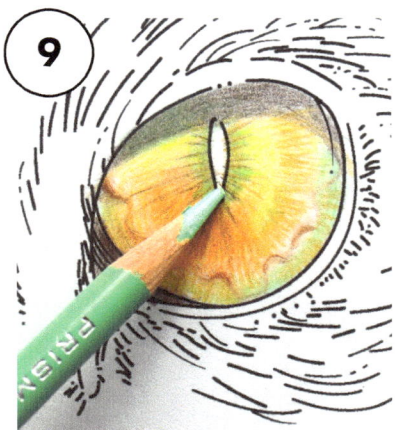

9

Now I add some minty green, Light Green 920, to create drama! It surrounds the pupil (drawn as rays) and fills in the outer edge too.

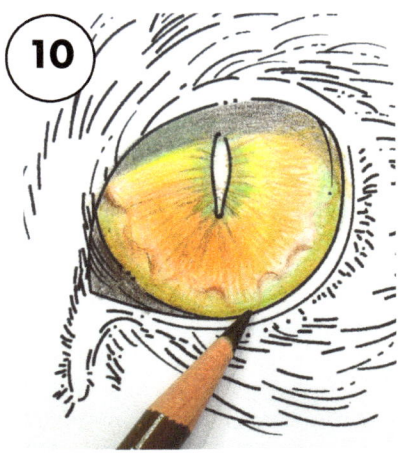

10

Next, I use some 1098 again to create a subtle core shadow on the bottom edge of the eye.

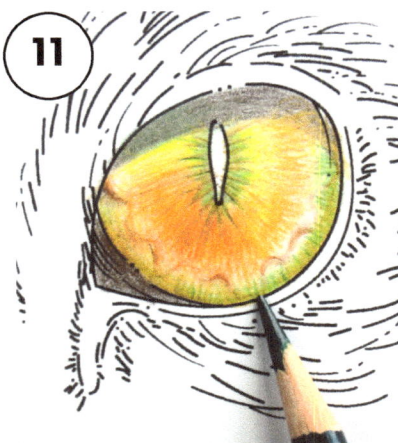

11

I add Dark Green 908 for a few ticks around the edge and I also lightly accent the wavy line a touch too.

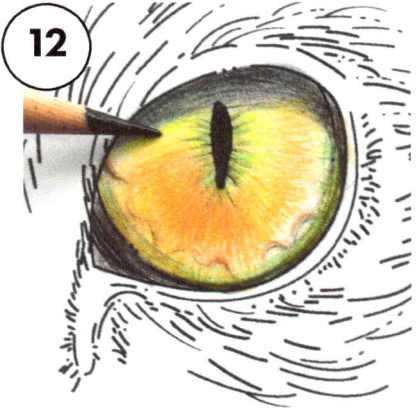

12

I fill in the pupil with Black 935 or if you wish a black permanent pen with blotter paper underneath. I also deepen the shadows.

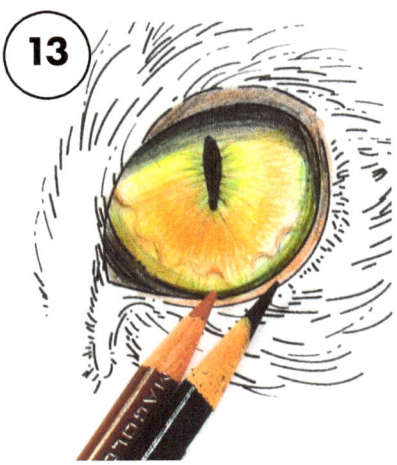

13

I blend 943 and 935 around the eyelid rim, with no black on the very bottom. Because it is facing the light, it will have lighter, more intense color than the upper lid.

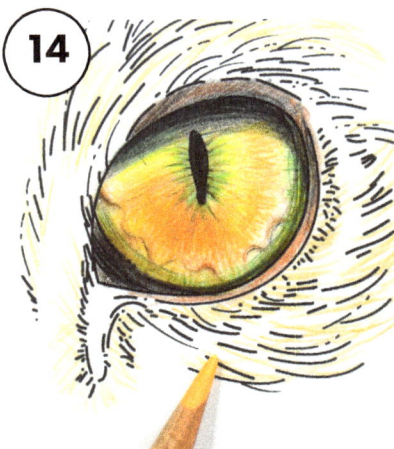

14

See Wolf Eye, Step 12. I use a sharp 940 pencil for quick bent hatch marks, with a bottom-up motion, for each piece of fur above the eye. I use the opposite motion below it. Don't blend.

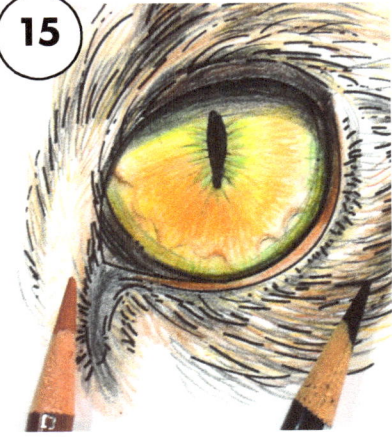

15

Finally, a combination of 943 and 935 is used. Using the same motion as the previous step. Use a white gel pen for a highlight below the top cast shadow, as seen in the finished picture.

Iridescent Beetle

You will need:

- The "Beetle" line art page
- Prismacolor Premier:
  1061, 916, 917, 918, 910, 992, 912, 989, 902, 907, 1065, 935
- Kneaded eraser to lighten (optional)
- Mono Zero eraser pen for mistakes (optional)

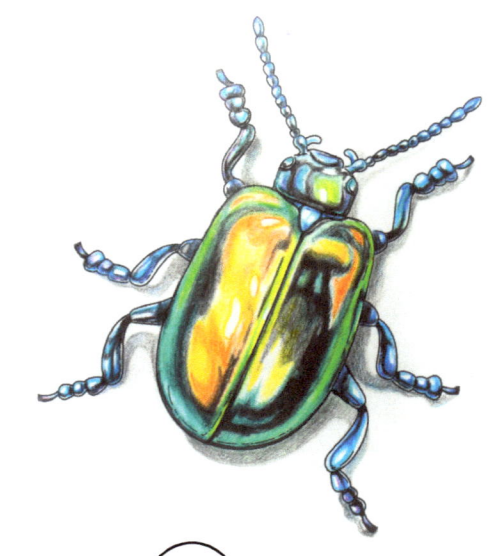

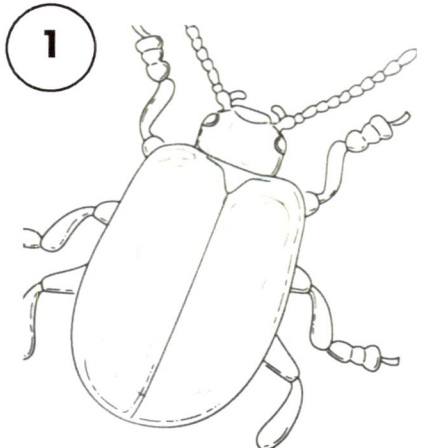

Step 1 is to use Cool Grey 20% 1061 or graphite pencil to "carve in" the individual shapes of reflections that will make up the beetle.

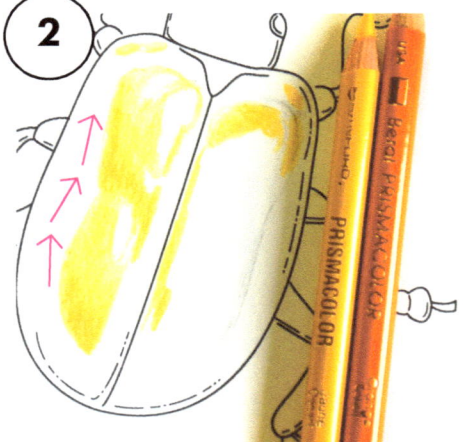

Next, I use Canary Yellow 916 and afterwards, Sunburst Yellow 917. I softly gradate the colors, as you see, directionally with the length of the shape.

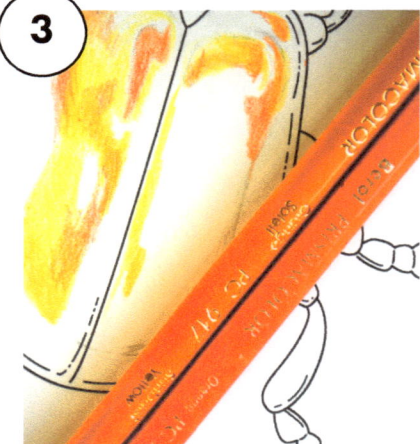

Then I deepen a portion of each shape, using stronger Orange 918, feathering it into the color below.

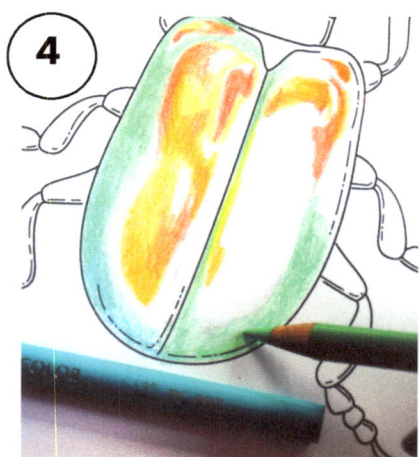

Next, I fill in the outer shape of the body with reflected light! True Green 910, with a hint of Light Aqua 992 (on the left side) works well because the shell is metallic.

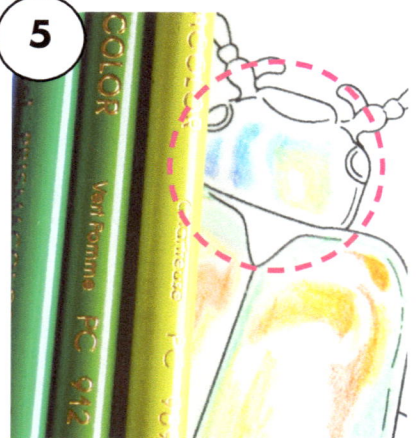

For the beetle's head, use 992, 902, 910, 912, 989. Darker and more blue on left, greens on right, with the Chartreuse closest to the highlight. I leave white spaces in between the shapes for now.

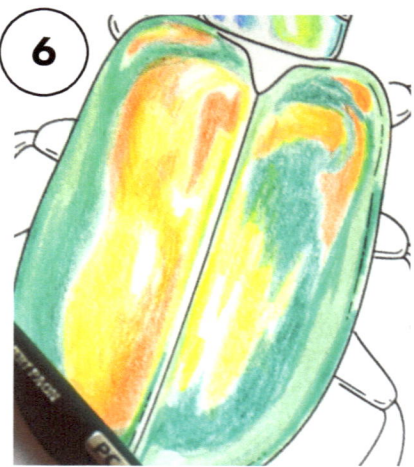

Next, I fill in the biggest shape on the right with the Peacock Green 907. I also add a layer of it, as a gradation, on the left side of the beetle by blending.

7

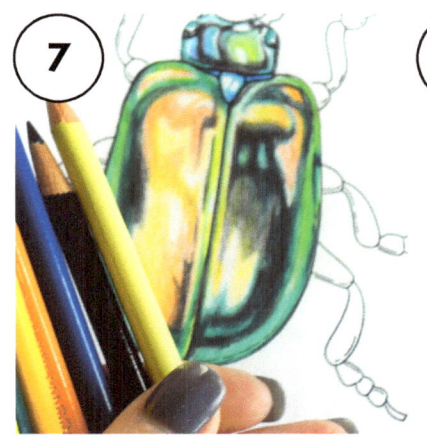

Time for contrast. A layer of Black over some of the 907 and a second layer to darken a few key spots needing more solid coverage, plus the white head.

8

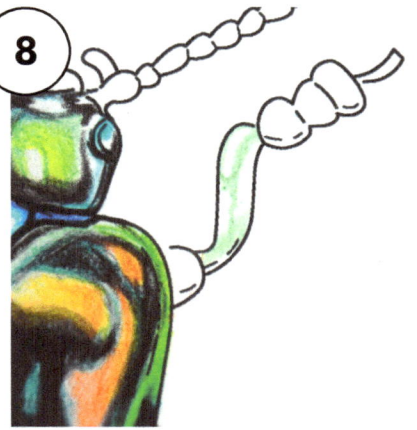

The legs! First step is to use the 910 to fill the middle segment, leaving a few curved white spots for shiny highlights.

9

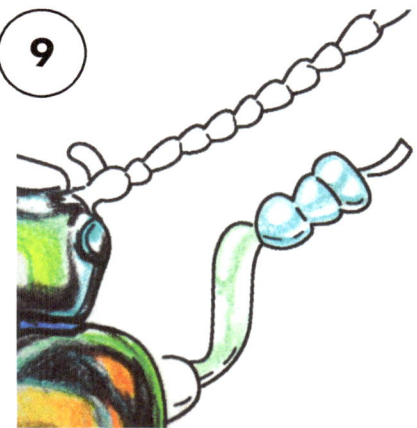

The next segment down I will do the same, but with 992. Since this is a rounder shape, I will make a round highlight next to the curved one. Color the eyes and mouth too.

10

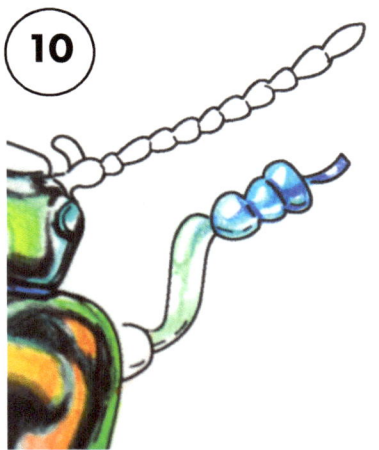

Now I use my Ultramarine 902 to deepen the last segment, right in between the two white shapes. I also fill the foot.

11

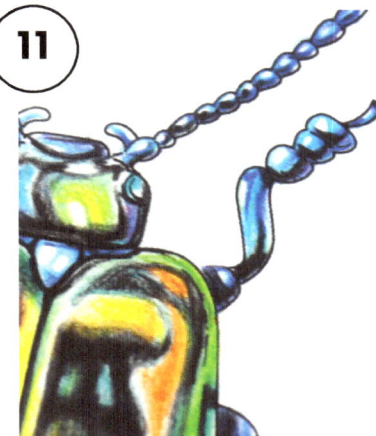

More 902 deepening color as I move towards the body. Don't cover up all your green. I use Steps 9 & 10 on the antennae also.

12

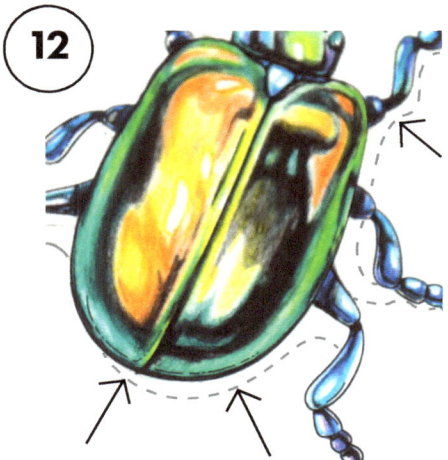

Now, if you'd like to make this beetle look real, give it a cast shadow. Use a light Grey pencil to draw a curvy line around the beetle as I did, to the right of each part of its body and downward a little.

13

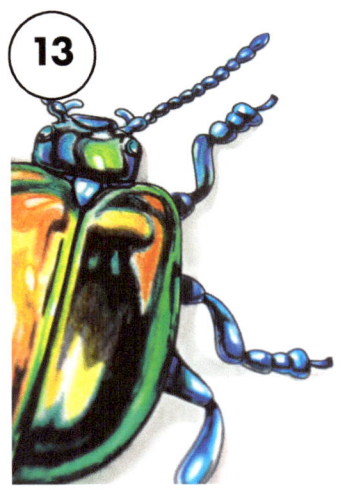

Fill in this shadow with a light but solid Grey 1061.

14

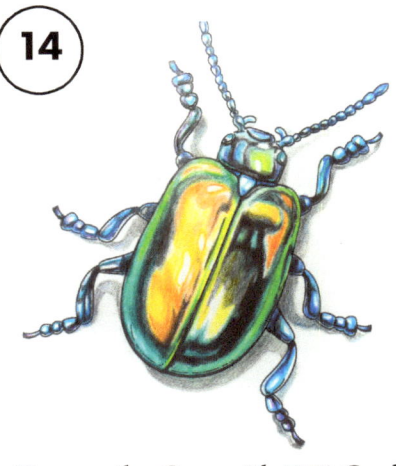

Deepen the Grey with 70% Cool Grey 1065 and a little Black 935 right under the bug! Vôila!

Coloring Bleeding Heart Flowers using Colored Pencil

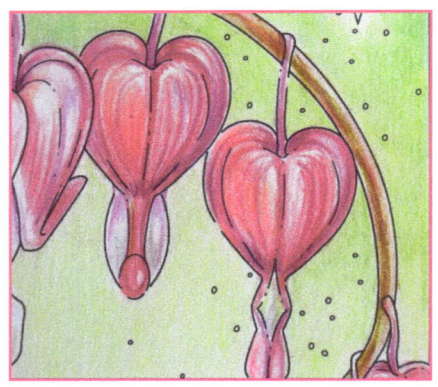

You will need:

- The "Bleeding Hearts" line art page

- Primsacolor Premier Pencils in 993, 994, 956, 995, 1038, 1009, 912, 943, 1098, 1061

- Optional: Mono Zero eraser pen, Kneaded eraser for mistakes

1

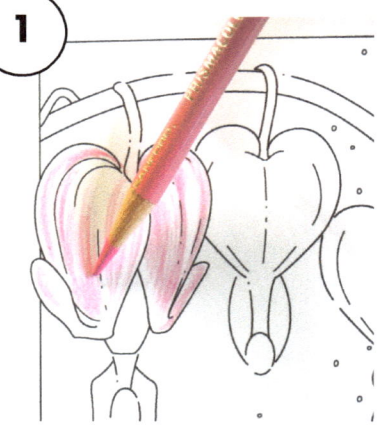

I begin directionally hatching with 993 from the bottom of the flower upwards, using a very sharp pencil. The marks shouldn't blend – we want to show texture.

2

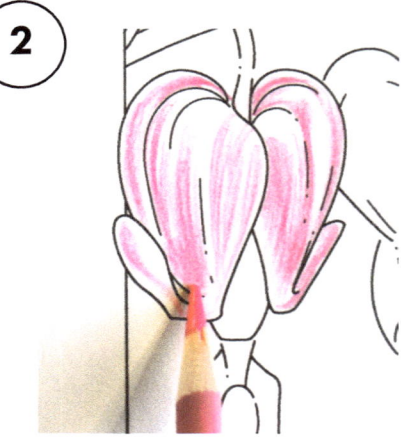

Using the same "bent" hatching motion, from the bottom – I add another layer. Perhaps these don't come up as high to keep the variation interesting.

3

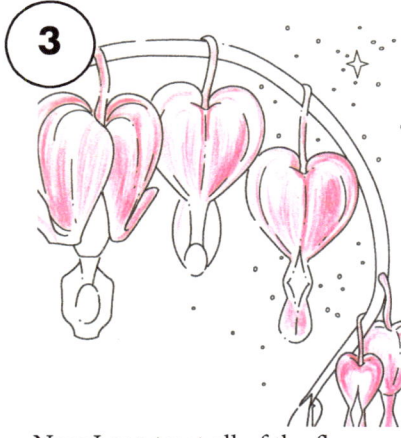

Now I can treat all of the flowers similarly, leaving some white spaces around some of the "bumps" and "ridges" of each flower that will be highlights. Don't forget the stems!

4

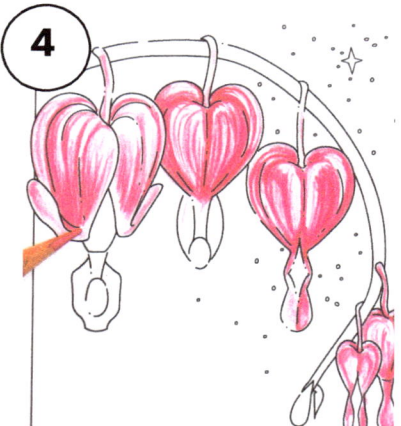

Next, I add Process Red 994 in the shadow areas and in the main valleys between ridges. This provides some contrast. I'm leaving the front flower a little lighter to emphasize it.

5

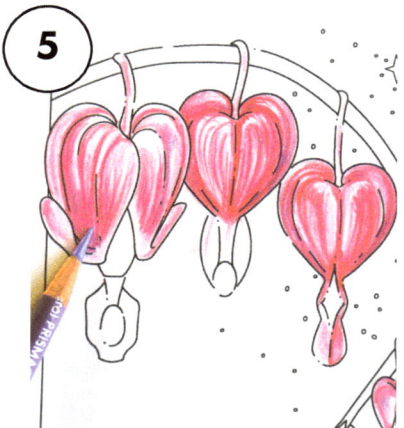

Now time for the cool color – reflected light. I add a little Lilac 956 around a few of the bumps. I overlap the last colors a bit. These marks should blend, so go softly.

6

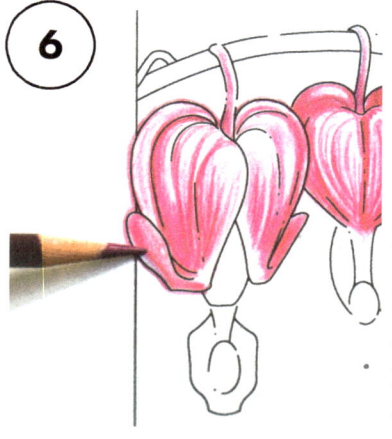

Mulberry 995, is used to take it a step further. I add a core shadow to the little "arms" of the flower. Notice I haven't made it dark all the way to the left edge – I leave some reflected light.

7

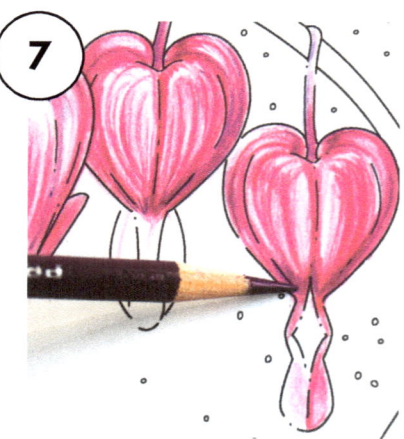

I deepen the deepest ridges with a Dahlia Purple 1009 instead of black. This way it is more vibrant. I deepen the top, where the stem sits for each flower, as well.

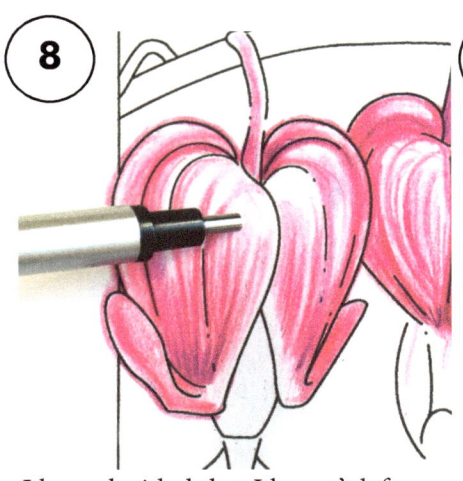

8

I have decided that I haven't left enough white for a highlight on the front flower so I am using a Mono Zero Eraser to gently remove some color. To learn more about this tool and other suggestions, go to:

moderncoloring.com/recommended-products

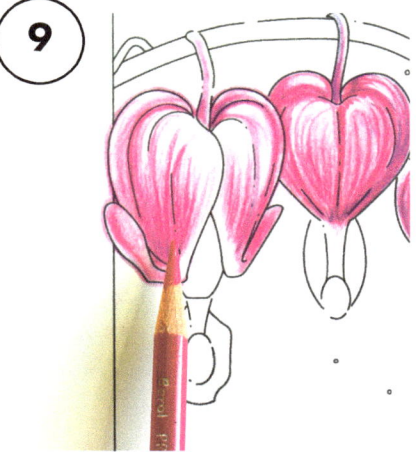

9

Now, using an upward sweep I'm gently blending some of the 994 from bottom upwards to make the color richer.

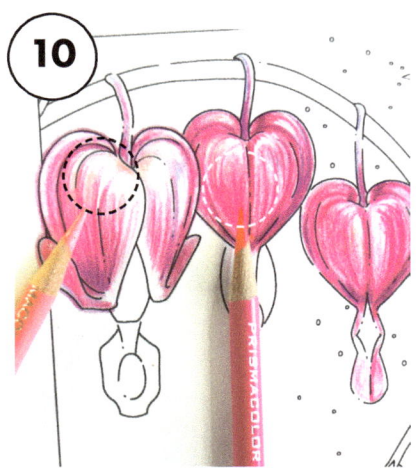

10

For some added punch I use a little bit of Neon Pink 1038 near the centers of flowers and Blush Pink to surround the white highlight. The Blush Pink 928 is a warm pink with some orange tones – adds dimension!

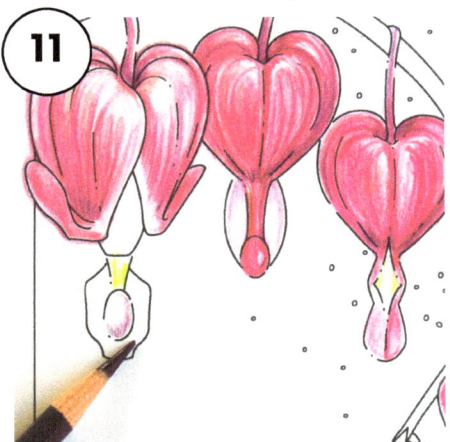

11

Dahlia Purple 1009 will fill in the bottom of the little egg shape and details on the left two flowers. Above it I add a little Apple Green 912, as well.

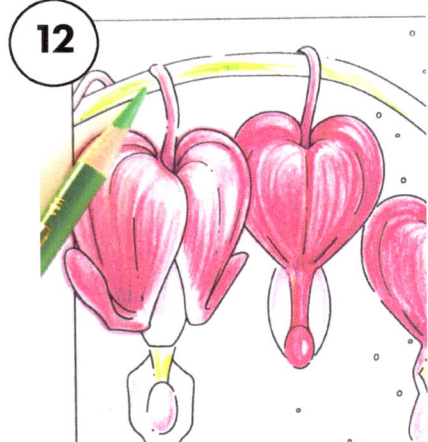

12

I use the same green to begin the branch itself. I have a very sharp pencil and don't blend my sideways hatches. Keep them scratchy!

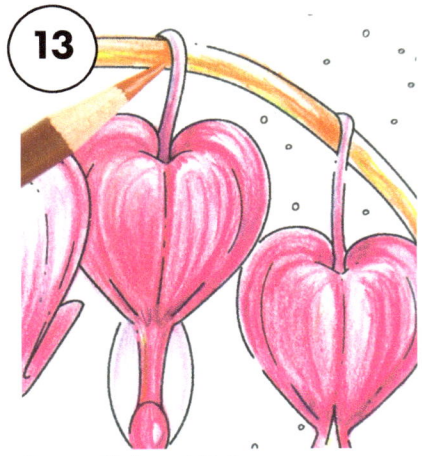

13

Burnt Ochre 943 is a warm brown that adds more texture to the branch. Same scratchy strokes with a sharp pencil.

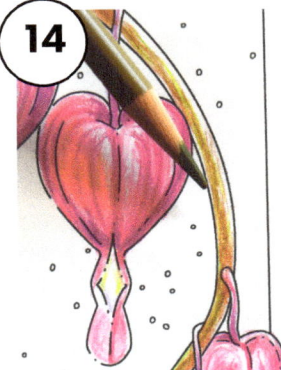

14

Now I go over the branch with a little Artichoke 1098 and establish a core shadow. It should be the darkest area so far.

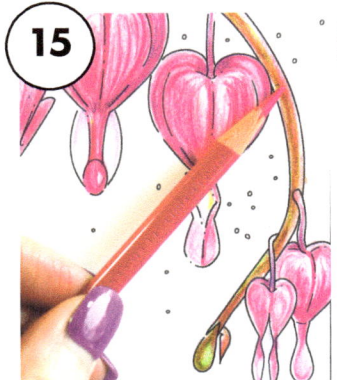

15

Optional: I add some 994 over the branch to give it a pink cast. Some Bleeding Heart plants look more pink than others, overall.

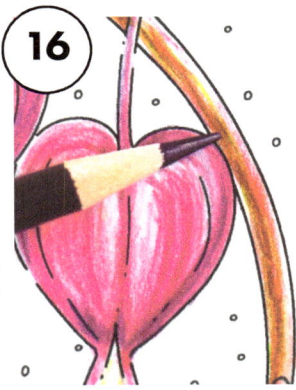

16

Back to the 1009 Dahlia Purple. I'm adding to the core shadow in patches so it looks more natural than an outline.

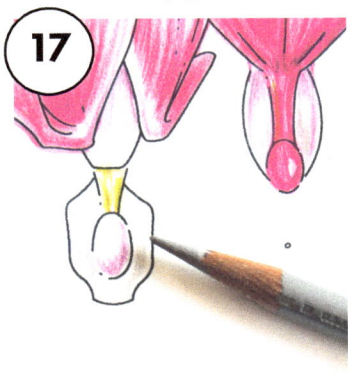

17

Finally, a few hits of Light Warm Grey 20% 1061 for the outside shapes on the bottoms of the blossoming flowers.

Metals

Metals are actually quite simple once you get the hang of them: Yellow Gold, Rose Gold, and Pewter

Shiny Yellow Gold and Rose Gold

To help you visualize, I will use a couple of analogies:

- Where to place your marks = hands of a clock, i.e., midnight would be at top

- The shape of the dark reflection = a shark egg (I know, strange, but search and you will see!)

For yellow gold, you will need:

- To download the **white version** of the "Sparkling Gems" line art page from ModernColoring.com/freebies. To access, enter the secret code found on the backside of one of the last pages of this book.

- Prismacolor Premier:
  940, 916, 1034, 946, 918, 935

- Optional:
  Mono Zero eraser pen or kneaded eraser for mistakes

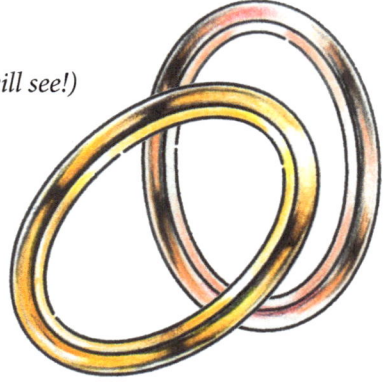

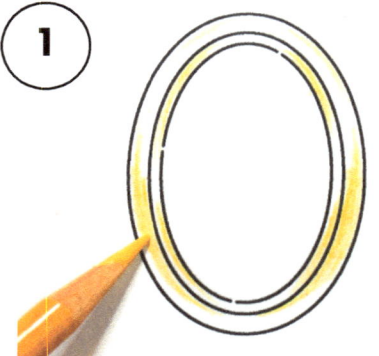

1

I start with Sand 940 to make it natural. I place it on both sides of the ring at "4:00" and "8:00" in the big ring and small, plus "10:00" and "1:00" for mostly the small ring.

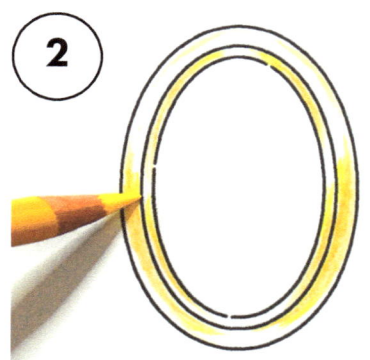

2

Just a touch of Canary Yellow 916 to extend the first color on both sides at 3:00 and 9:00 and a hint on the small ring on both *sides* of "6:00" and "12:00." Leave the centers white.

3

On top of the last color, add a shorter mark in the middle that looks like a "mermaid purse" (shark egg) on both sides, in all four spots using Dark Brown 946. Extend the legs of the shape out long.

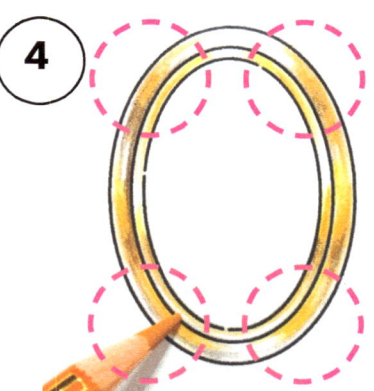

4

I use a long stroke of Goldenrod 1034 between "1:00" and "2:00" and "4:00" and "5:00" then the same on the opposite side. Leave white spaces you see here.

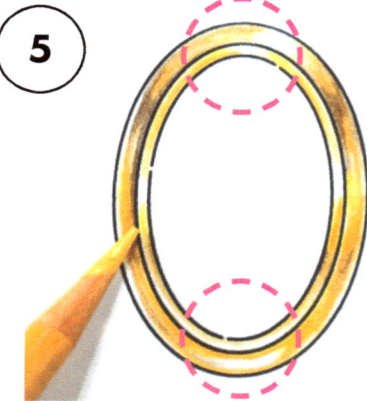

5

Now back to my 940 to fill in under the small ring and closer to the white at the top. Add a sweep of Orange 918 right in the center under the small ring (circled).

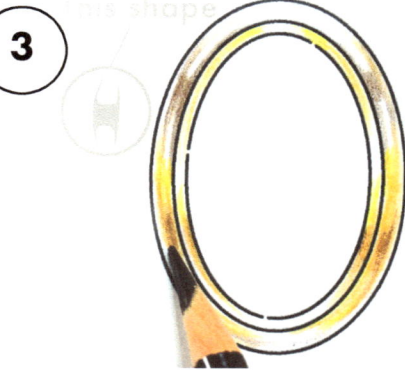

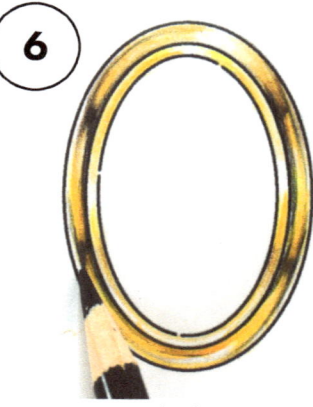

6

Now I use my Black 935 to add a thinner "mermaid purse" on top of the others. Use a very sharp pencil! Don't blend it. Give it long, skinny legs that fade. That's it!

For rose gold, you will need:

- To download the **white version** of "Sparkling Gems" line art page

- Prismacolor Premier:
  1013, 928, 1092, 993, 1076, 935

- Optional:
  Mono Zero Eraser Pen or kneaded eraser for mistakes

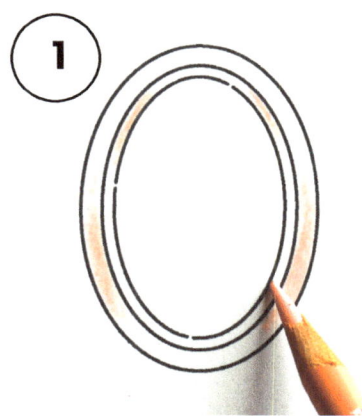

1

I start with Deco Peach 1013. I place it on both sides of the ring at "4:00" and "8:00" in the big ring and small, plus "10:00" and "1:00" for mostly the small ring.

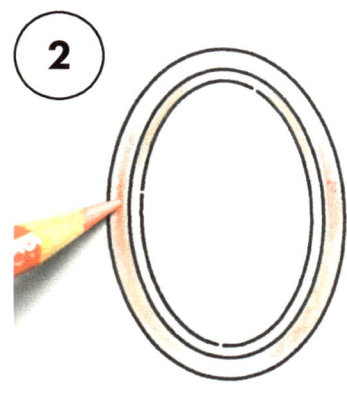

2

A hint of Blush Pink 928 extends the first color on both sides at 3:00 and 9:00 and a hint on the small ring on both *sides* of "6:00" and "12:00." Leave the centers white.

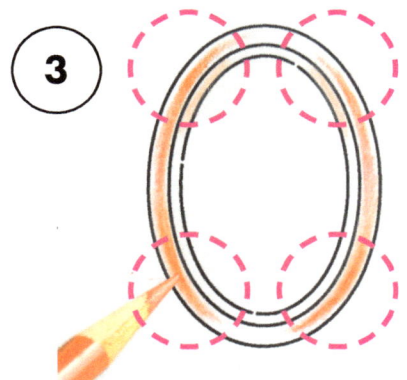

3

I use a long stroke of Nectar 1092 between "1:00" and "2:00" and "4:00" and "5:00" Then on the opposite side. Leave white spaces where you see them here.

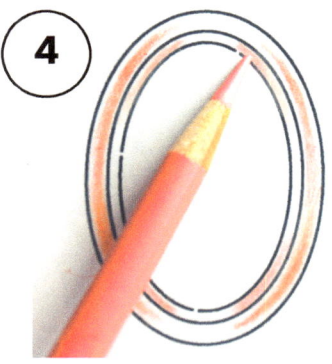

4

I'm extending the Blush Pink on both sides of "12:00" just a bit here. Add a sweep of 928 right in the center under the small ring too (not pictured here). For slightly more intense color, blend a hint of Hot Pink 993.

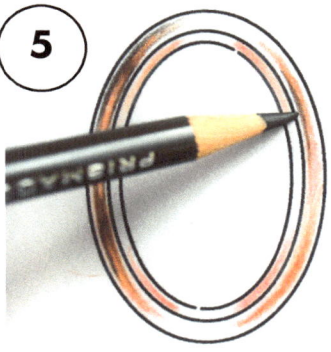

5

On top of the last color, add a shorter mark in the middle that looks like a "mermaid purse" (shark egg), like Step 3 – Yellow Gold, on both sides, in all four spots using 90% French Grey 1076. Use a very sharp pencil!

Did you know?

Yellow gold is not bright yellow and rose gold is not bright pink, as many new artists may think. Shiny metal is made believable by high contrast values and gentle shifts in color. The more contrast, the shinier something looks. Chrome is mostly black and white! Illustrators use tricks of the trade to render realistic surfaces. One of these tricks is dividing an object into top and bottom sections. The middle line is the darkest part (where your "mermaid purse" goes). The top half is light (to represent the sky) and the bottom is darker (like the ground), especially in the middle. A few white gel pen highlights and poof! Look at the ULTRA SHINY gold here. Do you see a blurry sky and ground reflected?

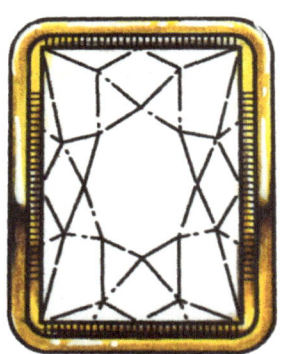

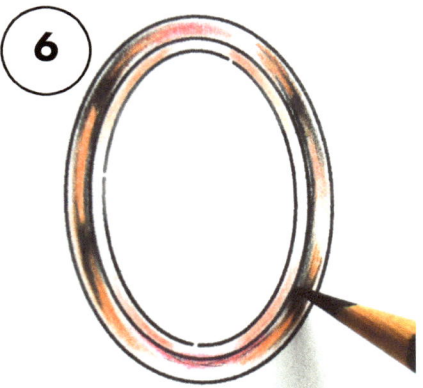

6

Now I use my Black 935 to add a thinner "mermaid purse" on top of the others. Use a very sharp pencil! Don't blend it. Give it long, skinny legs that fade. That's it!

Mirror, Mirror! Pewter

Finish your portrait page with this realistic mirror

You will need:

- Prismacolor Premier:
  1061, 1063, 1065, 919
- Optional:
  Mono Zero eraser pen or kneaded eraser for mistakes

Did you know?

Metals such as Pewter and brushed aluminum are somewhat matte, and less reflective. In drawing we can characterize this by using less contrast with soft transitions between colors. For this Pewter mirror, the range of values (darkness) is low. I am only using four pencils - three grey, and one blue – to complete it.

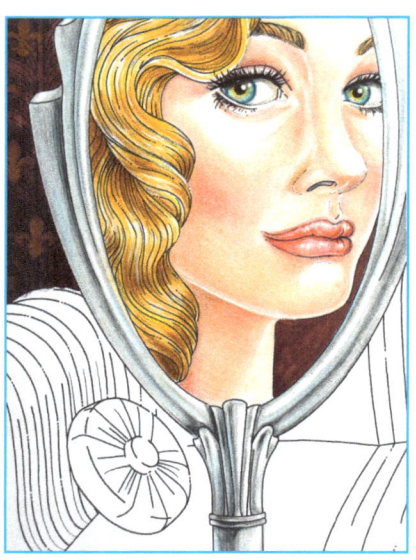

1

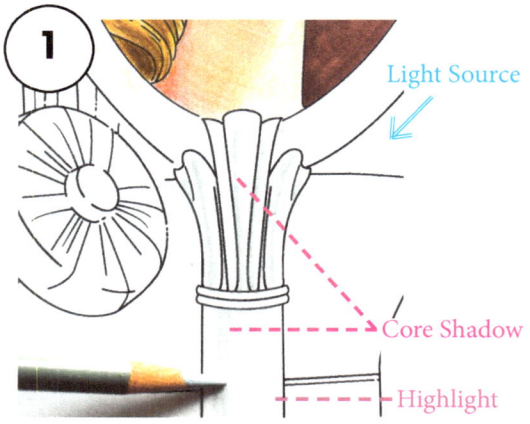

Light Source

Core Shadow

Highlight

I start with 30% Cool Grey 1061, using vertical strokes on the handle. Since the light is coming from the right, the highlight will be on the right side, while the core shadow and reflected light will be on the left of any semi-cylindrical part.

2

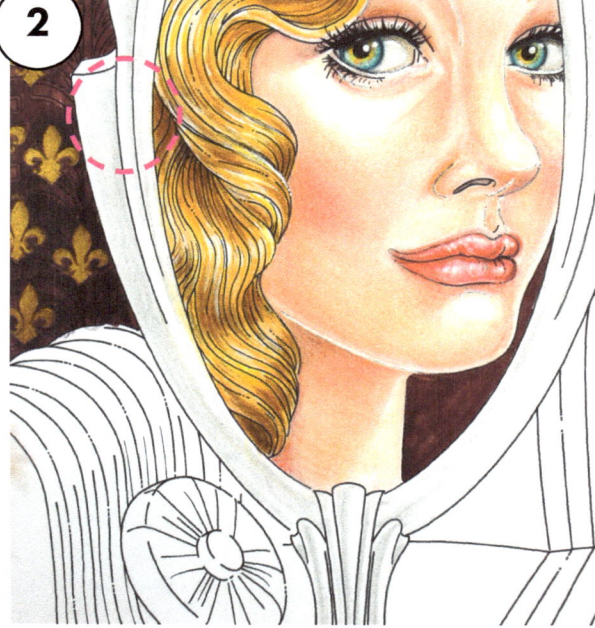

I use the lightest Cool Grey everywhere, only avoiding highlights and reflected light. Because the mirror is made up of flat shapes and cylindrical ones, the treatment is a little different. There is no core shadow showing on the flat areas. I use a second layer to darken any core shadows.

3

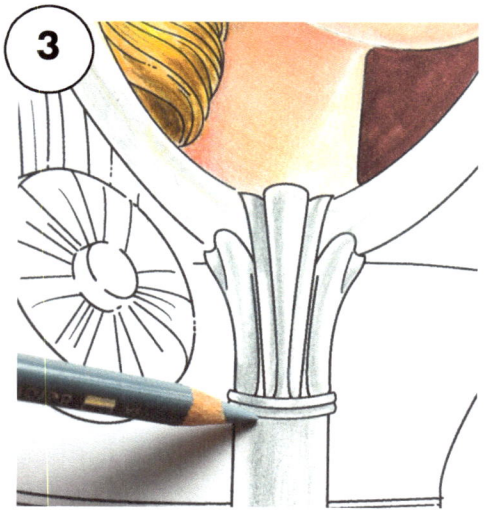

Now I deepen any core shadows by blending 50% Cool Grey 1063 on top of them. Again I'm using vertical strokes and not using much pressure.

4

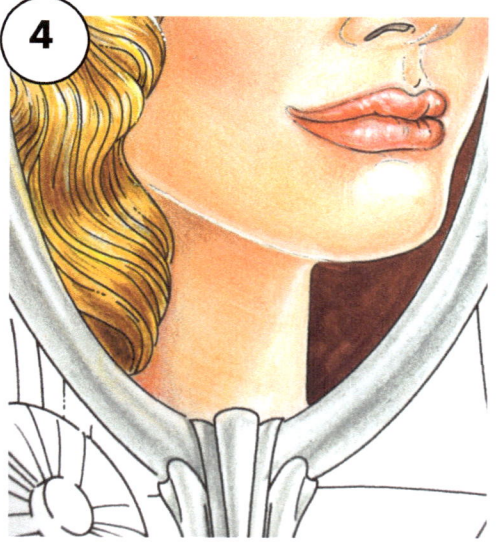

I've gone back in with both pencils and added more greys, and established core shadows for each shape, leaving a little white on both sides.

5

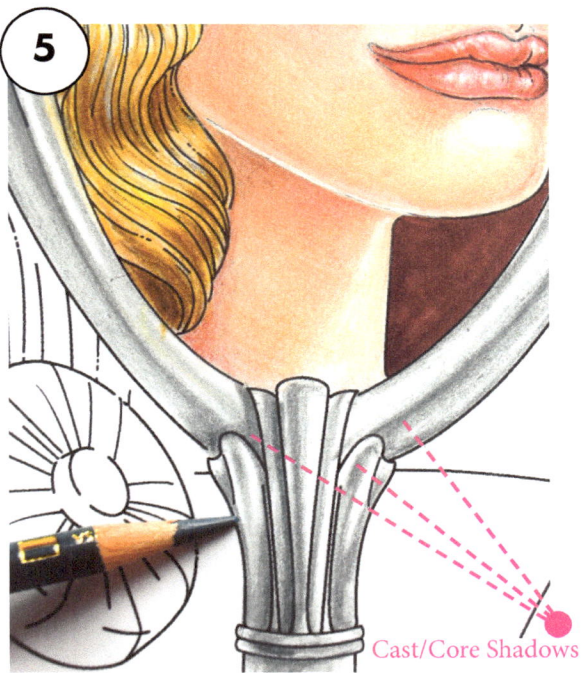

Cast/Core Shadows

Next I introduce some very subtle cast shadows (shadows from one part onto another), using my darkest color, Cool Grey 70% 1065. I bring this right up to the left edge of each part of the decoration on the handle of the mirror, and fade it as it moves to the left. I also deepen the center of each core shadow, just a touch.

6

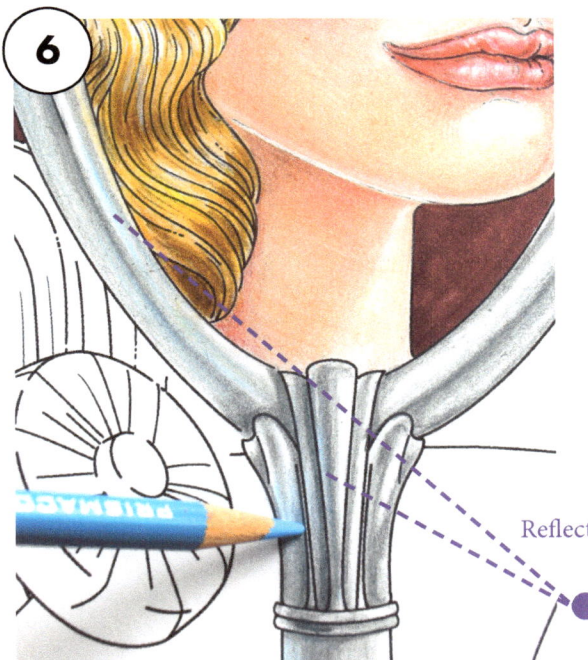

Reflected Light

Finally, it's time for a little reflected light to tie it all together and bring it to life! I use a subtle coating of Non-Photo Blue 919, to the left side of every deep shadow. This color is darker than anything on the light side of each part, just like in the "Darkest Dark in the Light" statement!

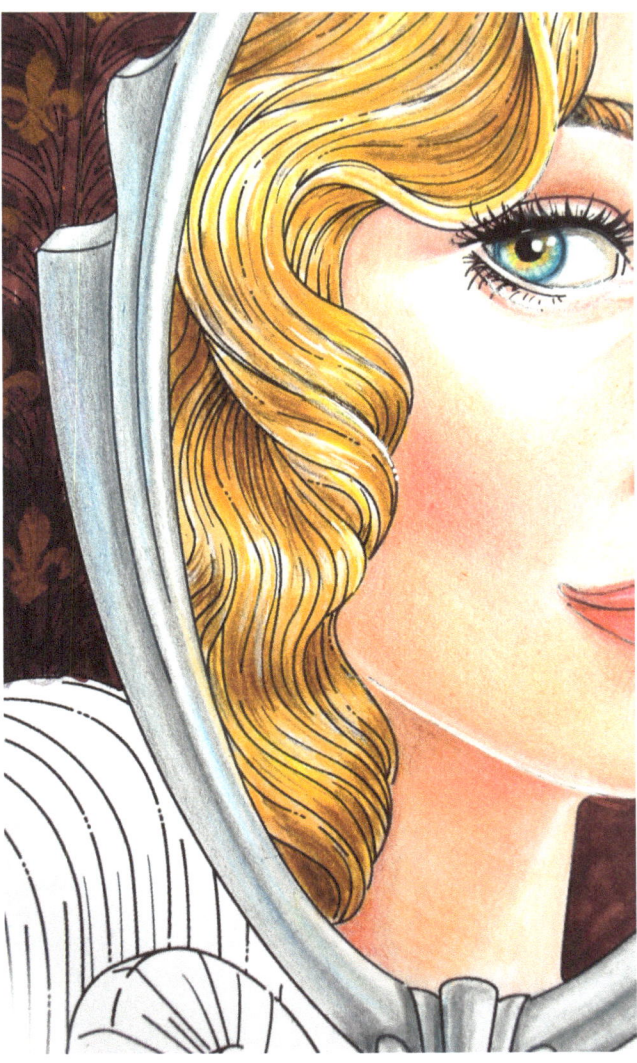

Your beautiful Glamourista's mirror is now complete.

Complex Pearls

I call these "complex", not because they are terribly difficult to recreate, but because of all the detail they come to life! They are definitely more elaborate than the "simple" pearls in my YouTube videos because they are large enough for the details. You can modify the colors for use with smaller pearls.

. . . .

Cobalt Blue Pearl on Toned Paper

You will need:

The "Sparkling Gems" toned paper line art page
-Prismacolor Premier:
  133, 956, 919, 901, 1086, 992, 938, 935
- Optional:
  Mono Zero eraser pen or
  kneaded eraser for mistakes

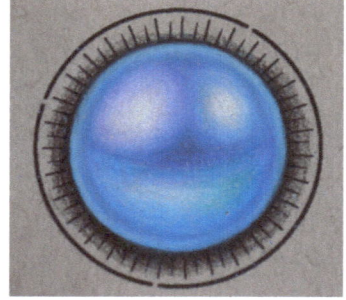 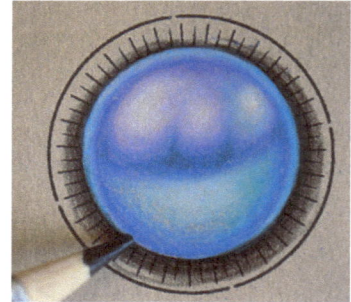

As seen above, there are two ways to begin the pearls - with two highlight reflections or three. Which do you prefer?

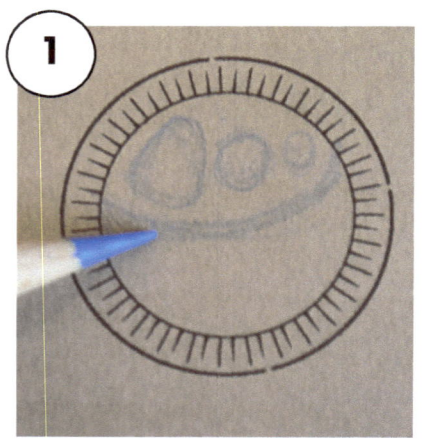

1 I have decided to do a three-reflection pearl and "carved in" 3 shapes plus a "belt" for the core shadow with Cobalt Blue 133.

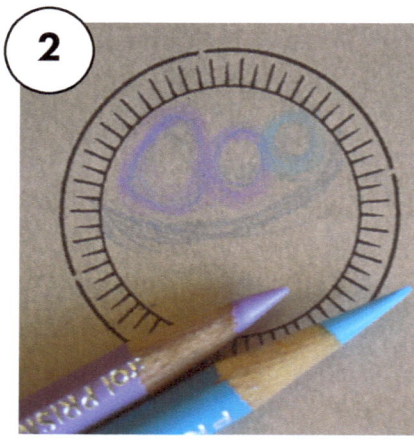

2 Now, I circle the highlights in either a Lilac 956 or Non-Photo Blue 919. I have chosen to do two Lilac, one Non-Photo Blue.

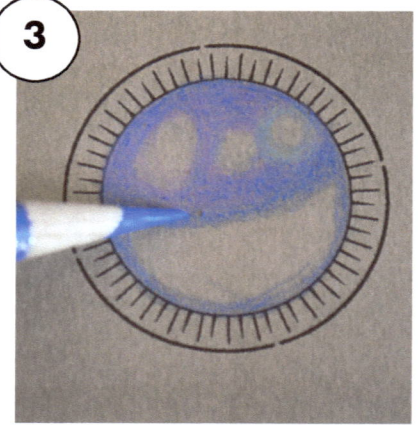

3 I fill the top section with a light coat of Cobalt, and make an edge on the bottom section which forms an empty crescent shape.

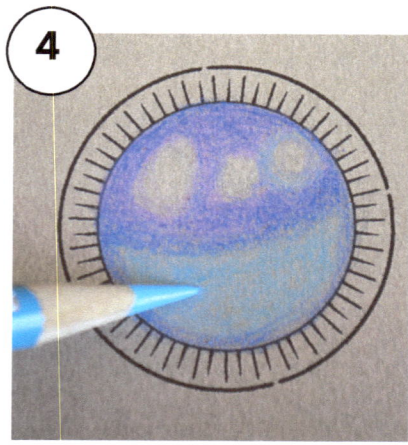

4 Next, I fill in the crescent with 919, lightly. As seen in the next step, I also make a ring of 919 around the whole circle up to the black edge of the line art.

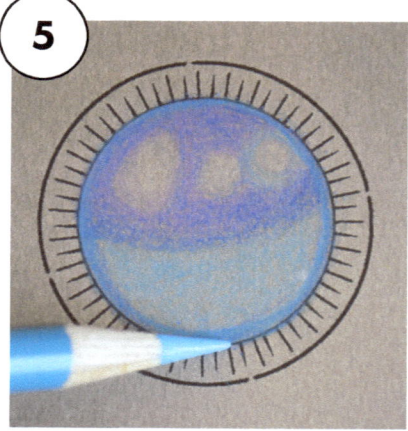

5 This is the reflected light. Sometimes it shows all the way around pearls, other times it disappears as it moves downwards. Either works!

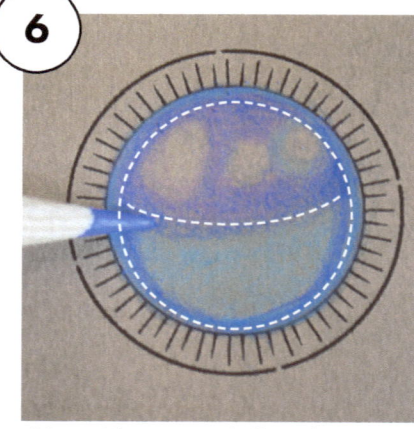

6 Now, I begin to define the core and the inside edge where the reflected light starts with a little more Cobalt 133.

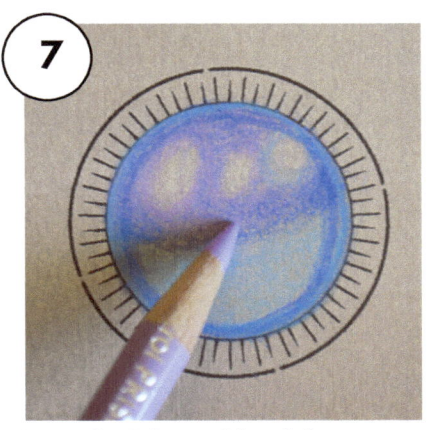

7

I use the Lilac to blend the top half of the pearl, using a "little circles" motion, filling in some of the tooth of the paper.

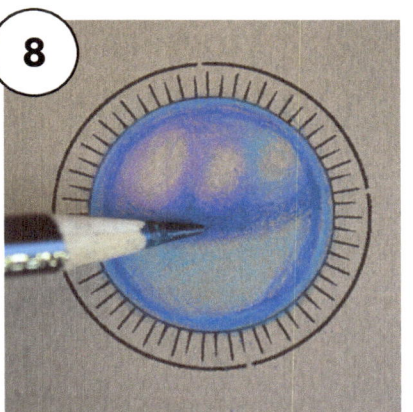

8

I next use some Indigo Blue 901, just in the center of the core and a hint over the darkest areas to deepen them just a touch.

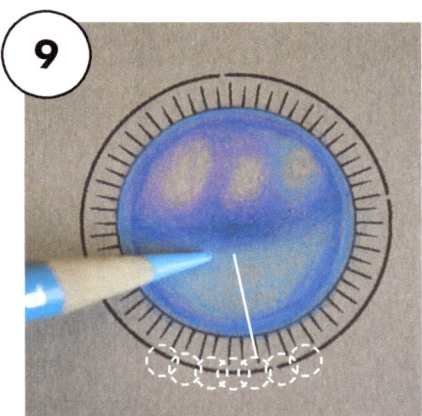

9

Another layer of 919 on the bottom half, all the way up to the core where I use it to soften the line that divides the two sections, by blending back and forth sideways in little circles.

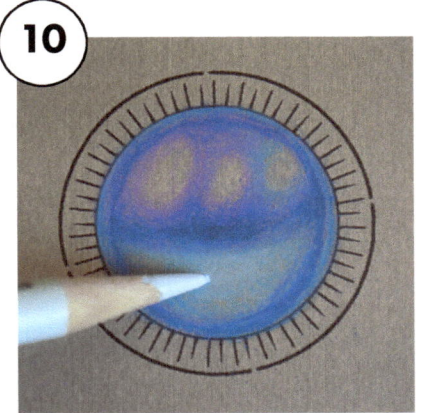

10

Sky Blue Light 1086 is added, only to the to the center of the lower half, to create contrast.

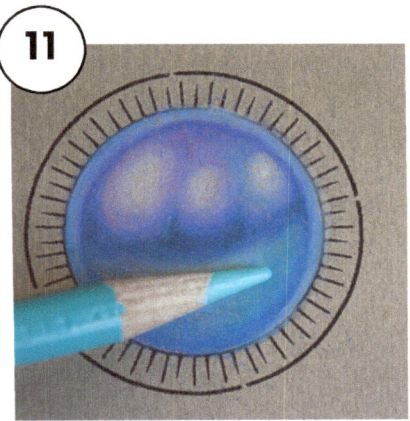

11

For more variation, I introduce a small amount of Light Aqua 992 on the right side of the lower half only, blending it below the core.

12

I go back in and tidy up the edges inside the reflected light with my Cobalt again, building up the layers. I use White 938 (not shown) in the highlights, circling outwards to blend with the 956 and 919. I also use it to lighten the reflected light around the pearl, just a hint.

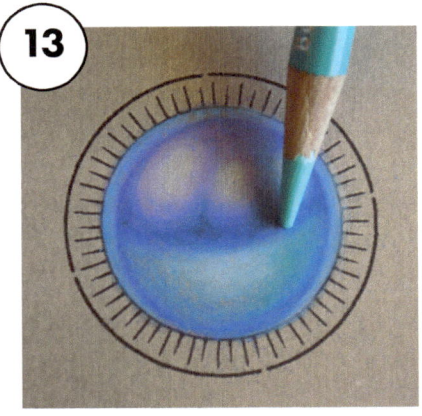

13

I use the 919 again to carefully blend around each section of the pearl and tie it together so that there are no stark lines.

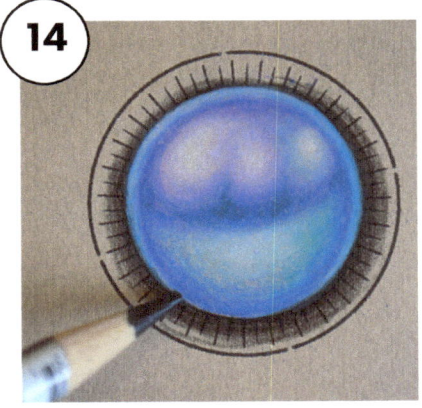

14

The final step is to place a cast shadow with Black 935 on the setting. You can finish the metal as you wish.

Iridescent Metallic Pearl

You will need:

The "Sparkling Gems" toned line art page
-Prismacolor Premier:
1080, 1008, 919, 916, 928, 1063, 993, 1065, 1086, 938 935
- Optional:
Mono Zero eraser pen or
kneaded eraser for mistakes

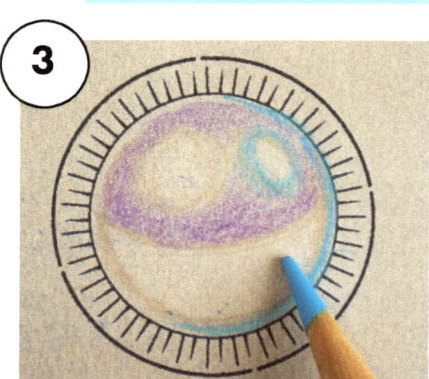

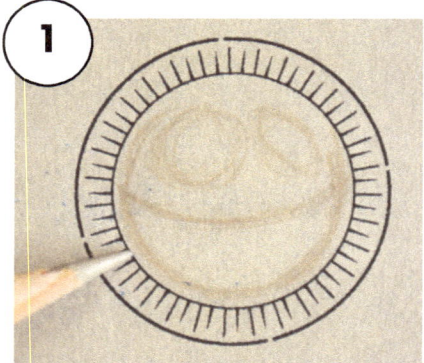

1 I'm starting a 2-highlight pearl and "carved in" 2 shapes plus a "belt" for the core shadow with space for the reflected light, in Beige Sienna 1080.

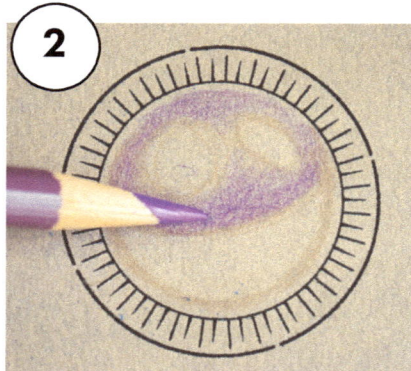

2 Now, I fill in most of the top portion around the reflections with Parma Violet 1008. I leave the edge blank.

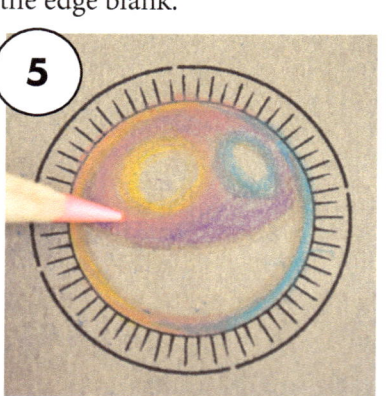

3 I use Non-Photo Blue 919 to fill in the right side reflected light and to form a glow around the right highlight.

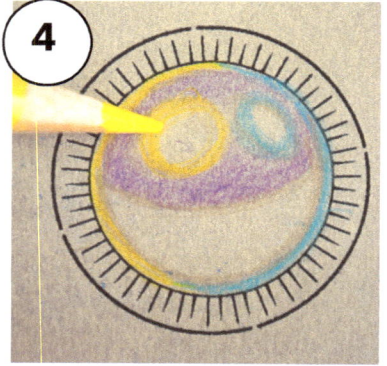

4 Now I do the same to the left with Canary Yellow 916.

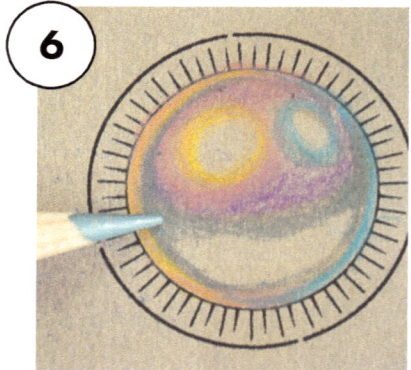

5 I blend the 916 into the 1008 with a little Blush Pink 928, using little circles and filling in the paper tooth.

6 For some contrast I use Cool Grey 50% 1063 along the outer original lines, defining the core shadow and up to the reflected light.

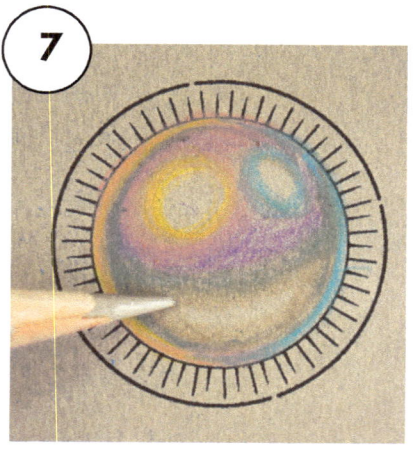

7 I introduce a small amount of 1080 inside the Grey lines of the sideways crescent shape, "fuzzing" it in to blend with the paper color.

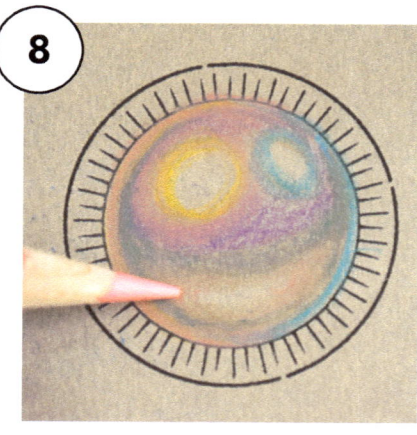

8 On both left and right of the lower half, I use a combination of 928 and Hot Pink 993 (not shown here), at both far ends of the crescent. I blend it again, leaving the very center empty.

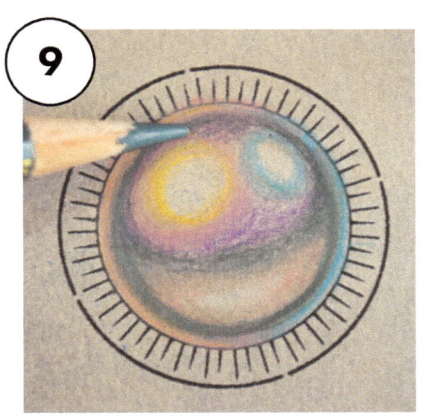

9

Next, I use some Cool Grey 70% 1065 to add more definition to the lighter Cool Grey in Step 6.

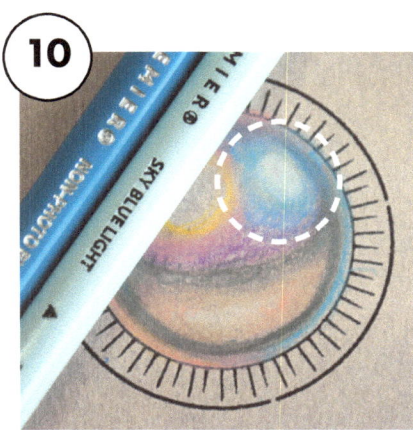

10

It's time to blend the right highlight. I use a combination of Sky Blue Light 1086 and then 919 to circle outward around the small shape.

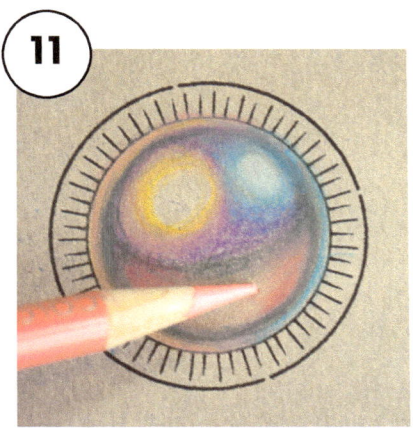

11

Another layer of the pinks on the lower half, with the brighter pink in the corners of the crescent shape. I will later lighten it again.

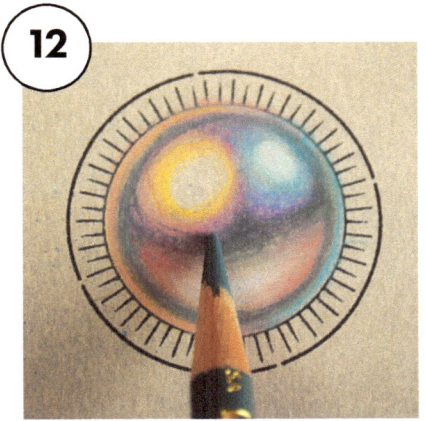

12

Once again, I deepen the core shadow with 1065.

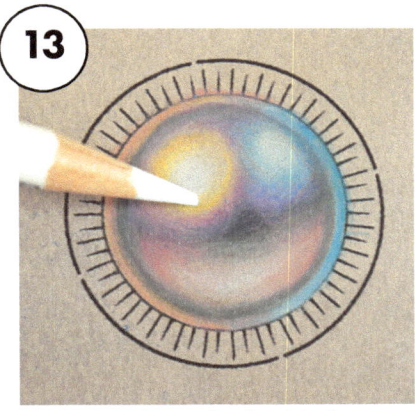

13

Now I brighten the highlights with White 938, circling outward to blend. I also use it to blend my core shadow, but with less pressure.

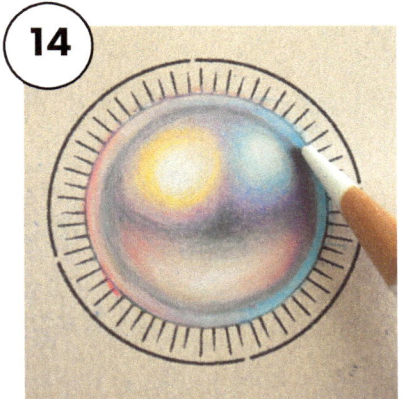

14

I use the white to smooth the reflected light around the whole pearl. Add a little more Hot Pink to the left side and a little more Non-Photo Blue to the right, if not bright enough. I blend here and there.

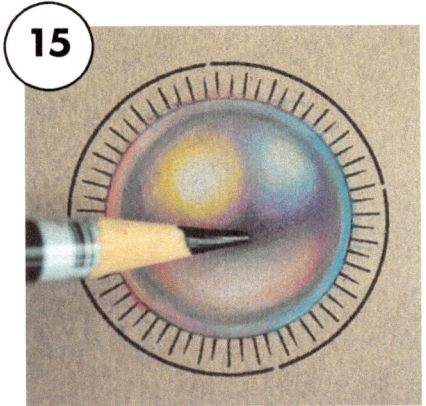

15

Only in the very center I use a hint of Black 935, with a super-light hand. This really makes the pearl start to look reflective!

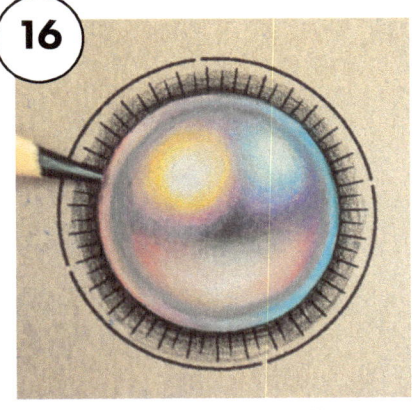

16

A Black cast shadow really sets my pearl off nicely. Darker right underneath the pearl; lighter as I move away from it.

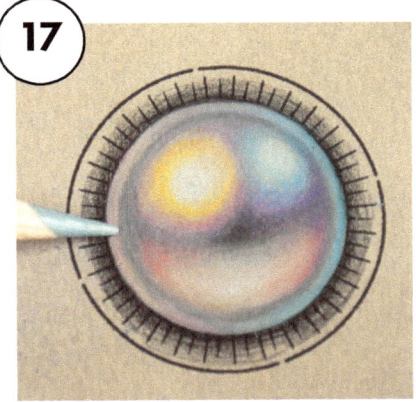

17

I've decided to add a coat of 1063 on the reflected light. It dulls the color a little and gives the pearl an amazing luminescence.

Satin Ribbon

You will need:

- The "Ribbon" line art page
- Prismacolor Premier:
  943, 945, 918, 1003, 1082, 914
- Optional:
  Mono Zero eraser pen or
  kneaded eraser for mistakes

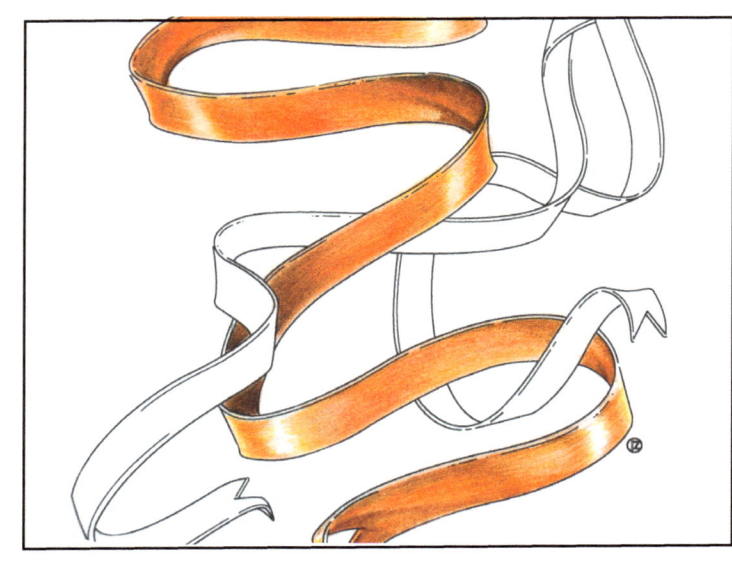

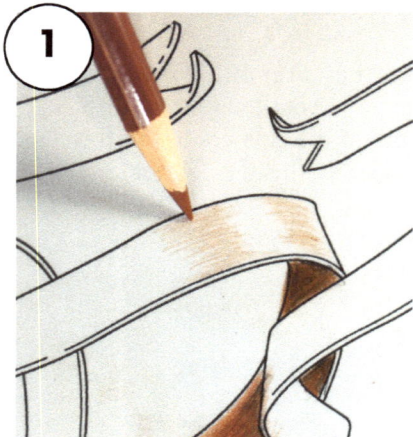

1 I start by turning my page upside down so that I can hatch with the direction of the ribbon. This section is bending outward so I will leave a highlight (white space). I am using a very sharp Burnt Ochre 943 pencil, so that my hatch marks will show at the bend. I will gradate this toward the inward bend (left in this picture).

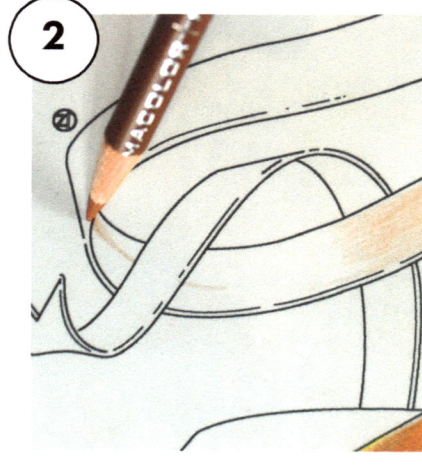

2 Next, I use a layer of pencil on the inside bend to create a crease in the ribbon. It basically starts as a line.

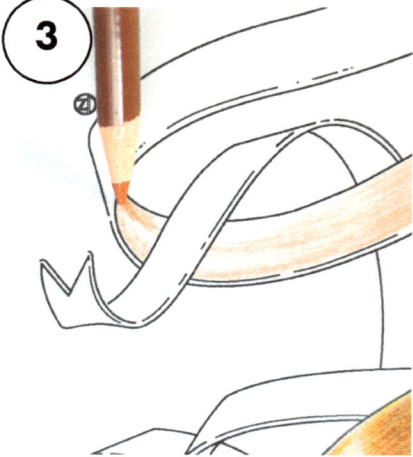

3 Next, deepen the color, start filling in the ribbon, and connect the two sections, leaving some white space for later.

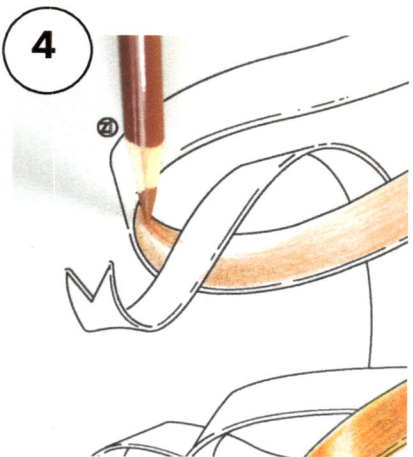

4 Sienna Brown 945 is a little deeper than the first color, so I darken the top part of the inner bend.

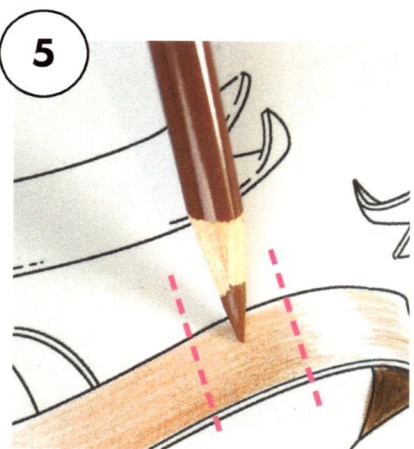

5 I use the same color to create a slightly darker, subtle core shadow to make it look more reflective.

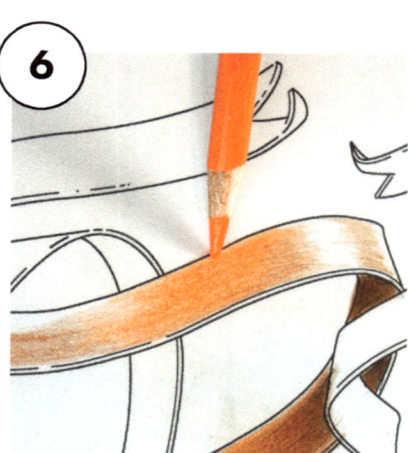

6 Next, I add some warmth using Orange 918 to the flattest middle area - a very light coat. I also add a little Orange to the crease of the white area, in the inner bend as you will see in step 9.

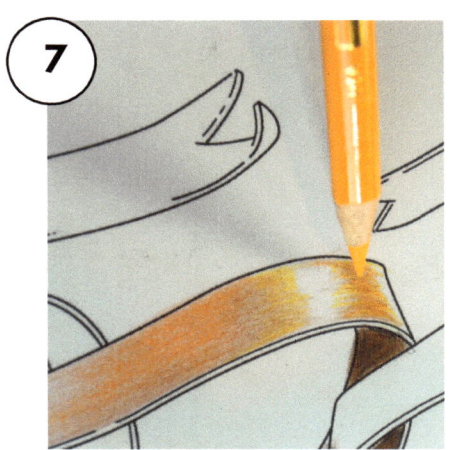

7 Now I use Spanish Orange 1003 to blend the hatches on either side of the highlight, leaving the center white. This makes it look reflective.

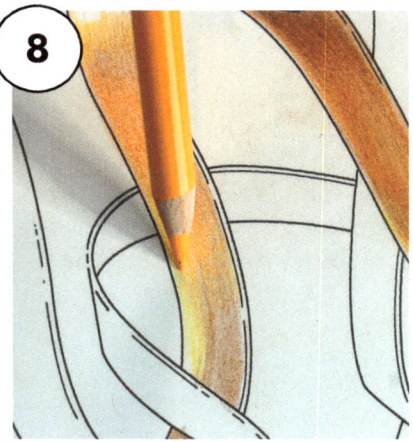

8 I rotate my page as needed and fill in the white space by the inner bend lightly.

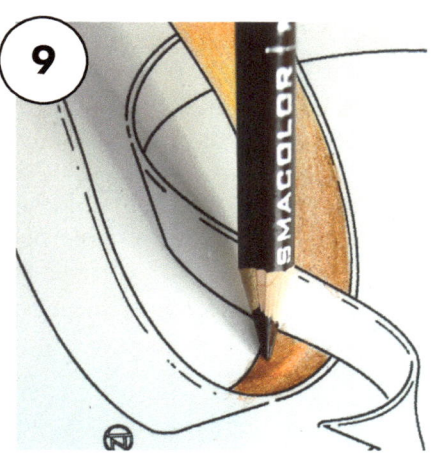

9 Chocolate 1082 is a rich brown which I will use in the shadow on the inside bend to make the crease more obvious. Note the use of Orange in the reflected light, to make the crease pop.

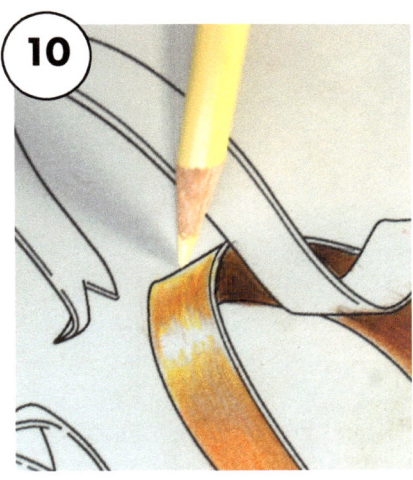

10 Now I add a little Cream 914 to the very edge of the side that bends out. This ties the whole ribbon together and gives it a finished look.

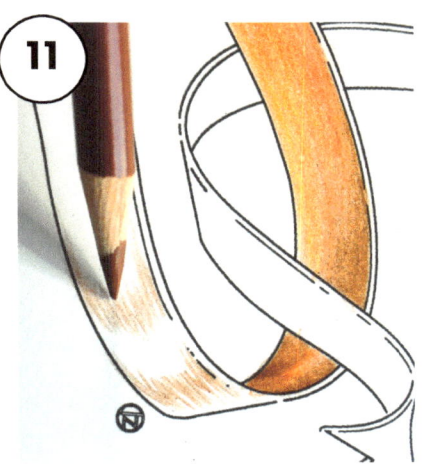

11 Next, I tackle the front outward bend of the ribbon, just like I did the first one. I used Sienna Brown instead here, to make the front ribbon stand out more – contrast.

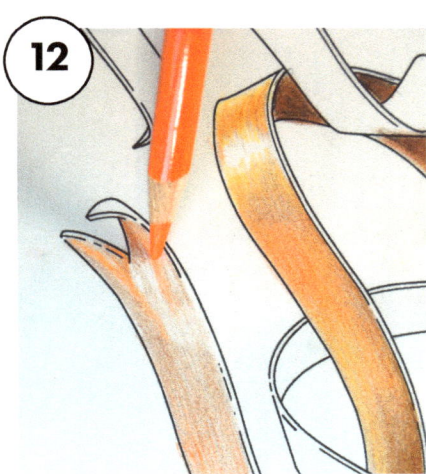

12 The end of this ribbon is tricky. I am creating a crease, just as I did before, but since it is split I am adding some orange below and on the tip of the ribbon end (next photo).

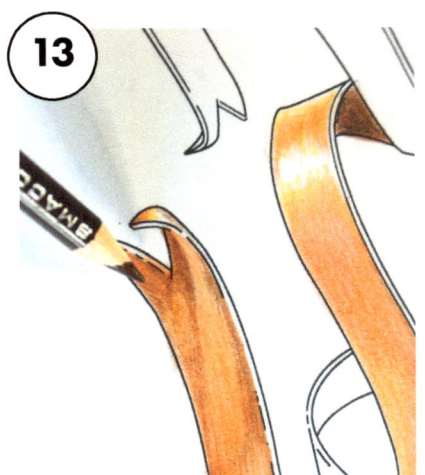

13 I am using 945 and 1082, like before, to darken the area below the crease.

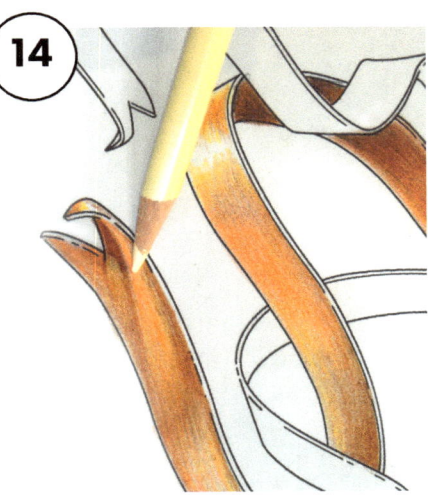

14 The final step is to blend with a little Cream and add some to the end of the ribbon, next to the Orange. Now you can use these techniques to complete this page.

Faceted Pink Diamond on Toned Paper

Facets are tricky – there is no doubt. If you have a page that is large enough and printed on toned paper, you can use this illustrator's technique. *The painting portion requires a steady hand.* A few gel pens may be used in place, however it may be difficult to find the exact colors you will want. If the gems you are coloring are very small, skip the painting part altogether and add just a few highlights with a white gel pen. You can use greys and blues for a white stone instead!

You will need:

- The "Sparkling Gems" toned paper line art page
- Prismacolor Premier:
  956, 929, 1092, 934, 1008, 933, 132, 1065
- Mono Zero eraser pen for mistakes (optional)
- Grumbacher, Winsor & Newton Cotman or other watercolor or gouache paint in White and Mauve or Violet. Uniball Signo white gel pen, if not painting
- Small round acrylic paintbrush (I'm using a #1) and a palette

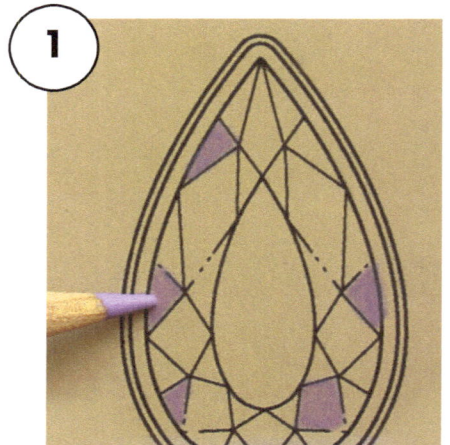

I begin by using Lilac 956 in several facets around the gem, filling the spaces carefully.

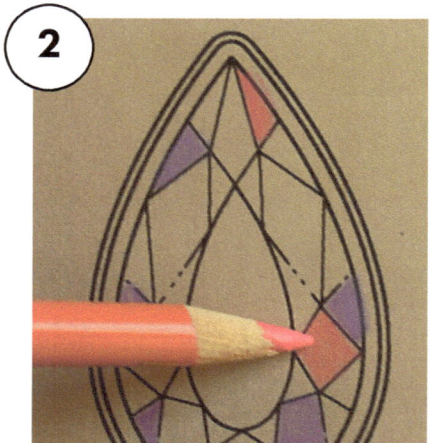

Next, I use Pink 929 for a warmer tone on just a few. This will be reflected light.

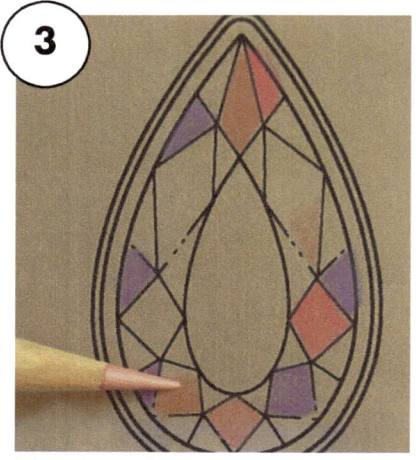

Then I gradate some Nectar 1092 on just a few facets, two of which are only filled halfway.

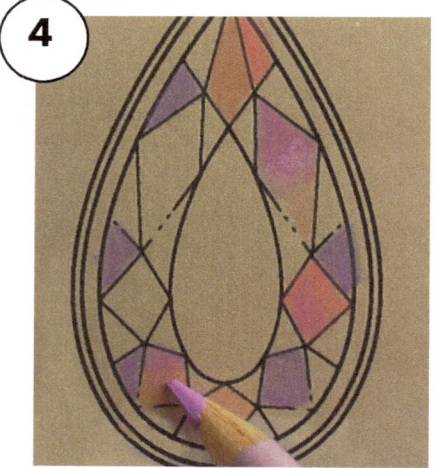

Now I add Lavender 934 to the other half of the gradated shapes.

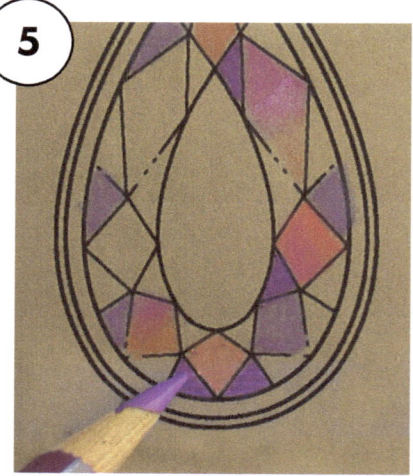

Next, I color a few slightly cooler, medium-value Parma Violet 1008 facets.

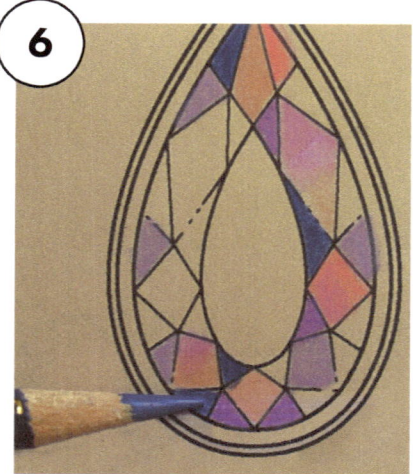

Then I fill in some very dark value Violet Blue 933 facets to create dimension and interest.

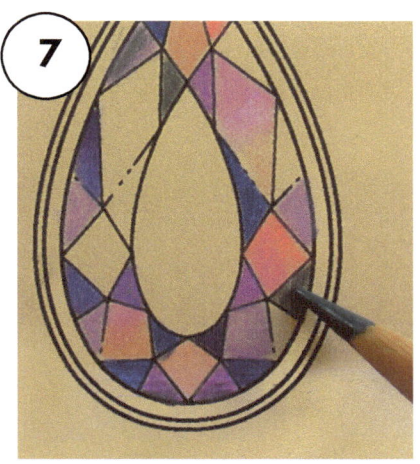

7

I use Dioxazine Purple 132 for a few facets, which is similar in value to Violet Blue but a bit warmer. Plus, I place just a couple of 70% Cool Grey 1065 shapes.

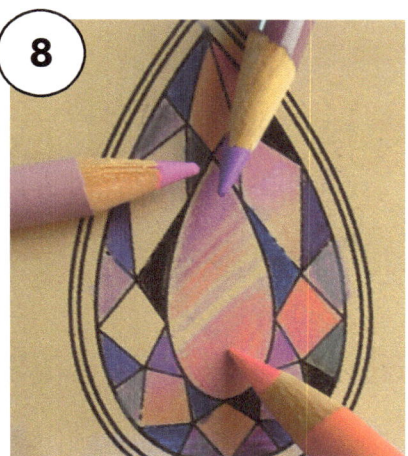

8

The center facet is primarily made of 3 colors: 934, 1008, 929. I color diagonally from the top down with the darkest color, leaving some blank areas. I blend 1008 and 929 in the bottom half.

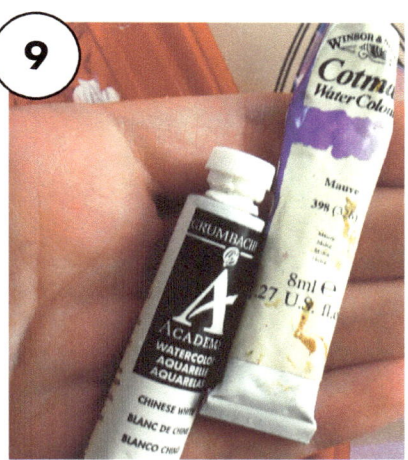

9

You can use any brand of watercolor or gouache paint. I mix a few drops of water into my paint to make it more spreadable. Not too much though or it will be too thin.

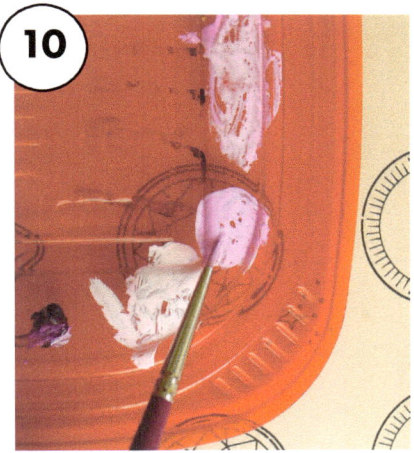

10

I am mixing on a plastic lid as my palette because it makes for an easy clean up. Combine two colors to get a light Lavender color.

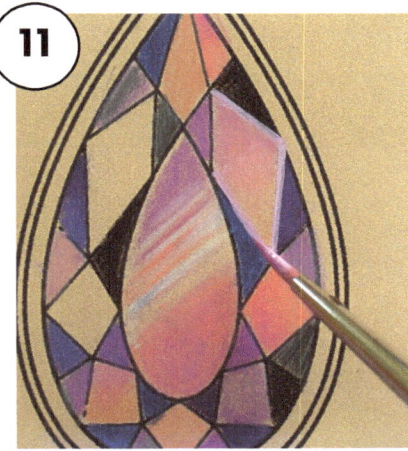

11

With a steady hand, I paint over most of the black lines (I like to leave a few of the ones closest to the edges to create depth).

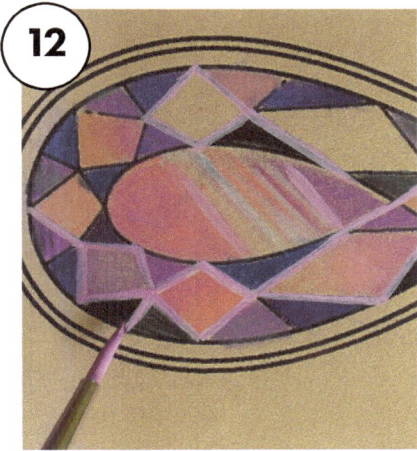

12

I prefer to paint away from myself because I have more control, so I keep rotating my page as I work.

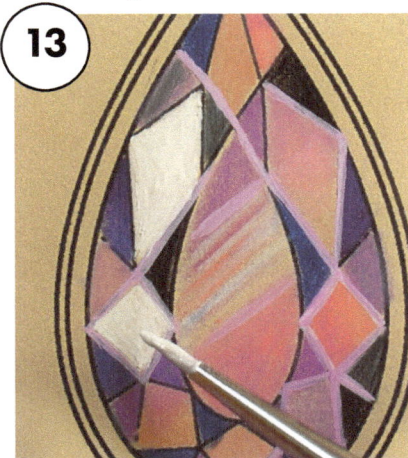

13

Now I mix up a batch of white. Make sure it's not too thick or it will look chunky, not smooth. I fill in both diamonds on the left.

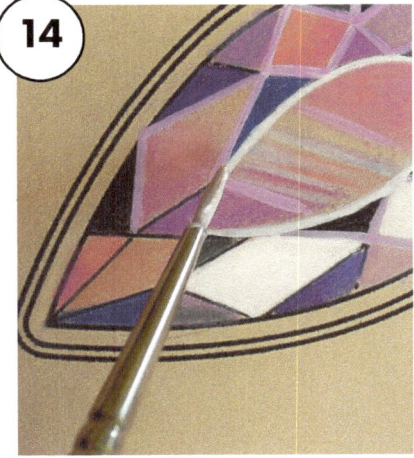

14

I rotate the page and go over a few of my Lavender lines with white to make them stand out, in the center and on the left side.

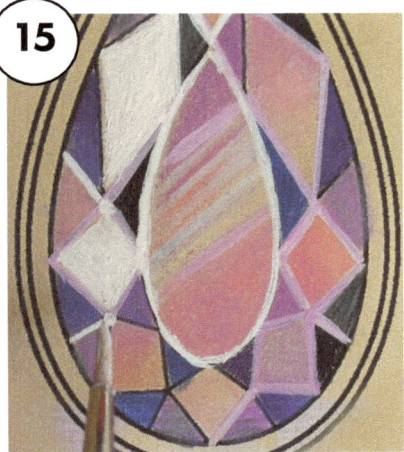

15

I add a few highlight "dots" and "pings" at intersections where facets meet. I go back with colored pencils to fix an overage of paint.

Golden Egg and Nest on Toned Paper

Haven't you always wanted a golden egg of your own?

For yellow gold, you will need:

- The "Golden Egg" line art page

- Prismacolor Premier:
940, 916, 1002, 941, 948, 935, 1098, 917, 943, 914, 1060, 938

- Uniball white gel pen

- Optional:
Mono Zero eraser pen or kneaded eraser for mistakes

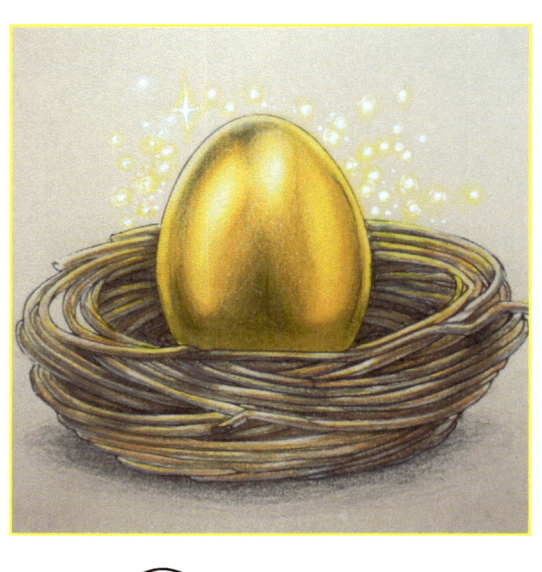

Golden Egg

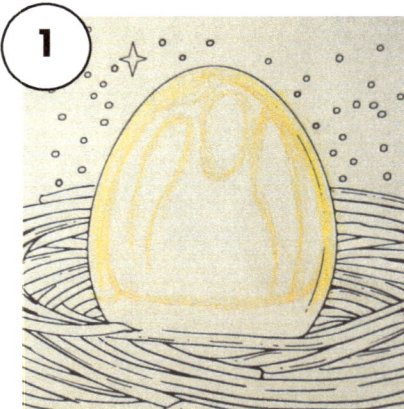

I decide the light is a diffused type, coming mostly from above. I start with Sand 940 to make a map of where my main reflections will be and a curved shape to close off the bottom. I very lightly color the area surrounding, for reflected light.

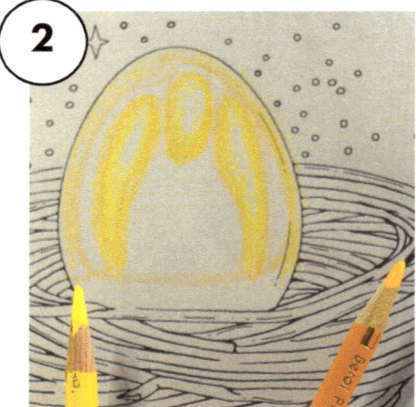

I begin the next step by gently filling in the "fang" shapes of the reflections with Canary Yellow 916, then going around the shapes with a fuzzy line of Yellowed Orange 1002. I leave the centers white.

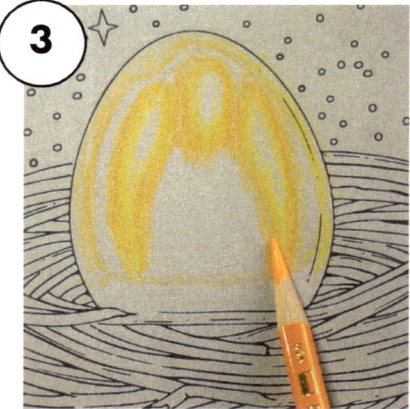

I thicken the 1002 by extending it outwards towards the edges of the egg. I leave the very edges of the egg alone until Step 5.

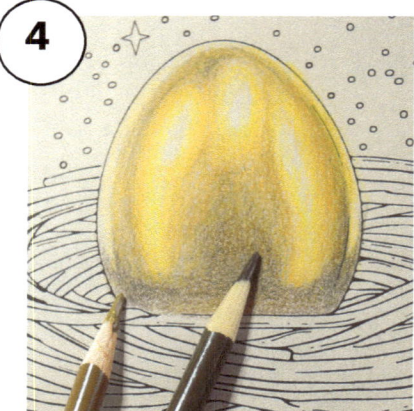

Lightly, I use Raw Umber 941 to fill in all of the blank space, except the reflected light on the edges. I use directional strokes along the side of the egg. I add Sepia 948, using circles, to the center and darken the edges of the brown.

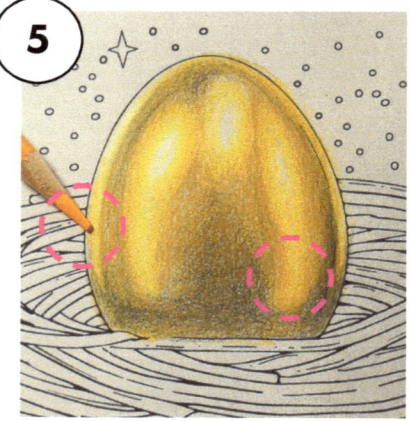

Now I can fill in some reflected light. I use 916 and 1002 to lightly fill in some at the bottom of the empty strip surrounding the egg. I boost the bottom of the right reflection (fang shape).

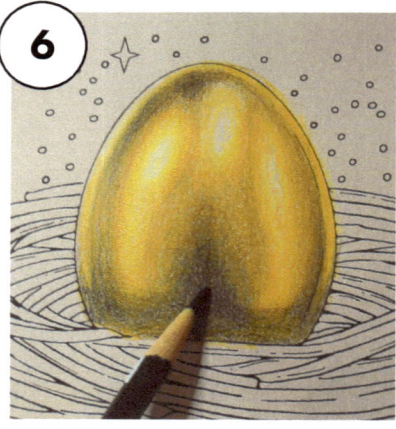

Now I use my Black 935 to deepen the center of the brown area of shadow in the lower middle of the egg. I use small circles, fuzzing outward to blend.

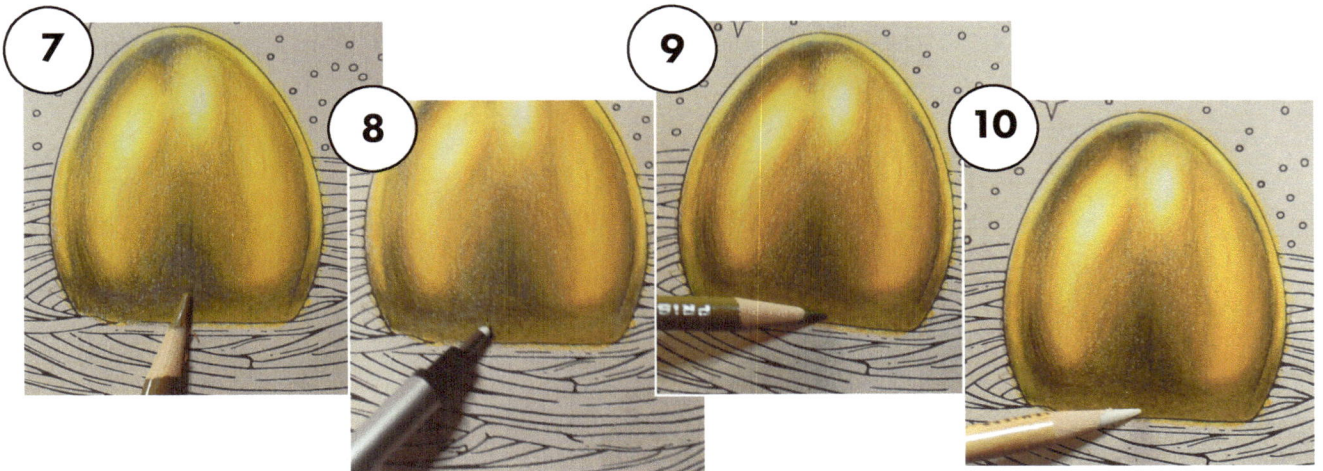

The last four steps of the egg include: 7. Going back into my 941 to blend in the Black 8. Using my Mono Zero to lighten the bottom 4 cm, just a little. 9. Adding a layer of Artichoke 1098 to the bottom area 10. And finally blending with my colorless blender where it looks grainy, on the entire egg (one small area at a time – being careful not to over-blend).

Nest

To create a dimensional looking nest, you will need to approach it as a whole object yet tackle some of the twigs, one by one. Remember what you learned in the Parts of Light lesson. To make something look real, it should have light and shadow. Each twig is treated as a cylinder, with a highlight, light/shadow, core and cast shadow, and reflected light. Take a close-up look:

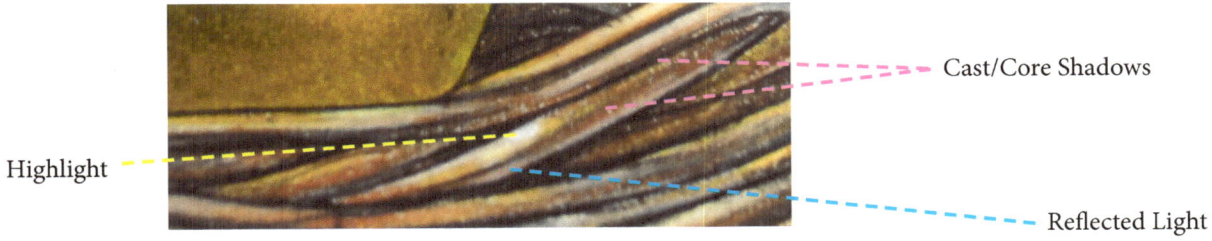

Highlight

Cast/Core Shadows

Reflected Light

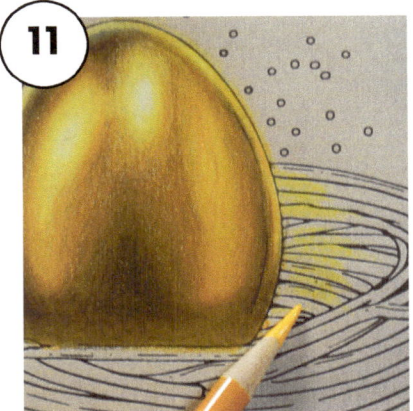

Behind the egg, on both sides, I add some gold tones to look like light is bouncing off the egg with Sunburst Yellow 917.

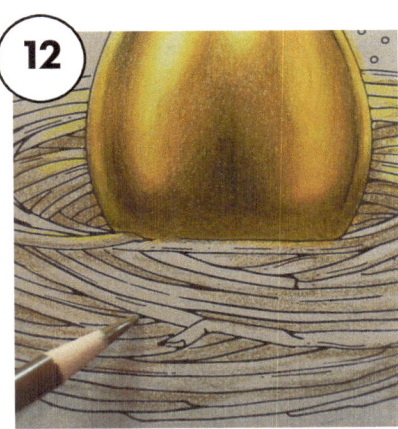

I move on to 941 to add a light coating of browns in any areas that look like they would tuck in – especially inside the nest.

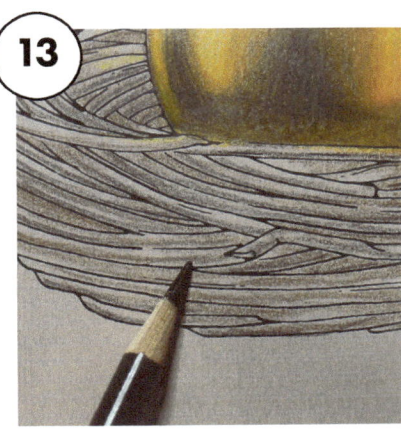

Now I use a deeper brown to add quick core shadows on the majority of twigs. This is simply a horizontal line below the middle of each twig, using a sharp Sepia 948.

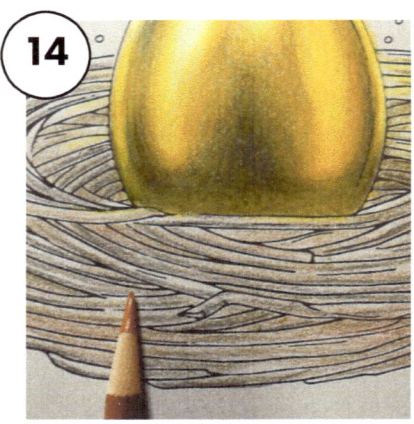

14 Now I apply a light layer of Burnt Ochre 943 on most of them, except the twigs that appear to be on top.

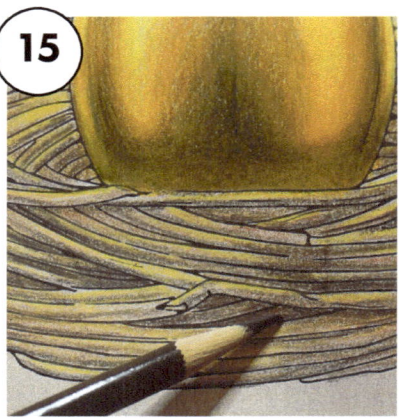

15 Back to Sepia 948 to get into the shadow areas to deepen them. I also add Sand 940 "light" on the tops of most twigs to liven them up.

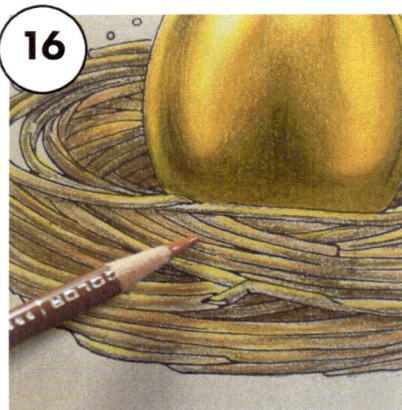

16 I warm up the core shadows and the middle tone areas (that aren't in direct light or shadow) with some 943. A thin coat all over.

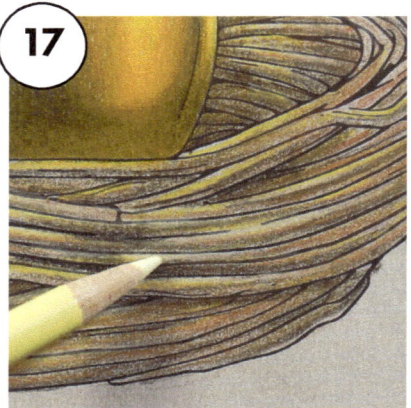

17 Next, I add some Cream 914 highlights to the top edge of the twigs that stick out. In Step 19 you can see I've added some to inside the nest as well.

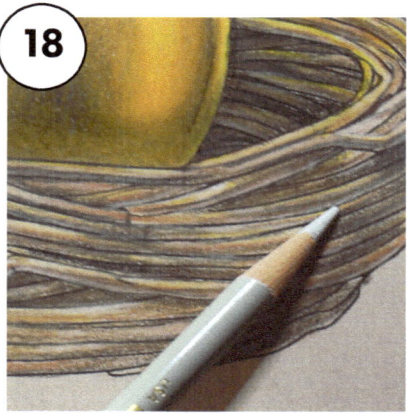

18 I add a light gradation of Black 935 (not pictured) inside the nest, darkest at the bottom. I use a sharp Cool Grey 20% 1060 as reflected light on the bottom of select twigs.

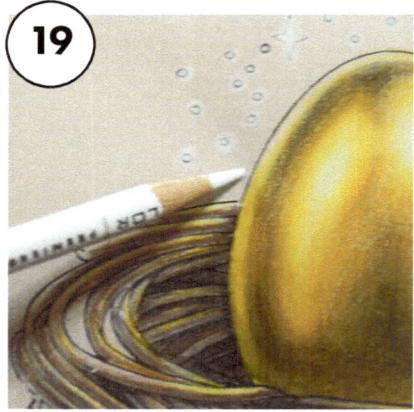

19 I increase the highlights in the reflections with White 938. For the "glimmer" above the egg, I color each little circle, and for some I go beyond the black outline to create a glow.

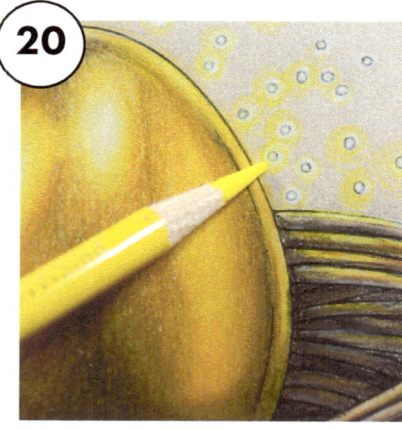

20 Now I circle some of the glimmer dots with a hint of Canary Yellow 916, to add to the sparkle.

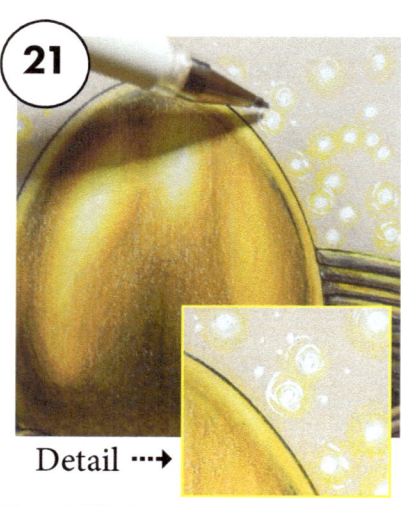

Detail ···➔

21 Then I fill the very center with a white gel pen, adding some quick "swirly" strokes around them to make them shine – see detail. I add a "ping" to the biggest star shape, as discussed early in the chapter.

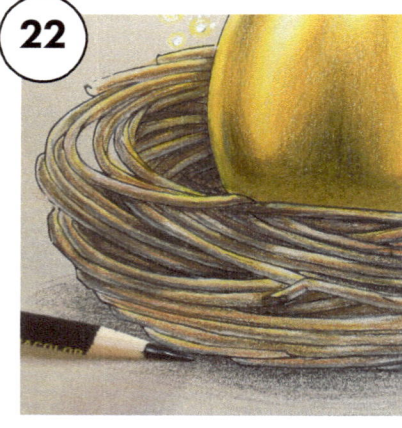

22 Finally, I touch up and deepen any core and cast shadow areas on the nest with a sharp Black pencil and add a cast shadow (darkest part right below nest) to ground it!

Mojave Turquoise Cabochon using Colored Pencil

This is fancy stone with lots of detail that can be created more easily than you might think!

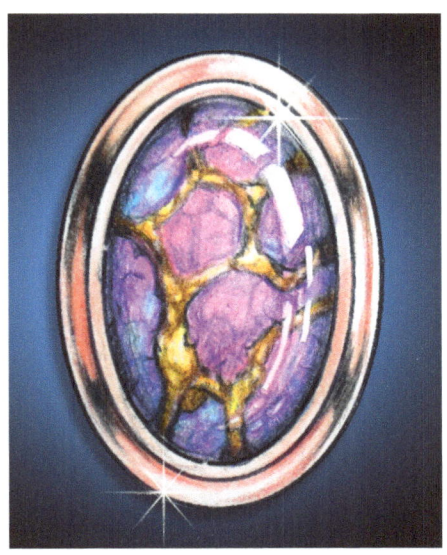

You will need:

- The "Sparkling Gems" toned paper line art page

- Prismacolor Premier:
  934, 919, 993, 1007, 932, 916, 1034, 918, 946, 935, 933

- Uniball white gel pen

- Kneaded eraser to lighten (optional)

- Mono Zero eraser pen (optional)

- A gold metallic or gold glitter gel pen for details on veining (optional)

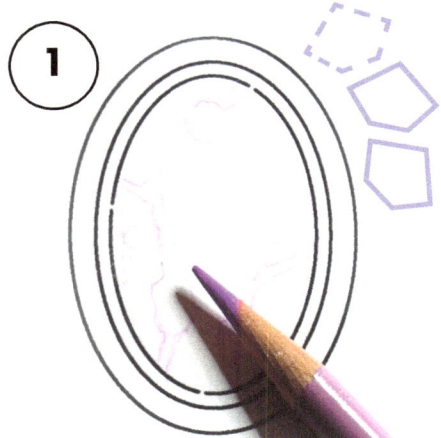

1 Using Lavender 934, I draw squished abstract pentagons, turning them to fit together like a puzzle, but leaving space for white outlines that form around them - making a pattern.

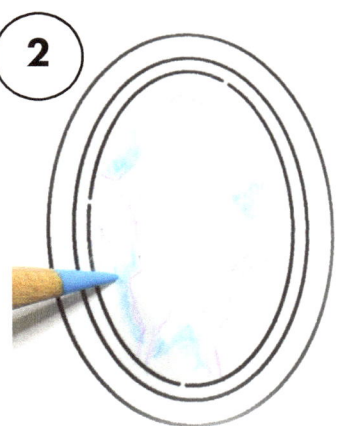

2 Once I've filled in the space with random shapes, the next step is to add a few splotches of Non-Photo Blue 919 in the bigger shapes.

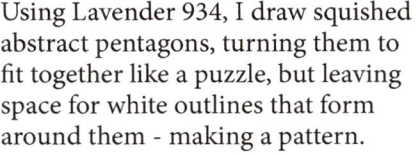

3 Next, I introduce some Hot Pink 993 to the center large shapes and a hint gradated into the other shapes. (Leave the center of 993 by itself.)

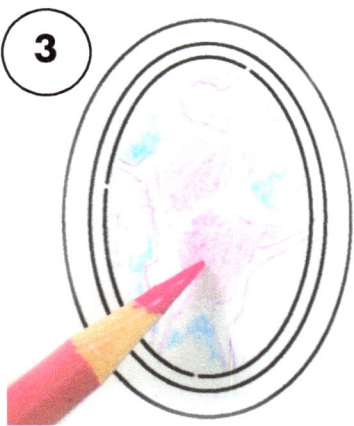

4 Now, I blend the edges of 993 with 934 outward and blend again with Parma Violet towards the edges, leaving the white veins.

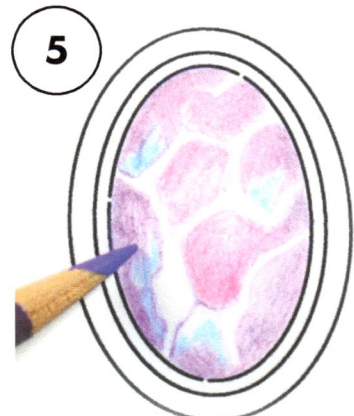

5 To make the stone look 3-D, I introduce some Imperial Violet 1007 from the black line towards the center of the stone.

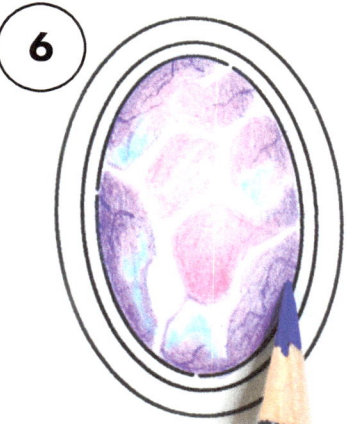

6 With a sharp Violet 932 pencil, I make some skinny short cracks around the edges only.

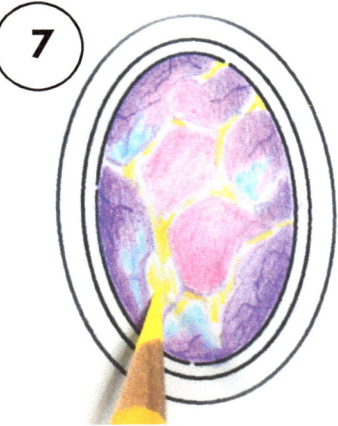

7 Now I begin the gold veining. I start with patches of Canary Yellow 916, all over, leaving some white.

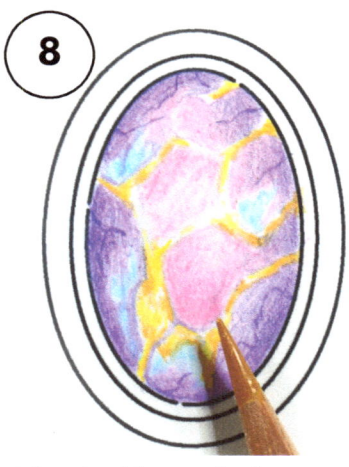

8 Then I add some little tiny patches of Goldenrod 1034 on top of the Canary, leaving the center-most part mostly yellow.

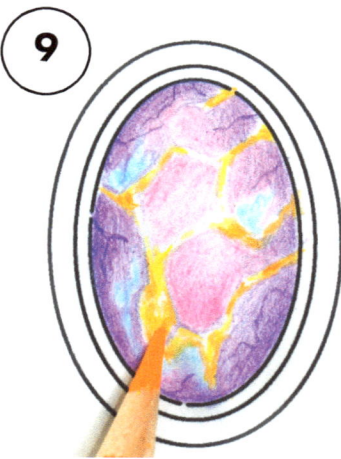

9 Next I use just a few hints of Orange 918 to warm up the gold.

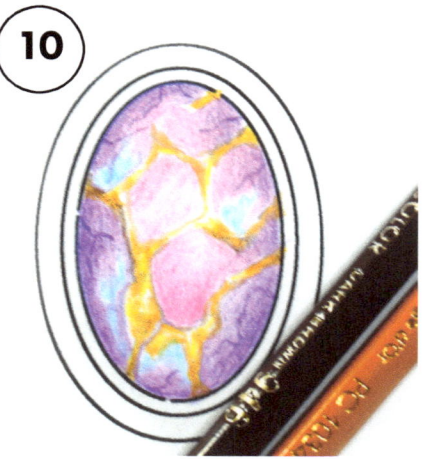

10 I deepen the gold veining by adding some more 1034. I accent some of the curves of the gold and darken the gold outside edges of the stone with a hint of Dark Brown 946.

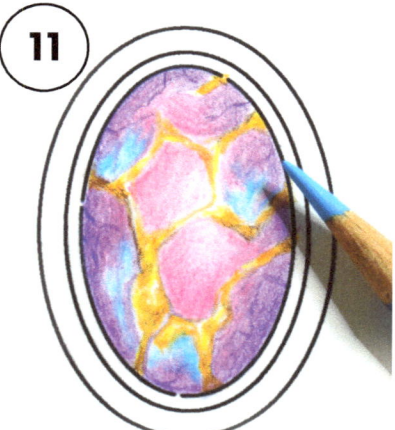

11 Going back to 919, I blend some of the blue into the mix of violets surrounding, by feathering it in.

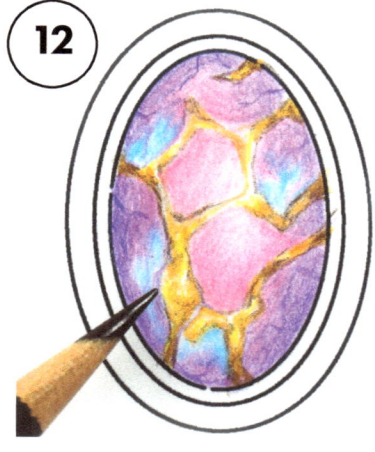

12 With a very sharp Black 935 pencil, I methodically accent some of the curves and deepen the edges of the gold – being careful not to overdo it!

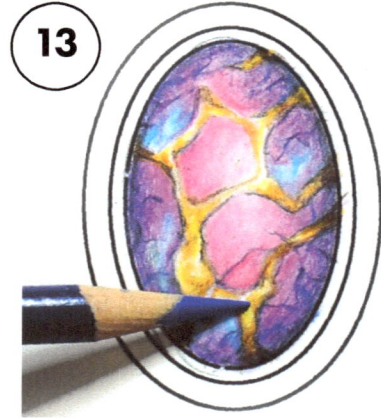

13 I begin to add a light shadow gradation that is heaviest at the edges, and then add a very small amount of Violet Blue 933 to edges and cracks.

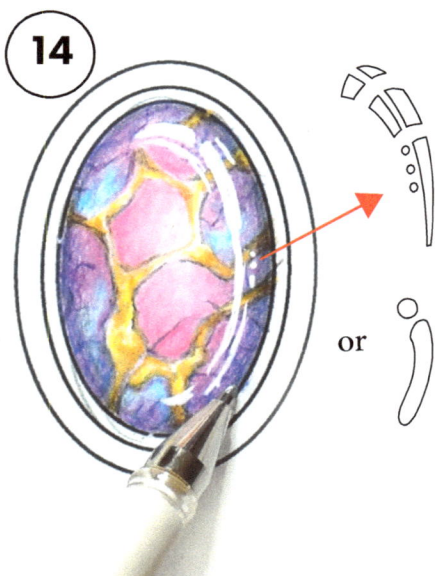

14 Add more depth and a few more details, as you see fit. For the reflection, choose between a stylized and simple "swoop" shape highlight or attempt to make your highlight look like a warped reflection of a window in the stone. It is just a preference. Use your gel pen to draw the shape you prefer. If you make a mistake, you can scratch it off with a colorless blender! Adjust it as needed. I did! Use a second coat to whiten. Optional: use some touches of metallic gold or glitter gel pen, in the gold, to make it sparkle!

or

The final chapter of The Secrets of Coloring consists of coloring pages that coordinate with Chapter 9 tutorials, an artist permission statement, a color organizer to test your supplies, and links to resources in this book. Your secret code for ModernColoring.com bonus download pages is found on the backside of a page at the end of the book. Don't forget to use it!

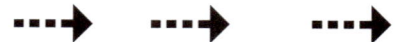

DIY: *Cmyk Color Wheel*

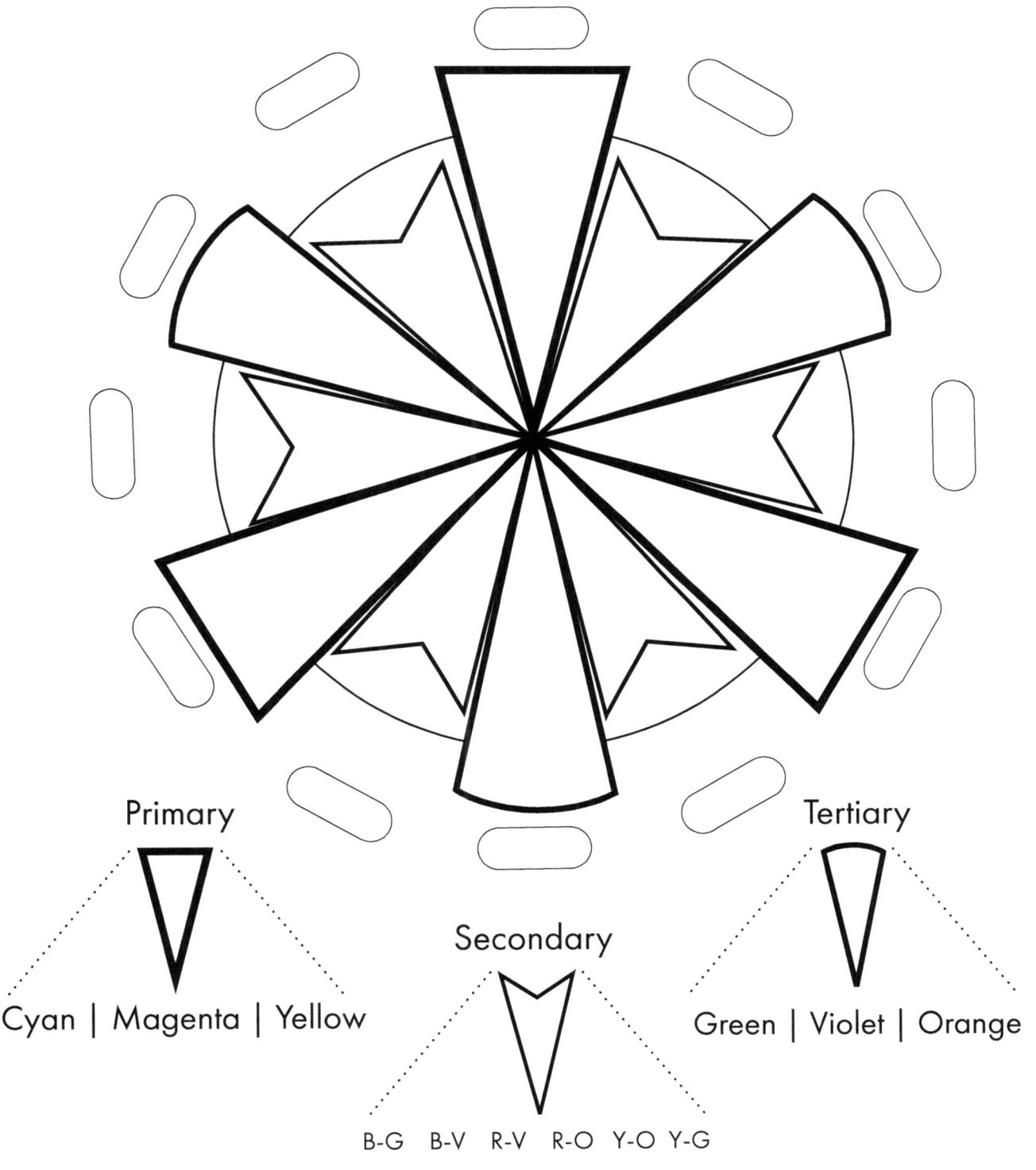

Primary

Cyan | Magenta | Yellow

Secondary

B-G B-V R-V R-O Y-O Y-G

Tertiary

Green | Violet | Orange

Use a blotter page under this page if you are going to
use marker on the previous page

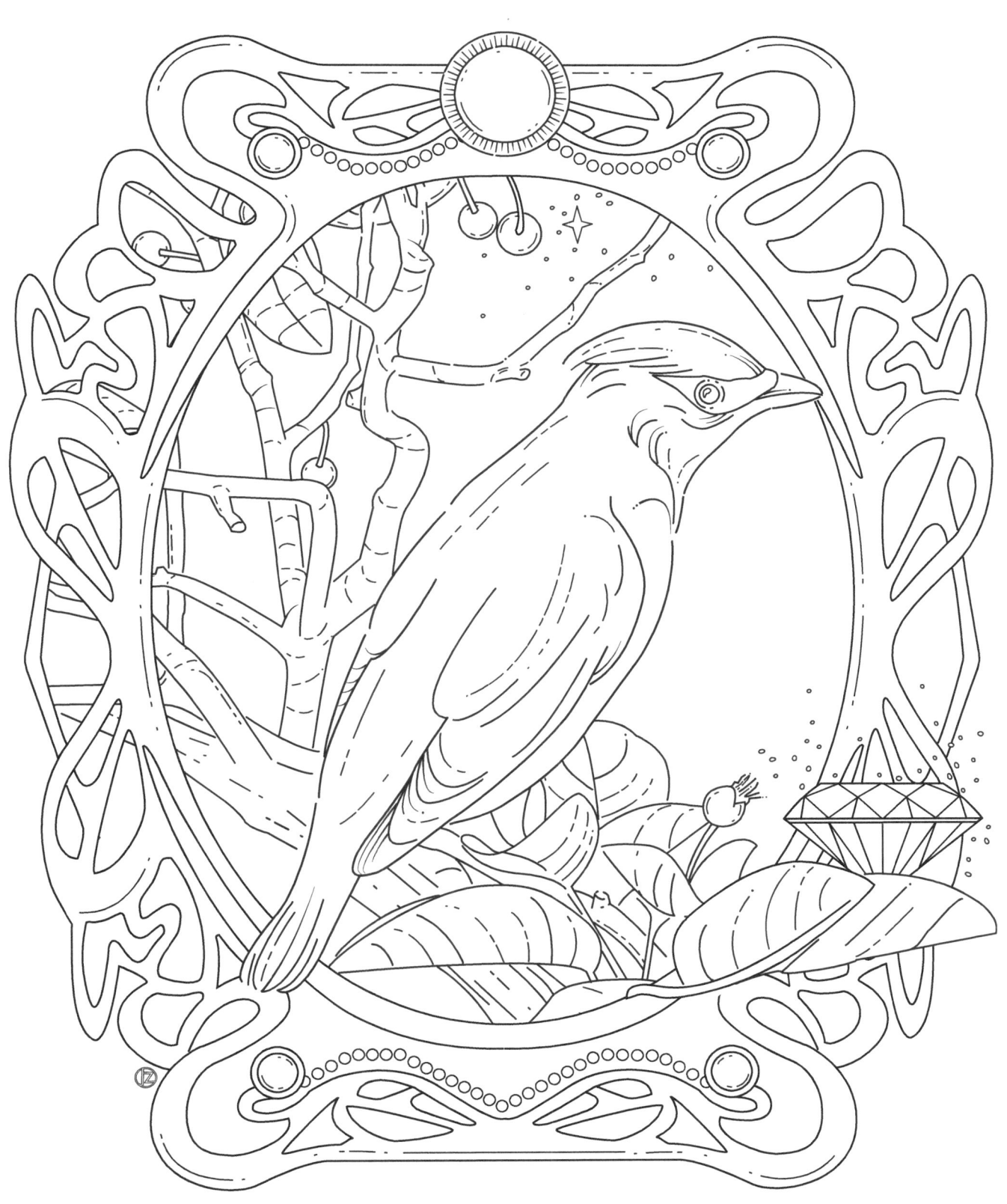

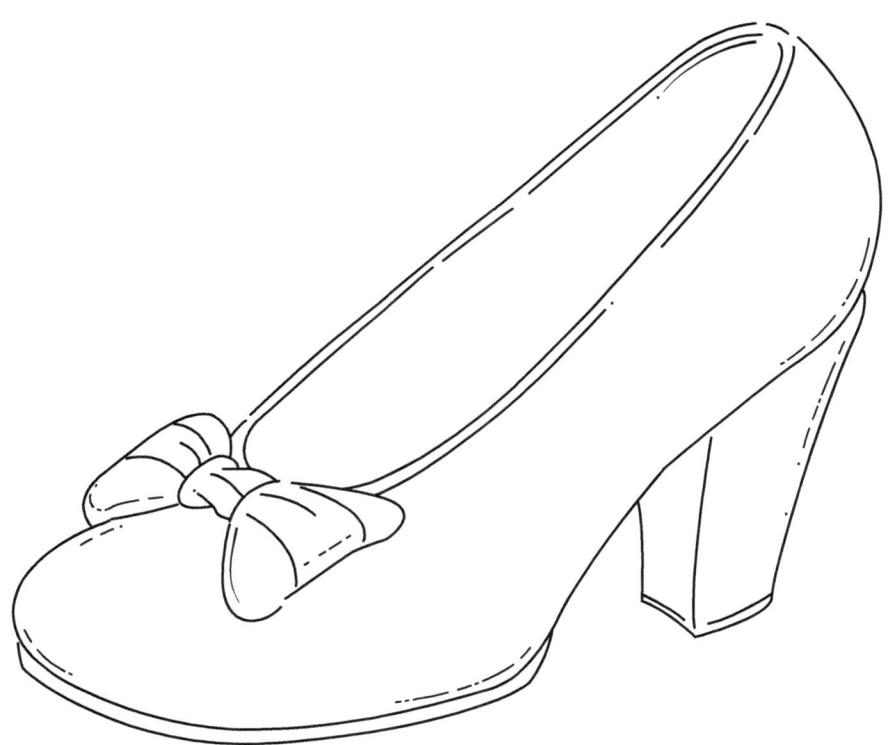

Use a blotter page under this page if you are going to
use marker on the previous page

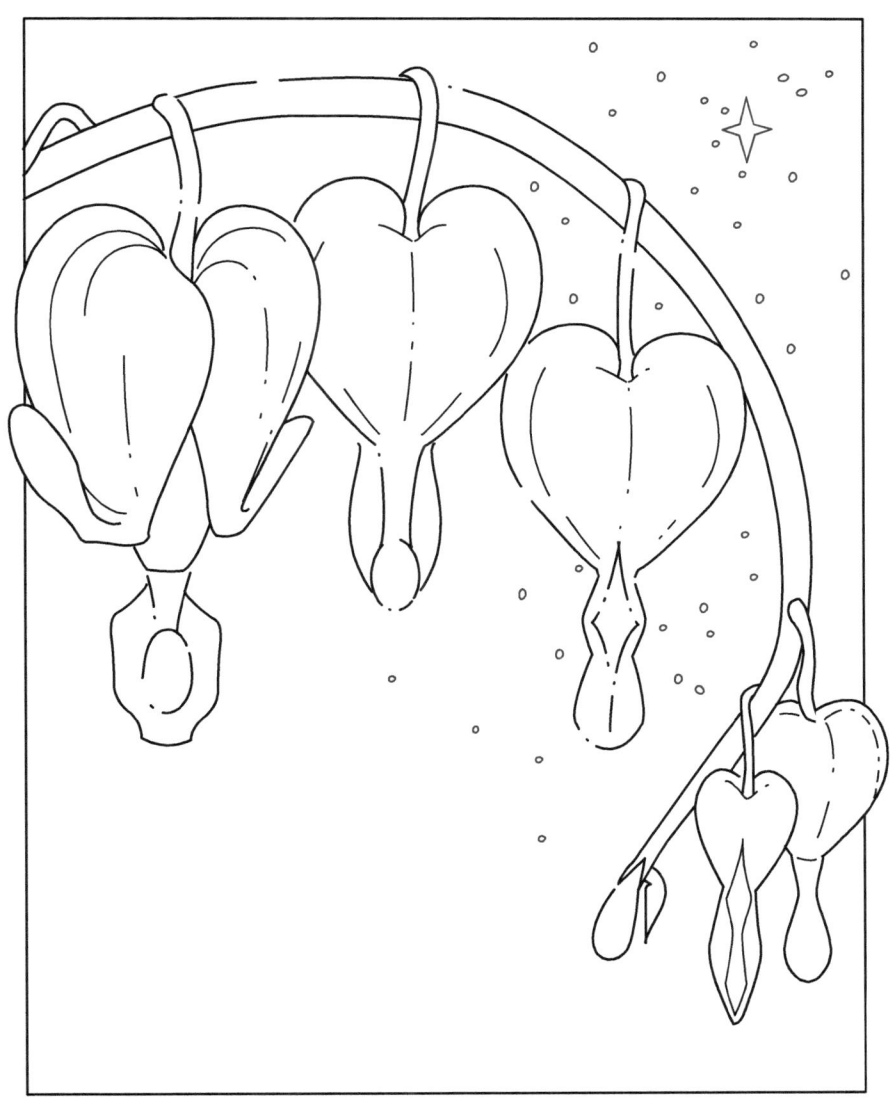

Use a blotter page under this page if you are going to
use marker on the previous page

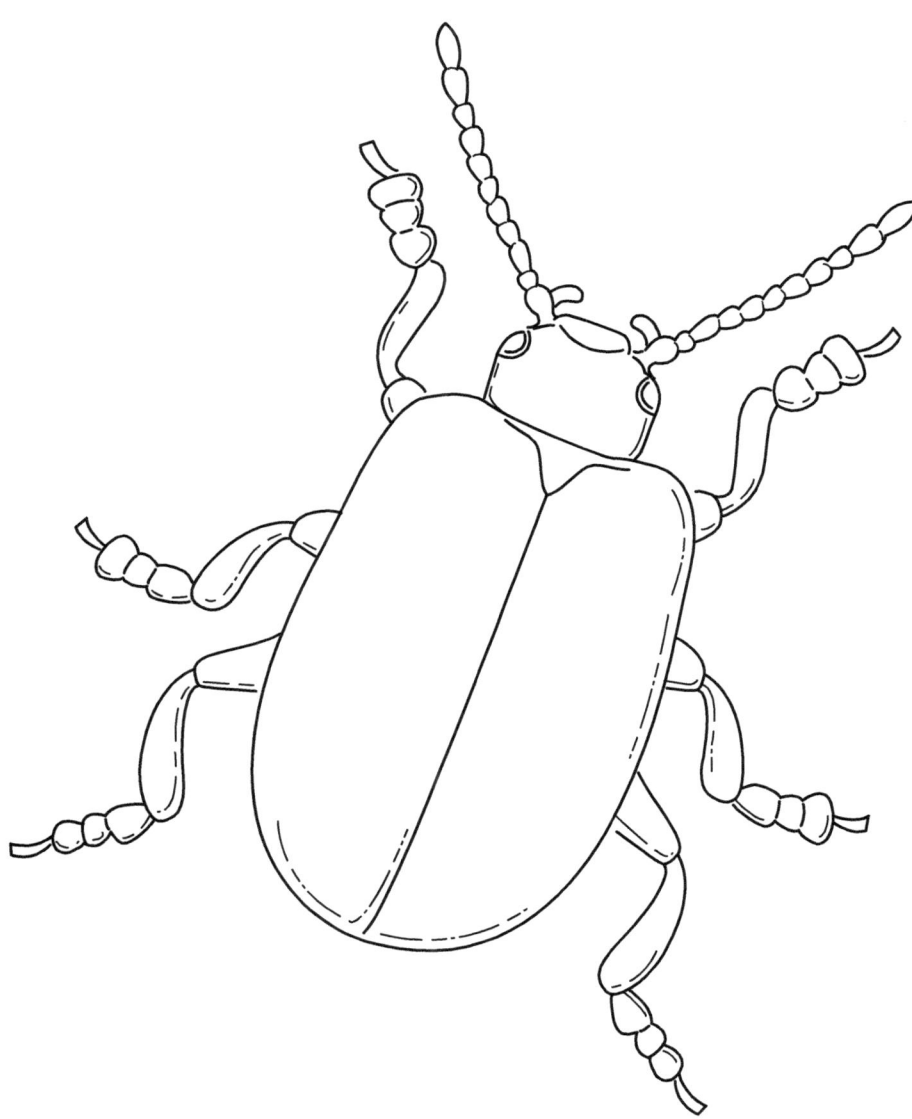

Use a blotter page under this page if you are going to
use marker on the previous page

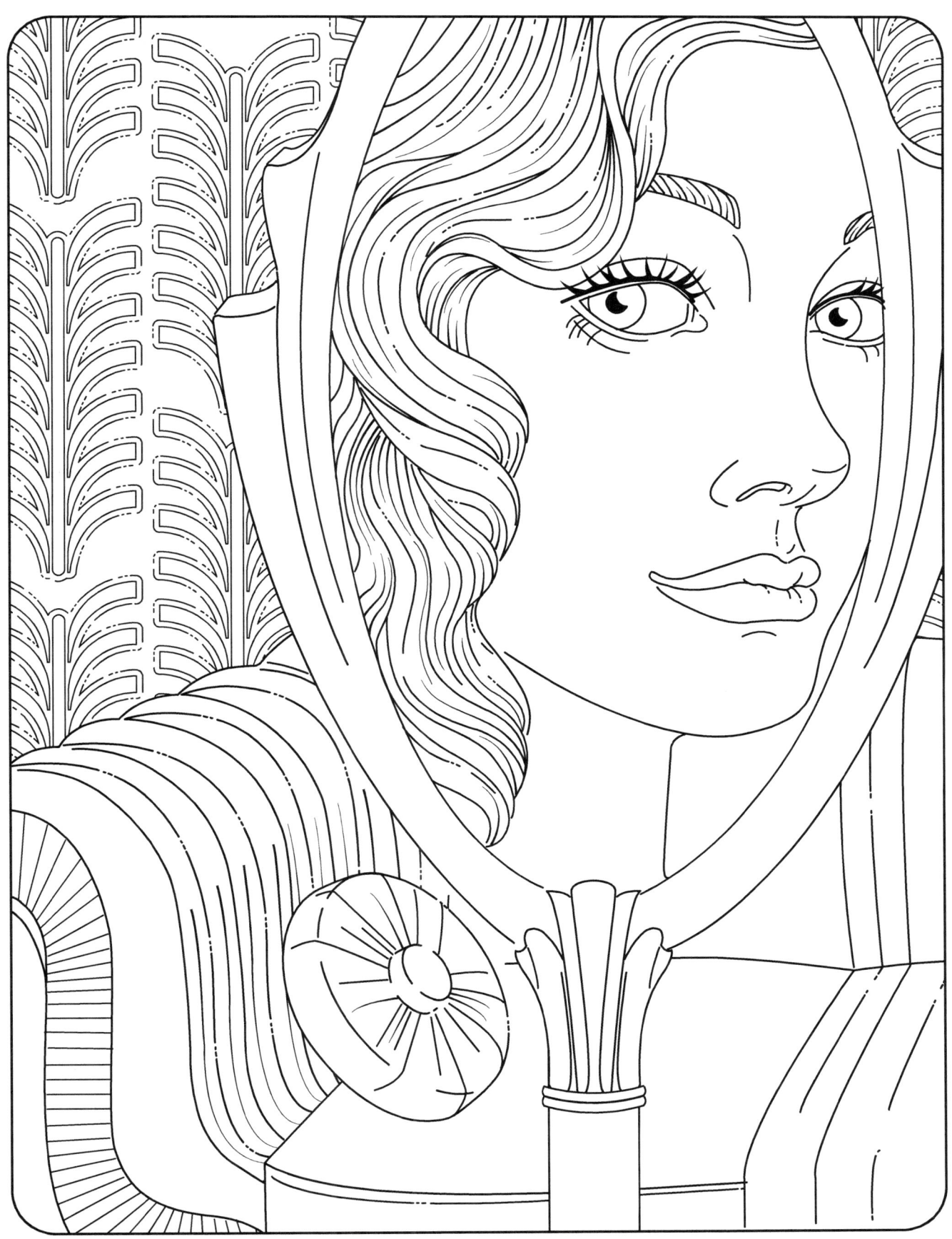

Use a blotter page under this page if you are going to
use marker on the previous page

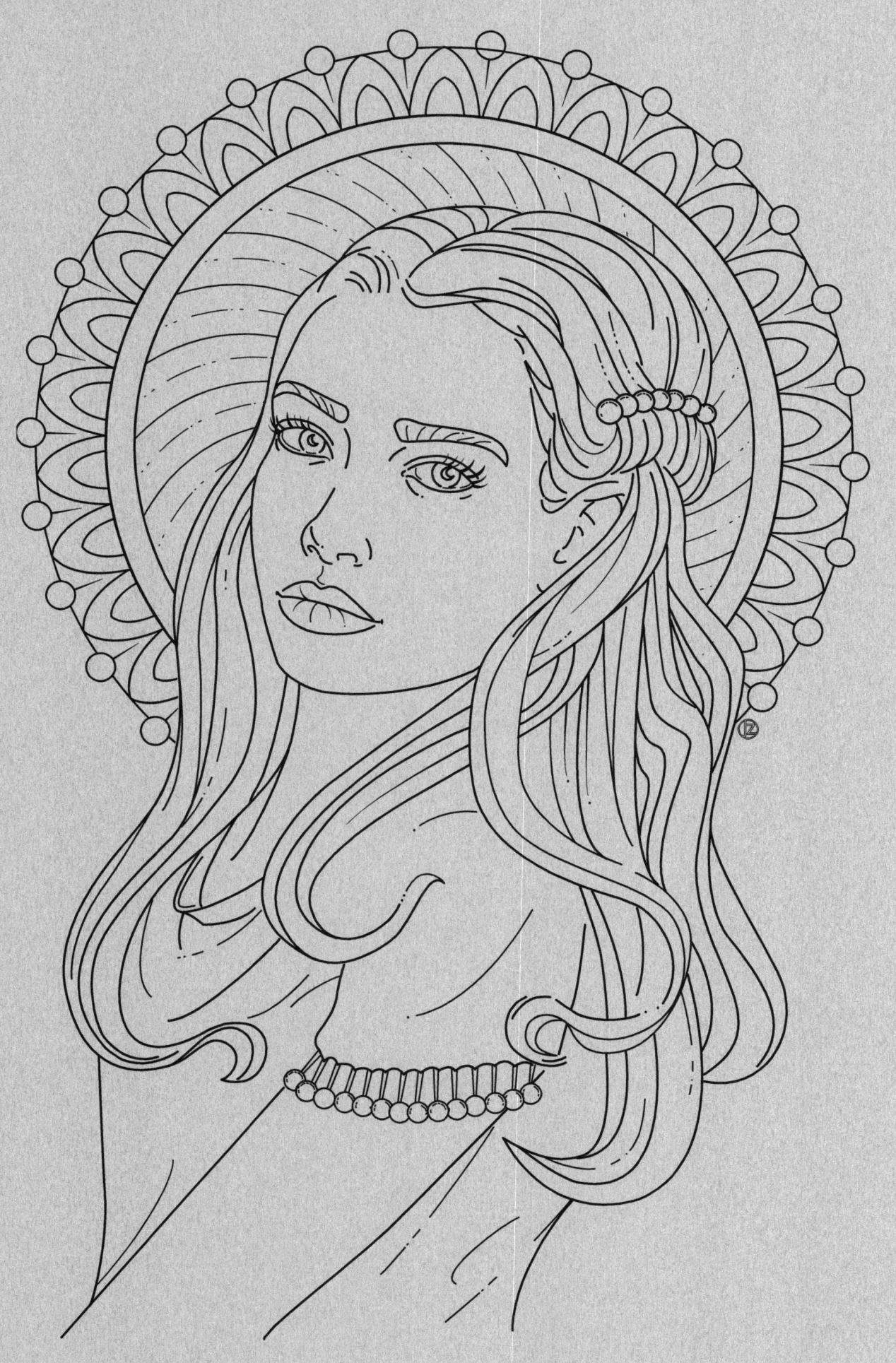

Cat

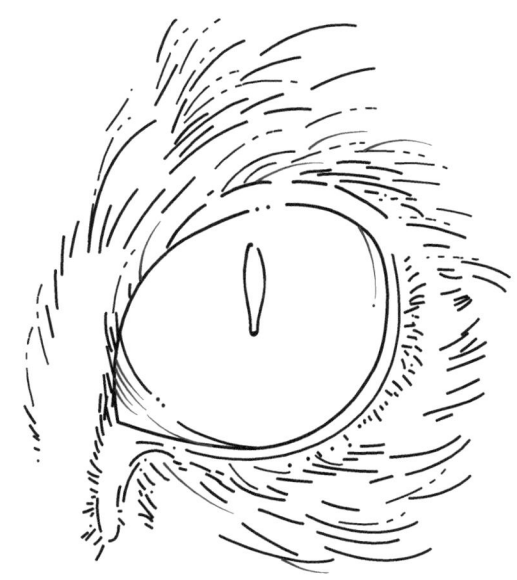

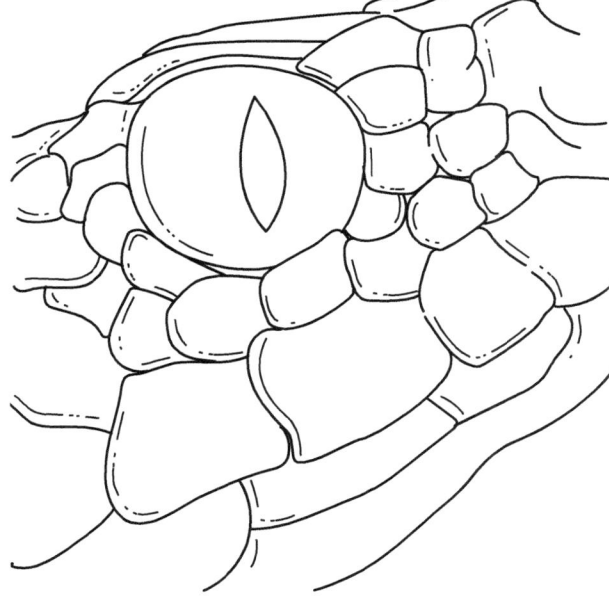

Snake

Wolf

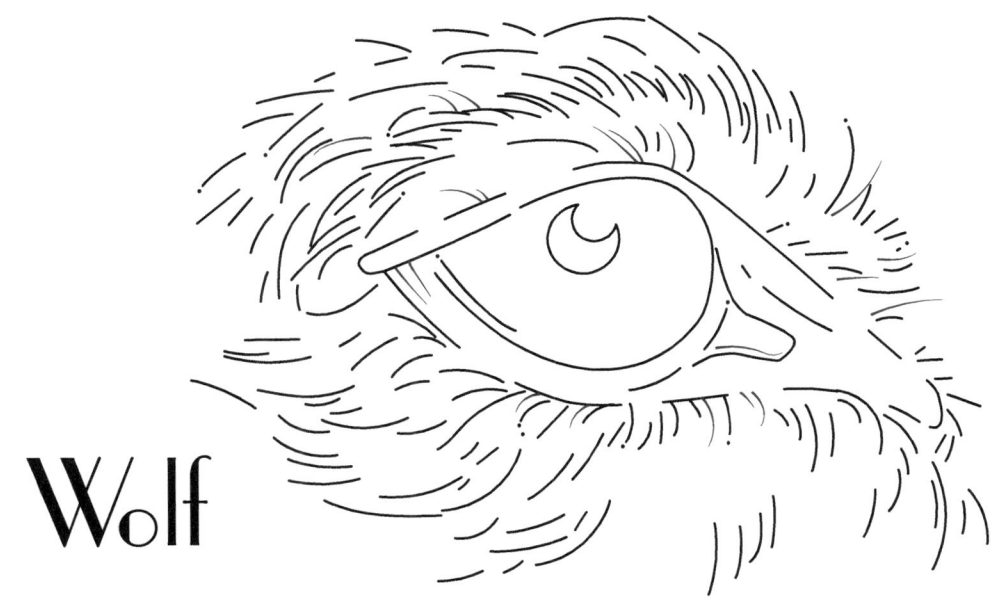

Use a blotter page under this page if you are going to
use marker on the previous page

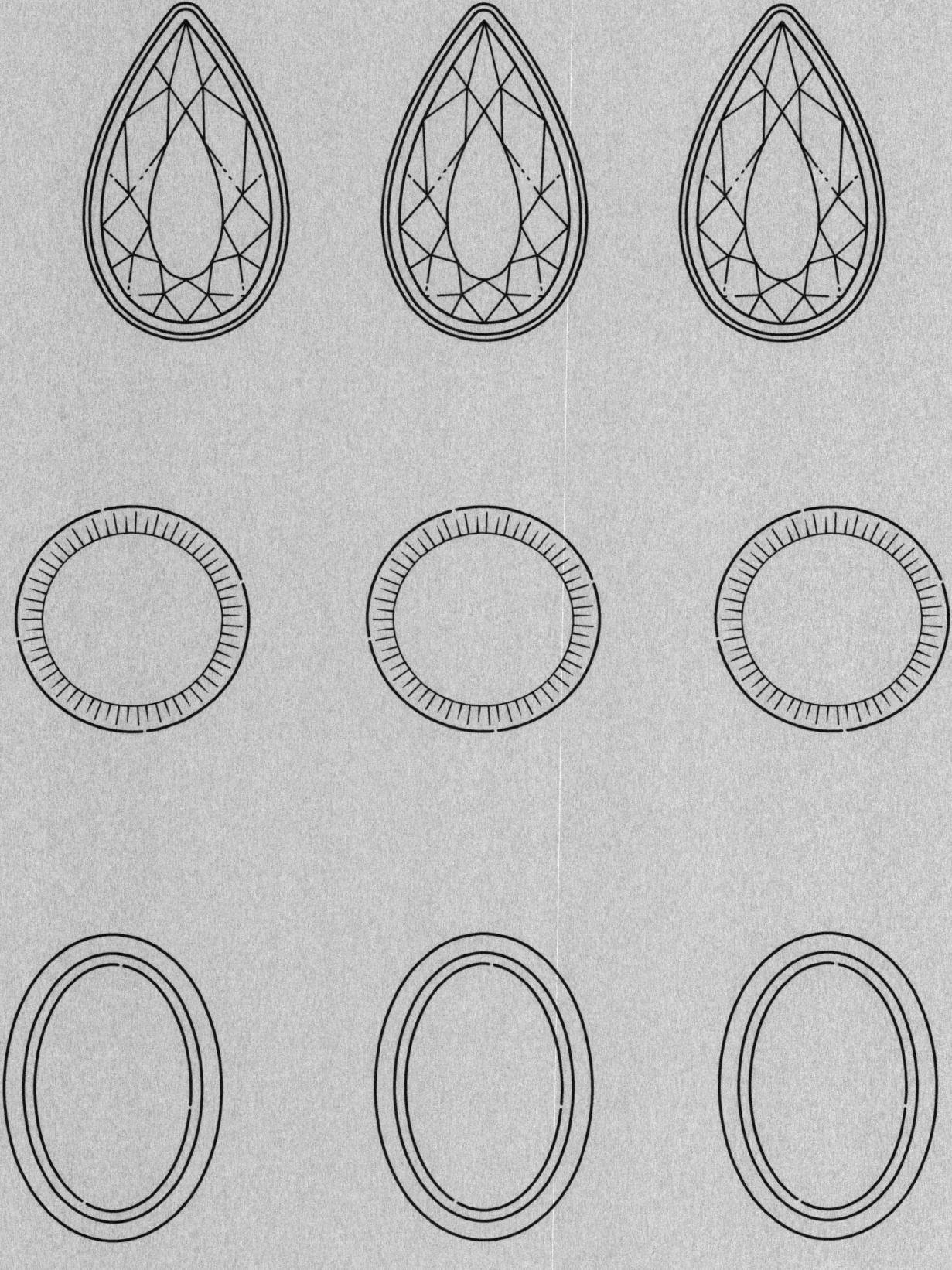

Use a blotter page under this page if you are going to
use marker on the previous page

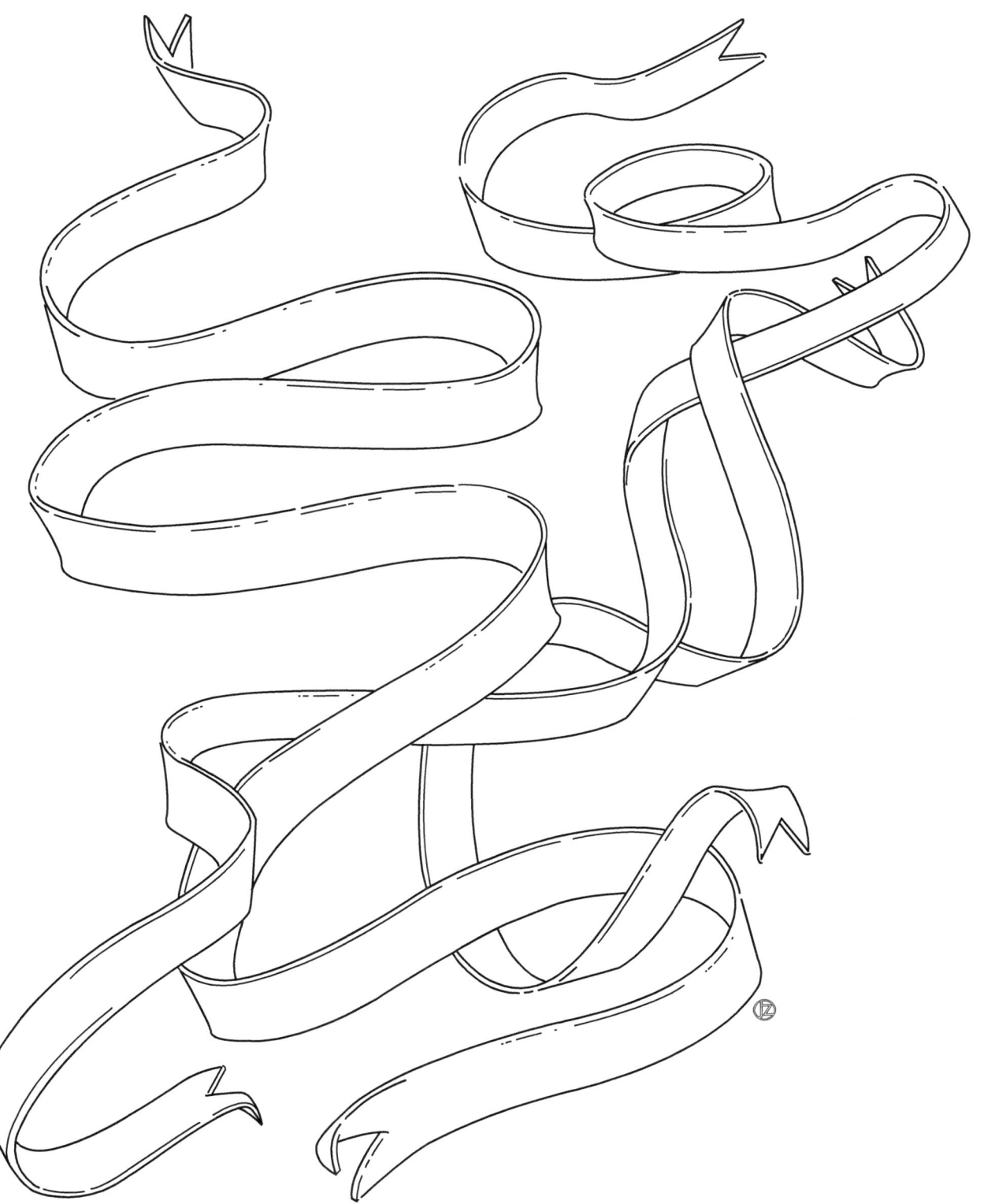

Use a blotter page under this page if you are going to
use marker on the previous page

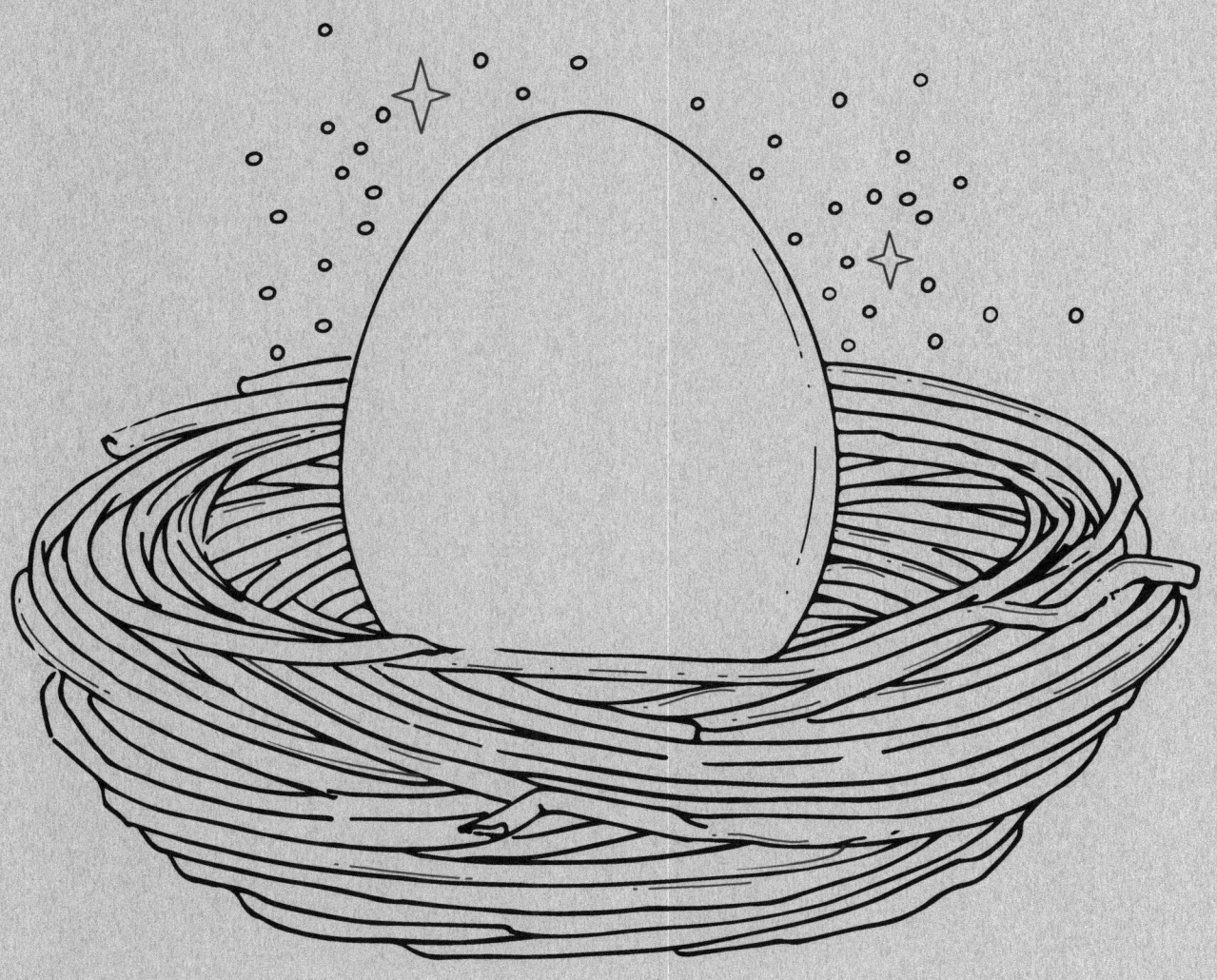

*Use a blotter page under this page if you are going to
use marker on the previous page*

Code: SHHH

Color Organizer

Page/Book		Brand/Color	#	Page/Book		Brand/Color	#
	☐				☐		
	☐				☐		
	☐				☐		
	☐				☐		
	☐				☐		
	☐				☐		
	☐				☐		
	☐				☐		
	☐				☐		
	☐				☐		
	☐				☐		
	☐				☐		
	☐				☐		
	☐				☐		
	☐				☐		
	☐				☐		
	☐				☐		
	☐				☐		
	☐				☐		
	☐				☐		
	☐				☐		
	☐				☐		
	☐				☐		
	☐				☐		

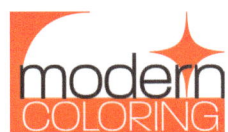

To Whom It May Concern,

Please allow the colorist _____,
to print the pages I've supplied strictly for personal use only.
Permission is granted to the colorist who has signed below, to copy
ten (10) pages from this book, *Coloring Secrets*, in a single visit to
your printing facility, for personal use only.
Mass production of this book is not allowed and business use is
strictly forbidden. If you have any hesitation, I can be reached at
FullCircleFineArts@gmail.com.

Best,

Jennifer Zimmermann
Author/Artist
ModernColoring.com

. . . .

Please defend the rights of artists and respect copyright law. Artists depend on the income
from the sales of their books and artwork to make a living. Misuse creates hardships for the
artists that produce the pages you love to color. Sharing of the colored pages in this book is
strictly forbidden, both by copying them for someone else, and posting them on social media.
The only exception is made for reviewers, whom are kindly requested not to display the book
in its entirety, but only portions of pages. If you are posting a review and including images of
the uncolored line art pages, please lay a pencil across the image to prevent theft. If in doubt
always contact the artist.

You, the colorist, are very welcome and encouraged to share your own finished coloring pages
from this book, and I kindly request that you list the book as the source if you do. Thank you
for your understanding, assistance and educating others in this matter.

I've read the above guidelines and agree to them.

Signed (the colorist):

_____ Date: _____

Resource Guide

Here you can find some of the materials used throughout The Secrets of Coloring. You can find links to many of these products at: **moderncoloring.com/recommended-products**

Sharpie - permanent markers .... sharpie.com

Prismacolor - colored pencils, blenders and kneaded erasers .... prismacolor.com

Caran D'Ache - colored pencils, blenders .... store.carandache.com/us/en/

Copic - alcohol-based markers and waterproof fineliners .... copic.jp/en/

Canson - papers .... en.canson.com

Strathmore - papers .... strathmoreartist.com

Georgia-Pacific - papers .... georgiapacificpaper.com

Faber-Castell - colored pencils, waterproof fineliners .... fabercastell.com

Bic - permanent markers .... shopbic.com

Tombow - brush and eraser pens .... tombowusa.com

Staedtler - fineliners, drafting stencils .... staedtler.us/en/

Krylon - fixatives .... krylon.com

SpectraFix - fixatives .... spectrafix.com

3M - safety masks 3m.com

Pentel - erasers .... pentel.com

T'Gaal - pencil sharpeners .... available online

Maped - pencil sharpeners, water-based fineliners .... uk.maped.com/en_uk/

Sofft - pastel knives and covers .... sofftart.com/products.html

PanPastel - pan-based pastels .... panpastel.com

Palette websites .... design-seeds.com
and colorpalettes.net

Signo - gel pens .... www.uniball-na.com/

Sakura - gel pens .... www.gellyroll.com

VersaMark - stamp pad .... tsukineko.co.jp/english/

Recollections - rubber stamps .... available in stores and online

Micron - waterproof fineliners .... sakuraofamerica.com

Grumbacher - watercolor paint .... grumbacher.chartpak.com

Winsor & Newton - watercolor paint .... winsornewton.com/na/

Q-Tips - Precision Tip cotton swabs .... qtips.com